CONSUMED

ALSO BY THE AUTHORS

Good for Business: The Rise of the Conscious Corporation (2009)

CONSUMED

Rethinking Business in the Era of
Mindful Spending

ANDREW BENETT AND
ANN O'REILLY

WITH STUART HARRIS

CONSUMED
Copyright © Andrew Benett and Ann O'Reilly, 2010.

All rights reserved.

First published in 2010 by
PALGRAVE MACMILLAN®
in the United States—a division of St. Martin's Press LLC,
175 Fifth Avenue, New York, NY 10010.

Where this book is distributed in the UK, Europe and the rest of the world,
this is by Palgrave Macmillan, a division of Macmillan Publishers Limited,
registered in England, company number 785998, of Houndmills,
Basingstoke, Hampshire RG21 6XS.

Palgrave Macmillan is the global academic imprint of the above companies
and has companies and representatives throughout the world.

Palgrave® and Macmillan® are registered trademarks in the United States,
the United Kingdom, Europe and other countries.

ISBN: 978–0–230–10178–4

Library of Congress Cataloging-in-Publication Data

Benett, Andrew.
    Consumed: rethinking business in the era of mindful spending / Andrew
    Benett and Ann O'Reilly ; with Stuart Harris.
        p. cm.
    Includes index.
    ISBN 978–0–230–10178–4 (hardback)
        1. Consumption (Economics)—United States—History. 2. Consumer
    behavior—United States—History. 3. Thriftiness—United States—History.
    4. Social values—United States—History. I. O'Reilly, Ann. II. Title.
HC110.C6B45 2010
339.4′70973—dc22   2010008504

A catalogue record of the book is available from the British Library.

Design by Newgen Imaging Systems (P) Ltd., Chennai, India.

First edition: July 2010

10 9 8 7 6 5 4 3 2 1

Printed in the United States of America.

CONTENTS

ACKNOWLEDGMENTS

There are many people to whom we are indebted for their help with this book, but none more so than Stuart Harris, CEO of U.K.-based strategic consultancy Meaning Business. Stuart came on board as we began to firm up our concept for *Consumed*, and his thinking is in evidence in every chapter. We thank him for his work in helping to draft and research the book and also for the enthusiasm with which he approached the project. It is a far better work for his contributions.

We are also grateful to our agency colleagues, especially to David Jones, global CEO of Havas Worldwide, of which Euro RSCG Worldwide and Arnold Worldwide are a part. Without his support, this project would not have been possible. Other colleagues contributed to every aspect of the book, from helping to craft our New Consumer survey, which underpins our arguments, to providing research, conducting interviews, and offering logistical support. Rose Cameron, who heads up strategy at Euro RSCG's Chicago office, was particularly helpful in the early stages, working with us to shape the direction of the book and offering up all sorts of ideas and insights on the topics we cover. Her assistance was invaluable, and we consider ourselves fortunate to have ongoing access to that incredible repository that is her mind! Many thanks also to Christian Travers, the very talented designer whose work graces our cover.

As a global company, we were able to call on great thinkers from around the world, and we extend our thanks to Matt Donovan from Euro RSCG's APAC headquarters in China, to Bronson Smithson in Brazil, to Zoe Decool in the United Kingdom, and to Marianne Hurstel and her team in France. We would also like to thank Julie Monroid, Noriko Yokoi, and Jamie Degiaimo at Euro RSCG Life for their contributions to our survey. Thanks also to Will Burns from Arnold's headquarters in Boston for his input.

From Euro RSCG New York, we received invaluable assistance from Phil Buehler and Harrison Schultz, who helped create the New Consumer study and offered help and insights throughout the process. Many thanks also go to Firoza Mehta, our most tireless and dedicated researcher; to Julianna Young and Paige Miller, for their research support; to Mariya Kutmanova, for cheerfully agreeing to create the appendix despite an already taxing workload; to Michele Deamer, for her constant help and support; and last, but certainly not least, to Julia Gates, for her intelligent input, her many hours of research, and her extraordinary ability to keep track of all those details that threaten to break loose on a project of this nature. Thanks also to Ross Nicolson, who joined our team for three months to help with writing and research.

The hard work of two other people can also be seen throughout this book: The first is Roxane Marini, who fact-checked the entire manuscript, always under impossible deadlines. We thank her for her tireless efforts and support throughout. We are also enormously grateful to W. Barksdale Maynard, who not only helped polish our prose but also contributed a good deal to the content. He came on to the project near to the eleventh hour and quickly proved himself utterly indispensable.

A special thank-you to all those leaders in business and academia who took part in interviews and helped us to refine our thinking and expand our scope: Alex Castellanos of National Media, Inc.; Carlos Abrams-Rivera of Kraft Foods, Inc.; Jim Fielding of Disney Stores Worldwide; Dr. Neal Hinvest of the University of Bath; Christian McMahan of Heineken USA; C. J. O'Donnell of Jaguar Cars, Ltd.; Dr. Scott Rick of the University of Michigan's Ross School of Business; Dr. George Ritzer of the University of Maryland; Becky Saeger of Charles Schwab Corporation; and Dr. Barry Schwartz of Swarthmore College.

This is the second book on which we have had the good sense to team with Laurie Harting and Laura Lancaster at Palgrave Macmillan. As our editor, Laurie was instrumental in bringing the book to life. We very much appreciate her support of the project and the discerning eye she applied to our early drafts. Knowing that Laura is on standby, ready to answer our questions and help shepherd the book from contract through to completion, made the entire process run smoothly. We are grateful to both and also to Yasmin Mathew, who capably and graciously guided us through the production process.

Last, we extend our thanks to all those—both individuals and companies—who are contributing to the shift from wasteful excess to a more mindful and sustainable approach to consumption and to business. We hope this book will play some small part in advancing that cause.

—ANDREW AND ANN

PREFACE: ALL MAXED OUT?

If you had to name the single most potent force that shook the world in the past half century, what would it be: technology? Gender shifts? Terrorism? Individualism? Globalization? Yes, each has had a massive impact on the way we live, but one phenomenon in particular has been especially pervasive and life altering: *consumerism*. Depending on one's point of view, consumerism can be seen as fundamental and benign (the purchase of goods and services that make us happy) or as rampant and dangerous (an out-of-control habit contributing to the creeping erosion of our environment, communities, and values). Along with its allied terms, *consumer* and *consumption*, it increasingly finds itself at the center of hot socioeconomic and political debate.

As professional marketers, we have a natural interest in the subject of consumerism. Along with economists, politicians, business reporters, and advocacy groups, we habitually describe our fellow humans as *consumers*. Of course, that term makes sense when applied to people wolfing down food and drink, but lately it has been extended to virtually every aspect of our lives. Nowadays we do not just consume hot dogs and Cokes; we consume services and environmental resources and media and durable goods and everything else imaginable, all with greedy gusto and a seemingly bottomless appetite.

Until recently, just about everyone accepted this insidious new moniker, perhaps not even noticing when the term *consumer* began to push aside references to ourselves as *citizens* or simply *men and women*. But that tacit acceptance is giving way now, just as attitudes toward mindless consumption are changing profoundly. In mature markets in which runaway consumerism has been the norm for generations, rebellion is in the air; there are stirrings of discontent and signs of insurrection:

> I Am Not A Consumer; I Am A Person....My sole purpose in life is not to buy enough stuff to prop up failing companies or line the pockets of some corporate big-wig.
>
> —"David," writing on mytwodollars.com
>
> The word "consumer"...completely disgusts me. It reduces all of us to market forces and resources to be bought and sold, and to be held in little more respect and with little more consideration than that which is granted to livestock, or ore bearing rocks.
>
> —"Indenturedebtor," on democraticunderground.com

Some of the credit for this pushback must go to the economic crisis and the pinch it has put on spending. Prior to the downturn, many of us saw no need to skip a beat between See, Want, and Buy. Caesar's famous *"Veni, Vidi, Vici"* (I came, I saw, I conquered) was readily supplanted by *"Veni, Vidi, Visa"* (I came, I saw, I charged it). But then came the economic meltdown—a crisis that caused sufficient anxiety to prompt hundreds of millions of us to pause, think, and even reflect before swiping our cards. This forced hiatus from the merry-go-round of mindless consumption has led many of us to question our old habits and, at the core, our consumerist identities.

Just a couple of years ago, we might have laughed unselfconsciously about our addictions to "retail therapy" as we swapped tales of shopping till we "dropped." But today, over-the-top consumption is more apt to elicit a sense of embarrassment or even revulsion. Increasingly, status is conferred by what we choose *not* to buy. Mega-SUVs seem almost preposterous all of a sudden, with their air of wanton waste and disregard for the planet. Sales of bottled water are at last declining as reusable containers become chic. Locally handcrafted goods have taken on an allure that once was the exclusive province of traditional luxury brands.

What is going on here? When did consumption become a political and even a moral choice? And why is this happening now? After all, there is nothing new in people making silly or extravagant expenditures solely to tickle a momentary fancy rather than satisfy a genuine need. Millions of dusty attics crammed full with the detritus of present and past generations pay testament to that. What is new, and alarming, is the hyperinflated scale of the excesses we have seen since World War II and especially since the 1970s, when our culture was thoroughly reconfigured to accommodate an apparently insatiable hunger for MORE STUFF. Imagine what archaeologists from an alien world might think were they to excavate the closets and garages of average households on shopping-mad Planet Earth—not to mention the billions (yes, *billions*) of square feet of rental storage space. What theories would they concoct to explain all the material goods that lie hoarded away, unopened, barely used, or just plain forgotten? What might they deduce from our big-box stores the size of football fields and the massive landfills built to absorb all the goods once sold there?

A particularly clever archaeologist might hit upon the truth: For decades, a relentless stream of container ships bursting with low-cost goods from cheap-labor countries engorged the shelves of fast-expanding shopping malls and online stores. During these heady years, mindful shopping gave way to mindless accumulation, with the full approbation of pointy-headed economists. Manufacturers and advertisers were there, too, gleefully rubbing their hands—pressing and prodding, messaging and motivating the masses to stay in the dance, to keep picking up the tempo and never stop to catch a breath or take in the larger scene. For millions of us on the whirling dance floor, shopping became a way to pick ourselves up after a tough day at work and a source of entertainment on weekends. Mindless accumulation proved as satisfying as any drug.

But suddenly reduced economic circumstances have slowed the dance to a crawl, and the winded participants are looking blearily around the room and wondering why they are here and whether this is actually what they want. "Can this be everything?" "Shouldn't there be more to life?" These are tough, unexpected, but highly welcome questions. And they have led us to wonder what lies ahead for these exhausted survivors of the buy-more era. As marketers, it is our job to understand consumers' growing discontentment, to probe their questioning mind-set, and to anticipate their emotional wants and needs as we all enter a new era that promises to be fundamentally different.

POSTCONSUMERISM: WHAT NOW?

Over the past couple of years, seismic changes have called into question western society's unspoken and often unconscious assumptions about consumerism. Some of these changes are beyond our control, such as the squeeze on credit and dwindling supplies of nonrenewable energy and other resources; others are more personal and include heightened global awareness, greater concern about green issues, weakened trust in institutions, and a growing weariness with the stresses of modern life. In this book, we will examine both categories of change, but with a special focus on the latter—on the small-scale, inward, and personal. And we will look at how emerging shifts in attitudes and behaviors will affect the way we live far into the future—how they promise to reshape the entire consumption cycle, from product development right down through sales and marketing.

Make no mistake: This shift away from the hyperconsumerism to which we have all grown accustomed promises to be big and lasting in its effects. The changes we are seeing will affect the entire global economy and virtually everyone who is a part of it, so all-encompassing has consumerism become. Consider this: In the United States, consumer spending regularly amounts to two-thirds of the nation's overall economic activity, according to some calculations. *Two-thirds!* Granted, that figure is lower in other economies, but even in developing markets consumer spending has been driving rapid growth. Going forward, key questions for businesses are: How much of that spending has been necessary, and how much has been compulsive, impulsive, or merely reckless? How much was intended to scratch a momentary itch rather than serve genuine, longer-term purposes? And, critically, how much of it is gone for good as a result of changed conditions and the new postconsumerist mind-set?

Our most recent studies at Euro RSCG Worldwide show clear and convincing evidence of a more mindful approach to consumption, one that we began to address in our earlier book, *Good for Business: The Rise of the Conscious Corporation* (Palgrave Macmillan, 2009). Whereas some observers dismiss current trends such as downsizing and sustainable shopping as no more than temporary aberrations brought on by the downturn, we strongly disagree: They are permanent. Indeed, we were already reporting signs of a major shift in values well before the economy tanked. The reality is that many people in developed markets have been burned out and turned off by their own gross habits of hyperconsumption for quite some time now. The recession simply served to exacerbate these feelings and provide the added impetus to turn doubts into actions and vague resolutions into concrete change. Whereas shopping and accumulation once promised a golden pathway to happiness, now consumers are getting unexpected pleasure hits from cutting back and making more considered consumption choices. They are profoundly reconsidering everything, from their personal definitions of value to the purity of product ingredients, from environmental impacts to provenance, from design and packaging preferences to brand integrity.

The impulses feeding this new, more engaged, and insightful mind-set spring from a myriad of sources and are tied to countless larger trends, including a growing hunger for community, the desire for vibrant authenticity and a sense of connectedness with the natural world, and the Internet-enabled upsurge in consumer empowerment. This book seeks to demonstrate how each of these overlapping and mutually reinforcing trends is reshaping how consumers make choices and has the potential to revolutionize their relationship with brands. It offers a map through surprising new terrain in which the old landmarks of consumerism have been blasted away and strange new ones have emerged. Shoppers may have been thoroughly, grotesquely *consumed* by the age of excess, but now they emerge chastened and more thoughtful, ready to partner with brands that understand their transformed needs.

In this bewildering environment, only brands that *get it* will survive; and only those smart marketers who are willing to replace old, threadbare assumptions with new, creative thinking will manage to reconnect with a savvy and skeptical public. It is dangerous out there and disorienting in its unfamiliarity. As we grope our way forward, only true and committed innovators have any hope of achieving success. These pioneers are facing tough, exciting challenges—and our book is meant to help.

Part I

UNLEASHED: THE SHOPPER WITHIN

Chapter 1

THE BIRTH OF CONSUMERISM

We used to build civilizations. Now we build shopping malls.

—Bill Bryson

Everyone consumes, even the most impoverished of humans. Strictly speaking, *Homo sapiens* could not exist otherwise. Our physical organism survives by taking in food and drink and extracting what it needs. We must consume natural resources, such as trees and coal, to shelter us from the elements and keep us warm. At the most basic level, we consume oxygen to breathe.

So, in a literal sense, we have always been consumers. We have not, however, always lived in a consumerist society. What is the difference? *Consumerism* is not about the fundamental, inescapable need to gather resources in order to survive. Rather, it refers to the act of consumption as a behavior in itself: consuming not to live but for other, less functional and indeed less rational ends.

Nonfunctional consumption is not entirely a new phenomenon—it exists even in nature. Scientists theorize that fancy phenotypic displays, such as the flamboyantly shimmering tail of the peacock, have evolved as proof that the displayer is so fit and healthy, he or she can afford to invest resources in superfluities. (A diamond-encrusted gold chain sends the same message on city streets.) In human communities in which scarcity is the norm, ostentatious consumption conveys a message of high status—hence the exorbitant sums emperors spent on gladiatorial combats in ancient Rome and the profligate giveaway of goods at potlatch festivals in the Pacific Northwest. Such over-the-top, status-driven behavior received a name from Norwegian American economist Thorstein Veblen at the close of the nineteenth century: *conspicuous consumption*.

In his book *Culture and Consumption*, cultural anthropologist Grant McCracken describes the "consumer boom" in sixteenth-century England, just as the little country was beginning to strike it rich from overseas trade. Landed gentry began to spend ruinously on housing, hospitality, and clothing. McCracken points to the abetting role of Queen Elizabeth I, who expected the nobility to pay for spectacular ceremonies at her court in order to earn her fickle favor.[1] The upper classes went to ridiculous extremes to maintain the appearance of wealth—regardless of how destitute they were all the while becoming. As Veblen noted in *The Theory of the Leisure Class* (1899), "Conspicuous consumption of valuable goods is a means of reputability to the gentleman of leisure."[2] Paradoxically, the more wasteful an Elizabethan gentleman could afford to be, the stronger his reputation.

WE'VE COME A LONG WAY, BABY: FROM SCARCITY TO THE SCIENCE OF PLENTY

In recent decades, conspicuous consumption has been on near-constant display, with blaring media accounts of celebrity excess and CEO profligacy, from multimillion-dollar weddings and Learjets to the buying up of Caribbean islands. But this is not the form of consumption that most interests us, nor is it the focus of this book. Rather than *conspicuous consumption* (the squandering of scarce resources available to a select few), we have chosen to examine *everyday consumerism* (the steady gobbling up of mass-produced goods readily accessible to most). Over the course of the last century, consumption managed to go from demand driven (businesses producing goods to meet people's genuine needs) to supply side (people buying goods to support business growth). This shift has had a monumental impact not just on business but on society as a whole, right down to how we interact and what we value and how we perceive ourselves. In the book *The Golden Cow*, John White decries the developed world's frenzied worship of material goods:

> Our grasping arms are being crammed with the produce of an age of abundance, our eagerness to grasp being more than matched by the zeal of the people who shower such produce upon us. Abundance in the West has become a menace threatening to inundate us under mountains of television sets, houses, clothes, flowery toilet paper, cars, snowmobiles, books, furniture....We need food, clothing and shelter. Even abundance and comfort are gifts of God.

> But we are no longer his creatures accepting and distributing the goodness he pours upon us but the feverish and slavish worshipers of abundance itself.[3]

Hyperconsumerism was no fluke, nor was it inevitable. Instead, it was conceived and promoted precisely as a means of growing wealth, primarily for the benefit of governments and corporations. As long ago as 1924—in another pre-catastrophe era in which the stock market seemed inexorably to rise—journalist Samuel Strauss first trumpeted the merits of supply-side consumerism. In an *Atlantic Monthly* essay, he fervently argued that civilization would perish unless citizens could be persuaded to purchase more and more of what modern-day factories were churning out:

> Through the centuries, the problem has been how to produce enough of the things men wanted; the problem now is how to make men want and use more than enough things—"the science of plenty," it has been called....Consumptionism is the science of compelling man to use more and more things. Consumptionism is bringing it about that the American citizen's first importance to his country is no longer that of citizen but that of consumer.[4]

Strauss's *consumptionism* is today's *consumerism*. The dynamic and logic are the same: in Strauss's prophetic words, "not how to produce the goods, but how to produce the customers."[5]

Over the eight intervening decades, consumerism has become so thoroughly embedded in our way of thinking and talking that the words *people* and *consumers* are now used interchangeably in numerous contexts. Consumerism is *what we do;* it is what is expected of us; it is our singular contribution and almost the chief reason for our existence—that is, if you believe Rudy Giuliani, whose post-9/11 mayoral exhortation to the citizens of New York was "Take the kids to the park, buy a pizza, see a show."[6] A few years on, in the face of growing world turmoil, people began to rein in their spending, and governments were desperate once more to stimulate consumption in order to stave off massive economic contractions. President George W. Bush's call to action at a 2006 news conference:

> As we work with Congress in the coming year to chart a new course in Iraq and strengthen our military to meet the challenges of the twenty-first century, we must also work together to achieve important goals for the American people here at home. This work begins

with keeping our economy growing....And I encourage you all to go shopping more.[7]

Much has changed in the years since Bush delivered that heartfelt appeal. We now face a situation in which the producer-side forces driving consumerism still apply but the conditions that made consumerism possible and desirable in the first place are unraveling. Before we look ahead to what is next, it is helpful to understand how we got to our current state of affairs. We look now at the origins of the strange alliance between government and retail.

THE POLITICS OF CONSUMERISM: MAINTAINING A STABLE SOCIETY

Be glad that you're greedy; the national economy would collapse if you weren't.

—Mignon McLaughlin, *The Second Neurotic's Notebook*

How did leaders in Washington and elsewhere come to be so interested in the contents of shopkeepers' tills? It all comes down to maintaining social order. Today, most people in developed countries have little experience with dramatic political or social turbulence. This is a far cry from a century ago, when civil unrest, riots, and revolutions were commonplace. To corral these dangerous forces, many countries established dictatorships; the United States and European capitalist democracies followed a more enlightened approach. In 1928, President Herbert Hoover became perhaps the first American politician to spell out the notion that producing and consuming should be the great driving forces of our national life. He told an audience of advertisers and public relations men, "You have taken over the job of creating desire and have transformed people into constantly moving happiness machines, machines which have become the key to economic progress."[8]

Hoover's reasoning, shared by forward-thinking economists of the day, was that the steady production and consumption of goods and services would spur ceaseless economic growth, which, in turn, would usher in universal prosperity—ever-greater joy for myriad "happiness machines." Basking in an improved quality of life, the everyman would never consider building a barricade, bombing a bank, or attempting to overthrow the state. What would be the point? This gospel of happiness through consumption was interrupted by an economic depression and war but flowered again during the Eisenhower years. World War II temporarily brought product scarcity and deprivation, but ultimately it boosted the standard of living thanks to the creation of new jobs that served the war effort. Between 1940 and 1947, the number of employed Americans expanded from 47.5 million to 58 million, and vast numbers of citizens were yanked out of poverty.[9] At war's end, Rosie the Riveter had cash to spare, as did returning soldiers, who benefited from low-interest loans available under the GI Bill of Rights. Corporations had been enriched by wartime profits, which they now plowed into new plants and equipment that churned out shiny consumer goods. As the 1950s unfolded, the goal of corporations and governments alike was to sustain throughout peacetime the same—or even higher—levels of production as during the war, for the benefit of all.

In a *Journal of Retailing* essay in 1955, economist Victor Lebow underscored the heightened imperative of consumption in postwar America and the extent to which consumers had already begun to internalize their purchases—deriving a thoroughgoing and satisfying sense of self from the material goods that filled their ranch-style suburban homes:

> Our enormously productive economy demands that we make consumption our way of life, that we convert the buying and use of goods into rituals, that we seek our spiritual satisfactions, our ego satisfactions, in consumption. The measure of social status, of social acceptance, of prestige, is now to be found in our consumption patterns. The very meaning and significance of our lives is today expressed in consumption terms. The greater the pressures upon the individual to conform to safe and accepted social standards, the more does he tend to express his aspirations and his individuality in terms of what he wears, drives, eats—his home, his car, his patterns of food serving, his hobbies.
>
> These commodities and services must be offered to the consumer with a special urgency. We require not only "forced draft" consumption, but "expensive" consumption as well. We need things consumed, burned up, worn out, replaced, and discarded at an ever increasing pace. We need to have people eat, drink, dress, ride, live, with ever more complicated and, therefore, constantly more expensive consumption.[10]

We need, we need. For business leaders, the imperative was clear: Take every measure available to turn citizens into full-time consumers. Make them see the link between consumption and happiness, between material goods and social status, and even between consumerism and good citizenship.

Turning sober citizens into hard-charging "happiness machines" required transforming the old exchange of goods and services for money from something purely practical into something far more pleasurable and enticing. It would mean creating an entire culture geared toward the promotion of shopping and spending, with all their thrilling concomitant delights. The first step in that process was already well under way (indeed, it had begun a century before): the reinvention of the retail experience from merely functional to extravagantly seductive.

"THE HAPPIEST PLACE ON EARTH": BIG STORES BRING OUT THE FUN IN FUNCTIONALITY

When a customer enters my store, forget me. He is king.

—John Wanamaker

Long before big-box stores were common, before shopping malls spread everywhere, customers visited local markets or specialty stores such as bakeries, butcher shops, perfumers. Take a look at re-created Colonial Williamsburg in Virginia, where numerous tiny shops (apothecary, silversmith, gunmaker, wigmaker, and a dozen more) are scattered along a dusty commercial street. The experience of shopping may have been sociable and a pleasure in itself; it may have been regarded as an important aspect of community life, much as going to church or synagogue was; but its primary purpose was functional. And retail was very much small scale and local, like the no-nonsense hardware store Jim Lowe ran in North Wilkesboro, North Carolina, sixty years ago—the seed from which eventually would sprout the modern Lowe's chain of more than seventeen hundred big-box stores.

The original, highly circumscribed retail scene already had begun to change by the mid-nineteenth century, with shopping becoming a more alluring, all-around experience in major cities. Established in 1838, Bainbridge in Newcastle-upon-Tyne, England, is one of several claimants to the title of "oldest department store in the world."[11] In Paris, Le Bon Marché was founded that same year, offering shoppers an environment so attractive it spurred, in the words of one historian, the "arousal of free-floating desire."[12] In New York City, A. T. Stewart, housed in the flamboyant Marble Palace on Broadway, was America's first department store. Built of shining white marble amid a streetscape of dull red brick, it devoured an entire city block—and caused a sensation.[13] Inspired by the innovations of Mr. Stewart's dazzling retail emporium, other businessmen followed suit, soon creating an entire district known as Ladies' Mile—an exciting arena where the top-hatted and bustled well-to-do could come to shop and socialize.[14]

The contrast between these palaces and their general-store precursors was stark. Where goods once were mere lumps of inert matter to be sold and bought, now they were romanticized and elevated to an almost ethereal status. As described by historian Richard H. Robbins:

> The department store evolved into a place to display goods as objects in themselves. When Marshall Field's opened in Chicago in 1902, six string orchestras filled the various floors with music and American Beauty roses along with other cut flowers and potted palms bedecked all the counters. Nothing was permitted to be sold on the first day, and merchants in the district closed so that their employees could visit Field's. Later elaborate theatrical productions were put on in the stores, artworks were displayed, and some of the most creative minds in America designed displays that were intended to present goods in ways that inspired people to buy them. The department store became a cultural primer telling "people how they should dress, furnish their homes, and spend their leisure time."[15]

And so it grew, with the notion of shopping as entertainment and spectacle spreading around the world. In 1909, American-born Harry G. Selfridge opened an exceptionally plush department store in London, paving the way for Oxford Street to become the world-class shopping destination it remains to this day.[16] In Paris, the Galeries Lafayette of 1912 sported a memorable steel-and-glass dome and twisting Art Nouveau staircases. That same year, the Bijenkorf in Amsterdam threw open its doors.[17] Many landmark department stores date from this period, including Harrods Buenos Aires (1912), Karstadt on Hamburg's Mönckebergstraße (1912), and Saks Fifth Avenue in New York (1924).

By the time motion pictures flickered to life, big stores and the notion of shopping for pleasure were already firmly implanted in the public mind. Several classic movies were actually set in them: In 1923's *Safety Last*, star Harold Lloyd (who famously dangles from the hands of a giant clock) is employed as a clerk in De Vore's Department Store. The Marx Brothers' 1941 romp, *The Big Store*, takes place in Phelps's. And who could forget Natalie Wood in *Miracle on 34th Street*, set in Macy's in 1947?

In many respects, big department stores achieved that modern goal, the industrialization and "massification" of retail. By virtue of their size, they were able to offer a gigantic selection of goods and services compared with traditional stores, and this enhanced selection meant they needed to be organized and managed in a far more systematic way. At the same time, they ushered in a deeply enriched, enhanced retail experience. They offered a cornucopia of wonderful stuffs laid out enticingly; they invited random wandering among the goods, exposing shoppers to things they may never have seen before—or even imagined. They offered firsthand epiphanies of abundance, luxury, and service that aligned with the ever-growing expectations of upscale customers (and anyone who aspired to be upscale). Most important, they made shopping a delightful activity in its own right.

The entrepreneurs who built these edifices had an intuitive understanding of shopper psychology—of how to get people to stop by more often, to open their purses wider, and to feel simply delicious while doing it. An imaginative story by novelist Kurt Andersen captures the sense of magic these vast emporiums held for the naive and uninitiated. He describes the reaction of a nineteenth-century working girl upon stepping inside A. T. Stewart:

> She turned left down Broadway, crossing Duane, crossing Reade, and felt the rising buzz of anticipation as she approached Chambers Street. She would be recognized by acquaintances in just the way she longed to be. They would treat her kindly and even, she imagined, with respect. Elsewhere, at theaters and saloons and ordinary shops, she was just another unattached young woman at large in the city, one among the new horde of maids and seamstresses, publishers' and daguerreotypists' assistants. But from the moment A. T. Stewart Dry Goods opened two years ago...Polly had been a habitué. She visited at least one afternoon a week, sometimes more often, and usually made a purchase—a hair ribbon, a piece of sheet music, perfume, a pen, nearly always something perfectly inessential....
>
> "Welcome back to Stewart's, Miss." As the boy in ludicrous blue livery heaved open the big front door, she stepped in and inhaled deeply: clean dry marble, expensive varnish, Oriental rugs, cut flowers, linen writing papers, powdered starch, lavender water, the latest crinolines fluffy as pastry, hundreds of pristine first-class calicoes, cambrics, balzarines, cashmeres, and muslins—the collective tonic aroma of so many good things all here together and all brand new. She shivered....Inside Stewart's the day always seemed brighter.[18]

With their retail emporia, bold entrepreneurs such as A. T. Stewart, R. H. Macy, and C. H. Harrod helped erect the basic infrastructure of modern consumerism. The next big milestone on the road to hyperconsumption, however, was laid not by a retailer but by a psychologist.

BERNAYS AND THE BIRTH OF MODERN MARKETING: TAPPING THE UNCONSCIOUS

People will buy anything that is one to a customer.

—Sinclair Lewis

Consumerism as we know it would never have arrived without modern marketing. Much of the thinking and practice that drives it can be attributed to the "father of public relations," Edward Bernays, who was born in Vienna in 1891 but almost immediately moved to New York with his parents. Propitiously, he was related to Sigmund Freud, the founder of psychoanalysis, on both his mother's and his father's side. In time he received a copy of *A General Introduction to Psychoanalysis* from Uncle Sigmund and began to consider the untapped potential of the unconscious as it relates to consumer behavior. He had the book translated into English and published in the United States in the early 1920s. Freud's theories were meant to be used in therapy, but Bernays had a more commercial outlook: He saw people's subconscious impulses as a golden opportunity for industry to connect with customers in new, more powerful ways and to convince them to buy. He had a special interest in public relations (as well as a gift for self-promotion), and he devised PR campaigns for his clients that incorporated Freudian methodologies.[19]

In his groundbreaking book *Propaganda*, Bernays showed his grasp of the subconscious motivations that underlie consumer choices:

> Men are rarely aware of the real reasons which motivate their actions. A man may believe that he buys a motor car because, after careful study of the technical features of all makes on the market, he has concluded that this is the best. He is almost certainly fooling himself. He bought it, perhaps, because a friend whose financial acumen he respects bought one last week; or because his neighbors believed he was not able to afford a car of that class; or because its colors are those of his college fraternity.[20]

Bernays had a powerful insight here: Shoppers' behavior is driven as much by unconscious impulses as by rational considerations; by understanding the associations and triggers that govern these impulses, marketers can sway people's choices. He recognized the potential immensity of this power:

> The conscious and intelligent manipulation of the organized habits and opinions of the masses is an important element in democratic society. Those who manipulate this unseen mechanism of society constitute an invisible government which is the true ruling power of our country....We are governed, our minds are molded, our tastes formed, our ideas suggested, largely by men we have never heard of.[21]

The implications of these ideas for twentieth-century government, business, and marketing were profound. Ever since, businesspeople have eagerly exploited the unconscious mind, and the field of consumer research has exploded. Today's marketers use a whole array of sophisticated psychological tools for the purpose not of healing patients but of manipulating customers—including projective and hypnotic techniques, semiotics, imagery, the psychology of color, and many more. To their way of thinking, functionality is a minor attribute of the products they pitch; more important are the nonfunctional, psychological dimensions—the ways in which a bar of soap or a pair of socks contributes to the buyer's personal identity and inward sense of well-being; the right toothpaste leads ineluctably to a passionate kiss; beer opens the door to warm friendships; an insurance policy is proud proof of responsibility toward loved ones. By moving beyond product features to communicate user benefits instead, marketers have turned even the most banal commodities into what historian Robbins calls a "source of satisfaction and a vital means of self-expression."[22]

Psychology spurs us to buy things we do not really need—such is the genius of modern marketing. The line between desire and necessity has become hopelessly blurred. Is emotional benefit somehow functional in itself? Which needs are real and which are merely perceived? Even in Shakespeare's day these matters were cloudy: "O reason not the need! Our basest beggars, Are in the poorest thing superfluous," says King Lear, arguing that even wretched people who lack basic necessities will choose to own a few useless things that happen to make them feel good.[23] Modern times have seen an explosion in the production of products that can make no claim to being absolutely necessary; instead, they are quasi-functional, filling needs more emotional than strictly real. Such is the terrain of today's consumerism. And it could not have developed in the absence of three critical postwar factors: rising incomes and easy credit combined with the octopuslike reach of television advertising.

PROSPERITY, TV, AND CREDIT: KEYS TO HYPERCONSUMERISM

Whither goes thou, America, in thy shiny car in the night?

—Jack Kerouac, *On the Road*

Consumerism is possible only when enough people are able to buy enough things beyond their basic needs. Automaker Henry Ford was one of the first to understand the importance of creating an "ever-widening circle of buying."[24] In 1914, he took the revolutionary step of nearly doubling pay for his workers, to five dollars a day, and reducing daily working hours from nine to eight. He reasoned that the only way to sell all the cars produced by his mass-production plants in Detroit would be to ensure there were plenty of working people with cash to spare—and time enough to go shopping.

It took a while for the Ford philosophy to catch on. The Depression pushed millions into unemployment and took billions of dollars out of circulation. There was not much scope for pleasure and consumption as World War II mobilized the western world into military production, combat, and mass destruction. Consumerism was sidelined (even as savings mounted in some markets); instead, the challenge for ordinary citizens was getting hold of basic food, clothing, and fuel. Hardship continued for several years after the war; in Britain, food and coal were rationed for much of the following decade.[25] Germany was of course devastated, and central and eastern Europe fell under the pall of communist central planning; decades would pass before they had a chance to join the banquet of western-style consumerism.

The situation was far rosier in the United States. By the early 1950s, it had become the first of the war economies to start enjoying a recovery, which soon turned into widespread prosperity. Real per capita gross domestic product soared from $6,857 in 1940 to $9,352 just a decade later.[26] Suddenly, hardworking families could aspire to more than just "a chicken in every pot": There could be a Sunbeam Mix Master in every kitchen and a Plymouth in every suburban driveway—or, even better, a whale-size Cadillac with an overhead-valve

V-8 engine, whitewall tires, and rakish tailfins to make a stunning statement to everyone it passed.

Thanks to the Economic Cooperation Act of 1948 (the Marshall Plan), the democracies of Europe finally began to enjoy prosperity by the late 1950s. For a large and rising generation born after the war, times were good: *La vita* was *dolce* in Italy, England was "Swinging Like a Pendulum Do," West Germany began cautiously building the economic miracle of the *Wirtschaftswunder*. The anthems of pop and rock music spread the rebellious, hedonistic spirit of youth culture around the world.

For the first time in history, large sections of the populations in western democracies and Japan had disposable income—bounteous money to spend. Having met their immediate need for food, clothing, housing, heating, and savings, they had extra cash for discretionary and even whimsical purposes. For older folks who had lived through the austerities of the Great Depression and war, the subsequent decades must have seemed like something out of the *Arabian Nights:* peace, comfort, sybaritic pleasures. By contrast, their children had been born into prosperity, and they found it normal and even boring; they craved bigger, wilder thrills. "We want the world, and we want it now," rocker Jim Morrison roared on behalf of his restive generation. Born in 1943 to a military family, his worldview was shaped by highway culture in a rootless childhood spent wandering from state to state. For the first time in history, teenagers were regarded as a demographic in their own right, and their wallets were full. With average spending money of ten to fifteen dollars a week, U.S. teens had a higher income than many *families* during the Great Depression, and by 1959, their spending had reached an extraordinary $10 billion.[27] This economic might—much of it expended on frivolities—laid the foundation for vast new fortunes in the music, movie, apparel, and consumer electronics industries. Teens and anybody else with extra cash to spend on indulgences truly served to set the great wheel of consumerism in motion. Around and around it spun: The more nonessentials we bought, the more scope there was to produce more of them, which provided the basis for new businesses, which in turn led to new jobs and new cash to be spent on even more consumer goods.

Enter the Boob Tube

By this point, another critical factor had taken hold: television. Full-blown, high-octane consumerism might have happened without it, but it would have taken much longer; by the same token, television might have developed without consumerism, but nowhere near so quickly, given that advertising dollars were the very backbone of the new industry. TV was phenomenally effective in spreading product and brand awareness; its scope and dazzle were far greater than anything heretofore possible in print, radio, or cinema. Salespeople of the slickest and most persuasive variety were teleported right into consumers' homes through the magic portal of the cathode ray tube. Over the course of the 1950s, TV viewing went from rare to ubiquitous as the number of sets in U.S. homes skyrocketed from 3.8 million to 45.8 million—that is, from 9 percent of households to 87 percent. TV ownership would reach 98 percent by the 1970s, where it remains today.[28] Having achieved total victory, television then launched a stealthy push beyond the living room; the 1.7 sets per home in 1980 grew to 2.6 by 2005, and there seemed to be TVs everywhere. These devices captured an enormous audience for marketers: By 2008, the average American was staring at a set for 4.7 hours every day.[29]

In 1941, the Federal Communications Commission began licensing commercial television stations. The first officially sanctioned TV commercial ran that same year, during a Dodgers-Phillies baseball game on NBC: Bulova paid the grand sum of nine dollars for the privilege of advertising its watches.[30] Five years later, the first commercially sponsored TV show, *Geographically Speaking*, debuted with the backing of Bristol-Myers. Numerous other sponsored shows followed, and by 1960, television accounted for 13 percent of all advertising dollars.[31] A few broadcasters were noncommercial, including the BBC in Britain and ABC in Australia, but the overwhelming pattern was for-profit, funded by advertising.

A cartoon tiger roars about Kellogg's Frosted Flakes, "They're G-r-r-r-eat!" An infectious jingle celebrates "Rice-A-Roni, The San Francisco Treat." Maxwell House Coffee is proclaimed to be "Good to the Last Drop." These and countless other 1950s commercials insinuated themselves into the heart of our culture and stimulated an upward spiral of consumption. At the same time, TV game shows contributed to the consumerist mind-set by giving "ordinary" people the chance to win the latest exciting products, thereby alerting viewers to what was especially desirable in the way of toasters, washing machines, and automobiles. The scale of everything was bigger on TV; the top prize on a popular radio show of the 1940s was sixty-four dollars, but when it was reinvented for television in 1955, the amount was boosted a thousandfold, making *The $64,000 Question*.[32] The following year saw the debut of *The Price Is Right*, a seemingly immortal program that perfectly embodies the alliance between television and marketing: Contestants "Come On Down!" and compete for prizes based on their knowledge of products' actual retail prices. Game shows multiplied throughout the 1950s, including *Queen for a Day*, on which players competed for prizes by telling sorrowful life stories, trying to earn the sympathy—and votes—of the studio audience; the subtext was that emotional catharsis lies in material things. The winner was apotheosized into nothing less than a consumerist king or queen—bedecked in crown and robe and seated on a throne, then showered with kitchen appliances, designer clothing, or maybe even a jet vacation.

Somewhat more subtly, television spread the consumerist attitude by osmosis. Soap operas and sitcoms opened the door into other people's homes, which turned out to be splendidly comfortable, well equipped, and thoroughly aspirational. And TV served the goals of marketers by sending the message that gratification ought to come easily; it reinforced the notion that lightweight commercialism and cheap laughs were an acceptable stand-in for real experience. Americans were deeply lulled: Why ponder things or engage in serious debate when it was so much easier to huddle in front of the boob tube for *Car 54, Where Are You?* Why worry about big issues when everyone on *The Donna Reed Show* overflowed with sunny optimism? In 1968, that disastrous year of Vietnam, assassinations, and rioting, the top-rated TV show was the silly *Rowan and Martin's Laugh-In*. The "thought-lite" trend continues today, when the top programs include *American Idol* and *Dancing with the Stars*. We are "amusing ourselves to death," according to the title of a famous book by media academic Neil Postman.[33]

The Rise of Easy Credit

> I'm living so far beyond my income that we may almost be said to be living apart.
>
> —e. e. cummings

No matter how enticing television come-ons might have been, modern hyperconsumerism could never have fully blossomed in the absence of easy credit. Hotpoint eighteen-cubic-foot refrigerators, General Electric P7 self-cleaning ovens, and matching suites of bedroom furniture from Marshall Field would have been outside the reach of most postwar families were it not for the availability of credit, generally in the form of installment payment plans. In a recent historical overview, the Federal Reserve Board of Boston notes:

> The big breakthrough came in 1919 when General Motors Acceptance Corporation (GMAC) became the first to make

financing available to middle-income car buyers. Instead of having to come up with the entire purchase price, prospective car buyers needed only a down payment and an income that was big enough to cover monthly payments over the life of the loan.

Before long, manufacturers of other "big ticket" items began to adopt the practice. And if consumers were hesitant to go into debt, the flood of advertisements in mass media outlets—newspapers, magazines, and radio—helped them to overcome their inhibitions.[34]

By 1957, a General Motors ad was boasting: "On the GMAC Plan, you get terms arranged to suit your needs—at reasonable cost. It's the way over 2,000,000 families bought their cars last year."[35]

Before the 1950s, those companies that extended the credit were usually the same ones that sold the product ("It can be yours for just a small up-front fee and ten easy monthly payments"). Credit cards issued by big stores and oil companies typically could not be used in other outlets, though some retailers established reciprocity agreements. The breakthrough idea for a general-purpose credit card belonged to Frank X. McNamara, head of Hamilton Credit Corporation. After embarrassingly finding himself without cash to pay for a meal with friends, McNamara came up with the idea of a card company that would act as a financial liaison between businesses and customers.[36] In 1950, he and dining companions Alfred Bloomingdale (grandson of the store founder) and Ralph Schneider (McNamara's attorney) founded Diners Club, marketing it to salesmen who needed to wine and dine customers. It filled an urgent demand: By the end of the year, 20,000 diners were using the card. Eight years later, American Express debuted its charge card; public interest was so high, a quarter of a million cards were issued prior to the official launch date.[37] That same year, Bank of America launched BankAmericard (precursor to Visa), and within months, 2 million of these cards were in the hands of consumers in California alone.[38] Merchants and retailers initially were reluctant to accept credit cards—they came with fees, and they competed against in-store cards—but they soon realized that general-purpose cards made it easier for customers to spend, spend, spend. The phrase "Charge it" soon entered the American lexicon.

Thus were established the two main forms of consumer credit: installment and revolving. These changed the way people defined what they could "afford"—and even their sense of what they deserved to own. As satirical *Mad* magazine put it, "The only reason a great many American families don't own an elephant is that they have never been offered an elephant for a dollar down and easy weekly payments."[39] Other countries took longer to accept the notion of consumer credit, and it was not until the 1970s that the Access card in Britain promised, in a controversial slogan, to "Take the Waiting Out of Wanting."[40] By that time, all the pieces were in place in the major democracies of the West: Hyperconsumerism was about to become all-consuming.

Chapter 2

EATING THE WORLD

Carrie: *Honey, if it hurts so much, why are we going shopping?*
Samantha: *I have a broken toe, not a broken spirit.*

—*Sex and the City*, "The Domino Effect"

With the stage fully set for consumerism following World War II, Americans eagerly embraced their new role as citizen-shoppers. By the mid-1950s, nearly 60 percent of the population belonged to the middle class.[1] They enjoyed the highest standard of living in the world, purchasing new cars in which to zip their families to new homes in newly developed suburbs, filling their private spaces with newly automated appliances, transistor-based electronics, and other "must haves" for themselves and their boomer children. By 1958, toy sales alone had reached $1.25 billion.[2] That is a whole lot of Hula Hoops, Matchbox Cars, and Frisbees. Shopping had become a crucial signifier of status and success; material goods were now part and parcel of what it meant to be "American."

The trajectory of consumerism did not follow a straight, ascending line from 1950 to 2000, however. While consumer confidence developed a perceptible swagger right through the early 1970s, it then tripped and stumbled—in a big way. The Carter years brought anxiety and turbulence, in some ways foreshadowing the economic crisis that launched a stealth attack in 2007. Far from slowing the consumerism juggernaut, however, the 1970s slowdown set the stage for the hyperconsumerist mania that exploded in its wake.

THE DECADE PEOPLE WANTED TO FORGET

Economically, the 1970s was marked by a dismal combination of high inflation and stagnant growth, making tough going for the newly expanded middle class. After the United States and other industrialized nations came off the gold standard in 1971, currencies rapidly depreciated. Adding insult to injury, the oil-producing nations of the Organization of Petroleum Exporting States (OPEC) chose that moment to start charging more for crude oil. Fuel prices shot up from around $2.45 a barrel in 1972 to more than $11.00 in 1974 and a whopping $39.00 by early 1981.[3]

Unemployment emerged as a troubling issue as well. The year 1975 marked the last time the value of U.S. exports exceeded the value of imports; every year since has seen a trade deficit.[4] In other words, the country had shifted from a production economy to a consumption economy. In May 1975, unemployment reached 9 percent, more than double the joblessness rate of five years earlier.[5] At the same time, prices in the developed markets of Europe and North America kept inexorably rising, prompting demand for higher wages, which in turn pushed up prices even more. The Misery Index (combining the unemployment and inflation rates) hit a whopping 20.76 in 1980; to give you an idea of how high that is, the index stood at 7.00 in 1960 and 8.92 in 2009.[6] It all seemed beyond the control of hapless governments. Throughout the decade, these economic woes gnawed away at consumer morale, which was also shaken by political turmoil.

In the political arena, the Watergate scandal gripped the United States from 1972 until the resignation of President Nixon two years later. The war in Vietnam dragged on until 1975. Terrorism was everywhere: At the 1972 Munich Olympics, that happy celebration of internationalism, militant Palestinians took Israeli athletes hostage, ending in a bloodbath. The Irish Republican Army repeatedly set off bombs in English cities, often targeting retail centers. In Italy, terrorists from both the left and the right committed outrages throughout the decade, including the murder of a prime minister. In Germany, the Baader-Meinhof gang committed numerous shootings. At decade's end, major oil producer Iran suddenly descended into an antiwestern revolution.

On the cultural front, this squalid decade brought a steady deluge of bad news. The U.S. divorce rate, which had stood at 2.5 per 1,000 of population in 1966, climbed to 5.3 by 1979.[7] In popular culture, a time of feel-good escapism (*The Waltons*, pop group ABBA) was incapable of blocking out the increasing sex and violence (porno-classic *Debbie Does Dallas*, .44 Magnum-wielding Clint Eastwood, self-destructive punk rocker Sid Vicious). The pervasive sense of malaise was encapsulated in an alarmist televised speech by President Jimmy Carter:

> I want to talk to you right now about a fundamental threat to American democracy.... The threat is nearly invisible in ordinary ways. It is a crisis of confidence. It is a crisis that strikes at the very heart and soul and spirit of our national will. We can see this crisis in the growing doubt about the meaning of our own lives and in the loss of a unity of purpose for our nation. The erosion of our confidence in the future is threatening to destroy the social and the political fabric of America.[8]

Like water building up against a dam, the pent-up consumer desires of millions were seeking an escape from the confines of dreary negativism and economic malaise. Explosive change was just around the corner. It began in 1979, when Margaret Thatcher was elected prime minister of the United Kingdom. Her election manifesto was a call for change and, like Carter's speech, reached out to a nation that seemed to have lost its way—and its will:

> No one who has lived in this country during the last five years can fail to be aware of how the balance of our society has been increasingly tilted in favour of the State at the expense of individual freedom. This election may be the last chance we have to reverse that process, to restore the balance of power in favour of the people. It is therefore the most crucial election since the war.
>
> Together with the threat to freedom there has been a feeling of helplessness, that we are a once great nation that has somehow fallen behind and that it is too late now to turn things round.[9]

The following year in the United States, Ronald Reagan was swept into office on a platform of lower taxes to stimulate the economy, less government interference in people's lives, and a strong national defense. When he ran for reelection four years later, his TV ad pointed to a dramatic change in the national mood:

> It's morning again in America. Today, more men and women will go to work than ever before in our country's history. With interest rates at about half the record highs of 1980, nearly 2,000 families today will buy new homes, more than at any time in the past four years. This afternoon, 6,500 young men and women will be married, and with inflation at less than half of what it was just four years ago, they can look forward with confidence to the future. It's morning again in America, and under the leadership of President

Reagan, our country is prouder and stronger and better. Why
would we ever want to return to where we were less than four short
years ago?[10]

Under the free market positivism that marked the leadership of
Thatcher and Reagan, their respective countries were ready to spring-
board into the final quarter of the century, with all its fuel-injected,
turbo-charged, high-octane consumerism.

SHOW ME THE MONEY(TARISM)

Before we look at how the New Consumerism took hold and took
off, it is important to understand the policies that encouraged it:
monetarism, supply-side economics, and deregulation.

The "stagflation" of the 1970s threw an entire generation of
policy makers off-kilter. Established economic theories were unable
to explain or cope with simultaneous inflation, unemployment, and
zero growth. Salvation of a sort came from the thinking of economist
Milton Friedman, who became regarded as a sort of prophet expound-
ing *monetarism*—a concept that became a household word. Having
published one landmark book in 1957 (*A Theory of the Consumption
Function*) and another in the 1960s (*Capitalism and Freedom*), Friedman
hit the big time in 1980, when *Free to Choose* (written with his wife,
Rose, to accompany a Public Broadcasting television series) topped
best-seller lists. As a curb to inflation, Friedman advocated keeping a
tight rein on the money supply.[11] He ushered in a new approach that
would underpin central bank policies for years to come. Monetarism
helped stabilize prices, which in turn enabled consumers to feel
confident about their purchasing power.

Friedman shared Reagan's enthusiasm for *free market economics*.[12]
He habitually considered all transactions to be beneficial to both
buyer and seller, provided they were undertaken freely and voluntarily.
A free market meant no government monopolies, no subsidies, no
burdensome regulations. This type of market was, of course, the
opposite of what prevailed in communist countries, where everything
was tied up in bureaucratic strings and corruption and where acute
shortages were the norm; it also differed from what prevailed in more
socialist-type capitalist democracies, where supplies and prices were
regulated by quotas and tariffs—a *controlled* market as opposed to a
free one. This embrace of free markets and free price systems during
the 1980s opened the door to a flood of consumer goods, even as it
gave corporations an incentive to come up with increasingly innovative consumer products, as fast and as cheaply as possible.

The third force at work, *supply-side economics*, promised to be the perfect catalyst for consumption. This approach favored lowering taxes in order to give people more incentive to work (boosting the supply of goods and services) and a greater willingness to spend (sparking demand), thereby ramping up the economy. Republican politician George H. W. Bush dismissed the concept as "voodoo economics" in 1980, but he lost the presidential nomination, and supply-side economics went on to become an essential component of what would be known as *Reaganomics*.

The final piece of the new economic puzzle was *deregulation*. Up through the Carter years, many aspects of economic life were constrained by governmental rules. These rules often created de facto monopolies or at least very limited choice for consumers. Increasingly, such restrictions came to be resented as impediments to growth. The Airline Deregulation Act of 1978 began to knock down this old order; it removed U.S. government control over fares, routes, and the entry of new airlines into commercial aviation. Soon trucking, railroads, banking, and telecommunications were deregulated as well, opening them up to increased competition and innovation. These winds of deregulation led to the dramatic 1984 breakup of the telephone service monopoly long held by American Telephone & Telegraph (AT&T). In the United Kingdom, deregulation was accomplished through privatization: selling state-owned or -controlled companies or transferring their assets to private companies. There, too, telephone service and airlines led the way; British Telecom and British Airways were privatized in 1982 and 1987, respectively. All told, between 1979 and 1991, more than 50 percent of the U.K. public sector went private under the laissez-faire policies called *Thatcherism*.[13]

Other countries proceeded more cautiously, but deregulation and privatization grew steadily ascendant around the world; both measures were advocated by the International Monetary Fund and the World Bank.[14] Deregulation and privatization meant organizations could no longer rely on guaranteed captive markets but would have to fight for their share. For consumers, heightened competition resulted in improved service, lower prices, and a steady stream of new and increasingly enticing goods. Consumerism also received a boost from the progress made in the General Agreement on Tariffs and Trade (GATT), a rolling round of negotiations aimed at reducing or eliminating trade barriers between countries. GATT was launched in 1947; after eight rounds of talks over a span of many years, it led to the creation of the World Trade Organization in 1995—a key factor in globalization and the accelerated pace of consumption.[15]

Thus, the forces of monetarism, free market economics, supply-side economics, and deregulation—plus globalization—created a new economic equation. Corporations were increasingly free to expand their businesses, invent new products, chase customers. They were also free to keep prices down by importing from cut-rate producers abroad. Cheap goods from Japan and Hong Kong helped feed the first great consumer boom of the 1960s–1970s in the mature markets of North America and western Europe; through the 1990s and into the 2000s, it was container-loads of goods from China and Vietnam and other low-cost countries that kept western consumers coming back hungrily for more. And they were seduced by an ever-wider selection of brands.

MY BOLOGNA HAS A FIRST NAME: BRANDING ON THE RISE

Brands and branding have played a critical role in fueling high-octane consumerism. Modern-day marketing has developed all manner of ways to instill desire in consumers' hearts for products they had perhaps never before heard of nor imagined they needed—a vital catalyst for today's increased spending. Miss Clairol convinced us of the dire importance of covering up those grays. DeBeers helped make diamond rings de rigueur for betrothals. And the likes of Frank Perdue and Orville Redenbacher made us realize that commodities we used to consider perfectly adequate simply *would not do.*

The modern iteration of branding goes back to the nineteenth century, when soap companies helped lead the way. In America, Procter & Gamble's Ivory Soap was first advertised in 1882, using full-color ads and catchy slogans such as "99 44/100 Percent Pure" and "The Soap That Floats," which are still featured today.[16] In Britain, Unilever's Sunlight Soap was launched in 1886, not sliced from a big bar in the store but rather purchased individually in a distinctive wrapper.[17] By the early twentieth century, branding was sufficiently far along for companies to engage in "trademark advertising," complete with slogans, mascots, and jingles. By the 1940s, professionals had come to recognize that consumers did not merely register brand messages; they actually developed personal relationships with brands, connecting with them on some deeper emotional level.

Through the formative years of television, branding was still relatively naive in its approach: "Brand X is good for you because it contains ingredient Y"; "Most moms prefer Z"; "You'll wonder where the yellow went when you brush your teeth with Pepsodent"; "There's always room for JELL-O." Moving into the 1980s, branding became much more serious and sophisticated: Academics started taking an interest, and numerous experts wrote books, including John M. Murphy's *Branding: A Key Marketing Tool* and David N. Martin's *Romancing the Brand*. As branding suddenly became the cool kid on the marketing playground, smart corporations aspired to build more-powerful brands and consumers grew increasingly brand conscious. Athletic shoe maker Nike illustrates the transformation: It first dipped its toe into the branding waters with its "There is no finish line" print campaign in 1977, then aired a national TV ad in 1982 (created by newly formed agency Wieden+Kennedy, which in 1988 thought up the unforgettable line, "Just Do It").[18] Apple was on board with brand advertising in these early years too; its 1984 Super Bowl TV spot promoting the new Macintosh computer was branding at its most memorable. Few recall which teams played on the gridiron that day, but "1984" by agency Chiat/Day and directed by Ridley Scott in the dark manner of his movie *Blade Runner* has never been forgotten.

Even accountants started taking branding seriously after 1988, when British confectioner Rowntree Mackintosh became the subject of a takeover battle between Swiss giants Nestlé and Jacobs Suchard. The winning offer from Nestlé valued the company at $4.48 billion[19]—far in excess of any possible valuation of its tangible assets. What Nestlé wanted was not so much the company as its *brands*, which included Kit Kat, Polo, Aero, and Fruit Pastilles.

For shoppers tiptoeing through the enchanted garden of consumerism, with alluring vistas of new products and opportunities in every direction, brands provide useful clues and signposts. Market researchers analyze shoppers' perceptions of brands and feed them through to marketers, who massage and amplify them, then feed them right back to consumers in enhanced, more potent form. By 1991, the cult of brand names was so deeply entrenched that Brett Easton Ellis parodied it in his gruesome novel *American Psycho*, in which the main character obsessively describes his and his fellow yuppies' material possessions in exhaustive detail. Strewn with brand names and prices, the book was less literature than shopping list.

CONSUMERISM CO-OPTS POPULAR CULTURE—AND VICE VERSA

Give the public the "image" of what it thinks it ought to be, or what television commercials or glossy magazine ads have convinced us we ought to be, and we will buy more of the product, become closer to the image, and further from reality.

—Madeleine L'Engle, *A Circle of Quiet*

As the dismal 1970s receded, marketers plied the public with what they wanted to see: flashy displays of wealth, hedonistic luxuries, designer names, and (in the title of the popular TV show) *Lifestyles of the Rich and Famous.* Prime-time CBS soap opera *Dallas,* with its deliciously aspirational brew of money, sex, and intrigue, led the pack. Through thirteen seasons starting in 1978, it delighted viewers with its portrayal of a heady milieu of big hats, big hair, and even bigger shoulder pads. The high-rolling world of the Ewing family soon became familiar across the planet as the series was dubbed into sixty-seven languages in more than ninety countries.

Even more influential and emblematic was the NBC cop show *Miami Vice* (1984–1990)—so effective at seeding and stimulating consumption, it might have been designed specifically for that purpose. The brainstorm brief for the show was "MTV cops," meaning that it would apply the slick, modish visual style of the wildly popular music video channel launched three years before, including fast cuts, thumping music, frenzied action, and a self-consciously "designer" aesthetic.[20] The setting was sun-kissed Florida; the lead characters (Don Johnson as Sonny Crockett and Philip Michael Thomas as Ricardo Tubbs) were gorgeous. As one commentator recalls it:

> The show had a huge impact on men's fashion, popularizing Ray-Ban sunglasses, T-shirts worn under suit jackets, and five o'clock shadow. A trend towards pastel colors and European fashion spread through America like wildfire. Designers like Gianni Versace and Hugo Boss kept Crockett and Tubbs' wardrobe on the cutting edge, as they generally appeared in up to eight different outfits on each episode.[21]

Eager to profit from the show's runaway popularity, designers and retailers vied to win over its fashion-hungry audience. As *Time* magazine reported, "After Six formal wear is bringing out a Miami Vice line of dinner jackets next spring, Kenneth Cole will introduce 'Crockett' and 'Tubbs' shoes, and Macy's has opened a Miami Vice section in its young men's department."[22] Don Johnson wannabes could even purchase the Stubble Device, an electric razor that enabled men to maintain just the right amount of facial hair to resemble their idol. *Miami Vice* sparked demand for more than just unstructured blazers and pastel T-shirts: Crockett and Tubbs drove the kind of cars that most cops only dream of, including Lamborghinis, Maseratis, BMWs. There was a replica Ferrari, until the automaker filed a suit to stop it—at which point Enzo Ferrari himself donated two brand-new 1986 Testarossas as replacements.

These two shows, *Dallas* and *Miami Vice*, marked the beginning of an era in which entertainment and retail finally fused into one. Having all the "right" things, consumers were told, required a steady flow of purchases. Those purchases were increasingly upscale and aspirational, and tradition rapidly gave way to trendiness.

CONSUMERISM COMES HOME

There is something permanent, and something extremely profound, in owning a home.

—Nevada Governor Kenny Guinn, 2005

Home ownership cannot be considered essential to consumerism. Even as hyperconsumption approached its peak around the year 2000, not quite two-thirds of U.S. homes were owner-occupied (65 percent), below the rates for Italy (78 percent), the United Kingdom (69 percent), and Canada (67 percent).[23] And yet the importance of owning one's home has been endlessly trumpeted, to the point at which it has formed, for many, a core ideological belief: Buying a house confirms a person as a steady and sober contributor to society rather than an underachiever, peripatetic leech, or shiftless soul. This attitude goes back many decades; in his memoirs, Herbert Hoover wrote that "a primary right of every American family is the right to build a new house of its heart's desire at least once. Moreover, there is the instinct to own one's own house with one's own arrangement of gadgets, rooms, and surroundings."[24] Under Hoover's leadership in the 1920s, the U.S. Department of Commerce churned out an array of public relations materials selling the idea of home ownership, among them a leaflet entitled "Own Your Own Home" and a film, *Home Sweet Home*. As historian Richard Robbins points out, these materials advocated "single-dwelling homes over multiunit dwellings and suburban over urban housing."[25] They also recommended separate bedrooms for each child, adding that it was "undesirable for two children to occupy the same bed—whatever their age."[26] The tendency of all these recommendations was toward freestanding homes for every family and for ever-bigger dwellings.

In Frank Capra's classic 1946 film, *It's a Wonderful Life*, hero George Bailey is the mainstay of a Building and Loan Association that helps the working poor buy homes of their own rather than cough up high rents to slum landlords. By that time, home ownership had become less about brick and mortar than about thrilling dreams of pride and independence. With the return of GIs from the war and a burgeoning middle class, the suburbs emerged as a centerpiece of the American Dream. Of the 13 million U.S. homes built in the 1950s, 85 percent were located in soon-to-be-sprawling suburbs.[27] William Levitt, developer of Levittown, the mammoth planned community on New York's Long Island, boasted that his company churned out a home every sixteen minutes of an eight-hour day between 1947 and 1951. These houses sold for as little as $7,000. What's more, for busy modern couples, the purchase process could be completed in just three minutes.

For the remainder of the century, the U.S. government continued to promote home ownership through mortgage lenders such as Freddie Mac, Fannie Mae, and the Federal Home Loan Banks as well as through a tax policy, still in effect, that allows a deduction for mortgage interest payments on a primary residence.[28] Similarly, in the United Kingdom, home ownership was a core tenet of Margaret Thatcher's political philosophy in the 1980s. She spoke passionately of a property-owning democracy, believing that citizens would take better care of houses if they owned them. She helped bring about "right to buy" legislation, whereby tenants in social housing were offered a statutory ability to purchase at a significant discount. Tenants who had lived at an address for up to three years earned a 33 percent discount on the market value of the home, while those in residence for twenty or more years qualified for a discount of half.[29] As in the United States, home ownership was expounded as a crucial key to prosperity and national stability.

More than Just a Place to Hang One's Hat

> A house is just a pile of stuff with a cover on it...a place to keep your stuff while you go out and get...more stuff! Sometimes you gotta move, gotta get a bigger house. Why? No room for your stuff anymore.
>
> —George Carlin, 1981

American satirist George Carlin's jaundiced view of *home* as a repository for "stuff" rings painfully true for many of us today. As one index of American "overownership," we can point to the current boom in self-storage facilities. There are about 58,000 of these worldwide—of which 52,000 are in the United States, ground zero for consumerism. Americans own so much stuff nowadays, they apparently need an extra *2.35 billion square feet of space* outside the home to keep it in. The Self-Storage Association reports that one in ten U.S. households now rents a self-storage unit, an increase of 75 percent since 1995. This despite the fact that the size of the average U.S. house has more than doubled since the 1950s and now stands at around 2,300 square feet, up from 1,660 as recently as 1973.[30] One begins to see how extraordinarily much we have accumulated.

Home is, of course, about much more than the storage of things. It is also about the careful placement and showcasing of newly purchased stuff—the endless quest to fashion interior settings that are continually updated and upgraded to meet our changing desires. As such, the home forms a central arena for the acting out of consumerism. Homes of the past were equipped with essentials, from chairs, rugs, and beds to oven, cooking utensils, and crockery; but today these have been joined by a massive list of new "can't-live-without-its": washing machine and tumble dryer (preferably front-loading), dishwasher, microwave oven, mixer, toaster oven, juicer, food processor, and coffee/espresso machine; not to mention widescreen TV, TiVo, home cinema, music system, Wii or other gaming consoles, desktop and laptop computers—and perhaps a security system to keep all these goodies from escaping the coop. These new "needs," many of them completely unknown to our parents or grandparents, suck us into a mad whirlwind of buying.

Then there is the social and communal element to consider: Our homes are not just for us but for those we invite over; they communicate our prosperity, our fitness as members of society, our dreams and heartfelt desires. Yes, the sofa may be comfortable, the refrigerator may hold plenty of food and keep it at the right temperature, the cutlery may handle well and stand up to the dishwasher—and yet nagging questions remain: Do all the elements fit together to form an intelligent and coherent style? Does that chair left over from grad school days communicate "retro chic" or merely poverty? What will the neighbors think when they come over for drinks?

House-proud is a term that has been around for generations. Venerable magazines such as *Better Homes and Gardens* (launched 1922) have long offered valuable advice to owners on how to achieve a seductive style. Early TV shows such as *I Love Lucy* (1951–1960), *Father Knows Best* (1954–1960), and *The Dick Van Dyke Show* (1961–1966) were notable for their domestic interiors, which were always perfectly maintained and filled with the latest products, artfully arranged. (The same holds true today on such shows as *Desperate*

Housewives.) TV producers knew that a shabby interior would immediately give viewers a jolt—such was the effect of the boorish Archie Bunker's battered easy chair on *All in the Family* (1971–1979).

Putting together a stylish home—up to the standards of the illusionary ones in TV Land—can be enormously expensive, and with so many choices now available, the most dedicated shopper may be pushed almost to the brink of madness. Nor (to manufacturers' delight) can a home ever be considered *truly finished*. In a phenomenon known as the Diderot Effect, a single, irresistible luxury purchase—a table, a cabinet, a new rug—has the potential to set off a chain reaction of new purchases to complement it. (The phenomenon is named for eighteenth-century French philosopher Denis Diderot, whose fancy new dressing gown inspired a runaway spending spree as he sought to live up to its high standard.) Once the new furnishings are in place, the room will need to be redone—with fresh paint or wallpaper and perhaps new flooring—to do justice to all it now contains. And now that the room is looking lovely—well, the rest of the house seems shabby by comparison. Better find the car keys, honey, we're off to the mall again.

The constant pressure to upgrade everything has helped fuel the current mania for big homes. In order to absorb larger appliances and more capacious cabinets and countertops, the size of the average American kitchen has doubled to nearly 300 square feet since the 1950s—even as there are fewer mouths to feed in the home now and prepackaged meals that take a fraction of the time (and space) to prepare. The same is true of bedrooms, which have expanded to an average of twelve by twelve feet, up from nine by ten just thirty years ago.[31] It is not just our appetite for stuff that is to blame; as we increasingly retreat from the public arena and sequester ourselves in the home, where 2.6 televisions await, we demand more comfort and spaciousness. Adding to the pressure for More is the portrayal of superaffluence we see on lifestyle shows such as *Cribs*, *The Real Housewives of Orange County*, and *My Super Sweet Sixteen*. Keeping up with the Joneses was a whole lot easier when the competition was limited to one's own block; now that Beverly Hills and the Hamptons have been brought into the mix, it is not just the Joneses against whom we measure our progress but also the Hiltons, Kardashians, and Trumps.

When those able to do so "trade up" to a larger home and more extravagant lifestyle, their peers feel pressure to follow suit—because the feeling of "having enough" is powerfully shaped by what we see happening to those around us. Trading up leads to a burst of consumption all around as a domino effect sets in: Not only is there more space that needs to be filled (and heated and cooled), there are also new spaces that beg to be outfitted with the sorts of equipment that "professionalizes" the home, including high-end apparatus for the in-home spa, gym, and media and game rooms. There is no end to the upward spiral, especially when second and third homes are added in—the number of U. S. vacation homes increased 25 percent between 1989 and 2004, to 5.1 million.[32] All this home-focused consumerism has come at a huge financial cost: The percentage of total consumer expenditures on housing-related matters in the United States increased from 24.8 percent of annual income in 1950 to 32.6 percent in 1999. Within this figure, actual physical shelter (mortgage or rent) accounted for 19 percent of income in 1999 compared with just 10.2 percent back in 1950.[33]

Few other countries have fully embraced the Uncle Sam-style McMansion. In most of Europe—where strict zoning, anti-sprawl laws, dependence on public transport, and population pressures produce high densities—new homes are tending somewhat bigger, but the averages are still way behind America's gargantuan 2,300 square feet. In France, the average new house has about 1,216 square feet of floor space, while modern homes in Spain are about 1,044 square feet. In Britain, new houses are even smaller, just 818 square feet.[34] But whatever the size of the western home, consumerism is likely to have engulfed it of late. This was strikingly illustrated in a BBC TV program, *Electric Dreams*, in which an ordinary British family was subjected to a strange kind of time travel. As the producers explained:

> In a unique experiment they were stripped of all their modern tech and their own home was taken back in time so that they could live with the technology of earlier decades. The family lived a year per day starting in 1970 right up to the year 2000. The experiment was designed to show just how much technology has changed the British home and the British family. How would a modern family cope with one black and white television set, one shared dial telephone in the hallway and no central heating in 1970?[35]

The striking lesson was how much more "stuff" accumulated around this family as the show went on: As the "years" quickly passed, they were bombarded with a microwave oven, videocassette recorder, game consoles, satellite TV, mobile phones, digital cameras, personal digital assistants, MP3 players, and much else (not to mention a mound of confusing instruction manuals). It was starkly emblematic of the explosion in consumer goods that has reshaped our lives.

One other aspect of the home-ownership trend as it relates to consumerism: Homes have increasingly provided a means of making money and (in an eternal feedback loop) of funding increased consumption. This pattern worked so long as home prices trended sharply upward. And they did: Starting with a base price of "100" in the first quarter of 1987, the *Economist*'s U.K. house price index showed an exponential rise to 180 in 1998, then to more than 450 in mid-2007. In the United States, Federal Housing Finance Agency figures showed a more gradual but still steady increase, peaking at 270 in 2007. At the same time, Australia peaked at more than 500 and Spain topped 700.[36] Growing populations everywhere demanded better and better homes, and so prices went up. Most consumers (and financial firms) assumed this trend was permanent, making it feasible for them to "invest" in properties well beyond their means and reap sizable profits at time of sale—a strategy that led to a boom in so-called house flipping. But there were even easier ways to wring cash from one's home: Some savvy folks sold at a profit, moved to a lower-cost area, then spent the difference; some remortgaged their homes for higher amounts, thereby releasing equity to spend as they saw fit; and others simply took out loans against their homes. In all these ways, properties served as a kind of personal automated teller machine, with many homeowners able to withdraw equity (typically because of increased value on paper) from the property at will, whether to finance home improvements or more general consumption. This giddy pattern of borrowing and spending continued until 2007–8, when real estate prices collapsed and the party abruptly ended. As 2009 drew to a close, nearly a quarter of U.S. homeowners—about 10.7 million households—were "underwater," owing more on their mortgages than their properties were worth.[37]

I BUY THEREFORE I AM

I can get no remedy against this consumption of the purse. Borrowing only lingers and lingers it out, but the disease is incurable.

—Falstaff, in Shakespeare's *Henry IV, Part II*

Over recent decades, philosophers, psychologists, and thinkers of all stripes have struggled to understand consumerism and its myriad implications. Clearly the practice has evolved—or perhaps devolved— into something far more than a purely functional activity. This much was obvious in 1975 when California ad executive Gary Dahl came up with what he thought was a joke: selling worthless little stones off the beach as Pet Rocks for $3.95, each packaged in a straw-filled cardboard box along with a "training manual." Little did he realize that he would become a multimillionaire in six months from what *Time* magazine called "1% product and 99% marketing genius."[38] Such fad toys have since become commonplace in our consumer-mad world: Cabbage Patch Kids, Tickle Me Elmo, or, most recently, Zhu Zhu Pets; and don't forget the Beanie Baby that sold, in the midst of hysteria in 1999, for $3,000 on eBay.

Hyperconsumption often seems wacky, even in its everyday varieties. Consider the suburban mom driving to soccer practice in her 2009 Cadillac Escalade: She has spent as much as $80,000 on a car her children have already christened many times over with Juicy Juice. More rationally, she could have bought a perfectly decent set of wheels for a quarter the price and socked the savings into a college fund or other investment account. How can such a decision be explained? To ethicist David Loy, it is not about rational thinking at all. He views consumerism as nothing less than a form of religion that attempts to fill a fundamental human need; it offers us meaning and props up our shaky sense of self.[39] Famed director and all-around existential mess Woody Allen describes consumption as an antidepressant, an activity that helps him get through the day:

> I like to buy things for the sake of buying them....When I get up in the morning and I'm depressed, it's hard to cope with things....Nothing to look forward to. I can always go down and walk down the street and BUY something. You go into a nice warm store and there's like four hundred record albums with covers, or gadgets—scissors and electric toothbrushes and things—and you can take out money and buy it, and go home and unwrap it. And just that—the mere act of doing that—is so pleasing, sometimes, and so relaxing, that it's a pleasure.[40]

In *Consumer Behaviour*, Ray Wright similarly likens the constant buying of ever-more-expensive products and services to the fundamental human quest for meaning.[41] Consumerism becomes a form of compensatory behavior, a compulsive and unhealthy way of making up for something that is wrong or missing in one's life. Yet the psychological effects of consumption are fleeting; no sooner is the object brought home and ensconced in the closet than we crave the fix of something else gift-wrapped. Psychologists who work with shopaholics routinely advise them to "fill the void" in their lives.

As many shoppers have discovered, buying things in order to feel better often produces the opposite effect. We step onto a fearsome treadmill that propels us toward more purchases, more debt, more dissatisfaction as today's hot items are soon rendered obsolete by the next model, the improved version, the upgrade. Maintaining a consumerist lifestyle magnifies the strain of everyday living—we must work harder to bring in more income, choose careers that pay well but do not necessarily satisfy. Heaven forbid there should come a setback or moment of reappraisal. "Many of my friends hate their jobs," a banking executive in Delaware told us confidentially, "but they can't afford to make a change. They are terrified of losing their lifestyle." They are stuck on that treadmill, the angle of which has gotten much steeper lately; as Merrill Lynch vice president Ajay Gupta says, for those chasing the American Dream, "the new $1 million is $5 million. Everything costs more—gas, housing, education, health care, food—everything. A million dollars used to be the magic number."[42] But for soccer moms driving Escalades, such riches do not go very far anymore.

As irrational as hyperconsumerism sometimes appears, Americans embraced it wholeheartedly and, until recently, spent like there was no tomorrow. Savings rates dwindled to less than nothing. As of August 2009, this nation of consumers had a collective credit card debt of $899.4 billion.[43]

Many observers felt that consumers were drowning in overconsumption, citing the fact that the average American consumes fifty-three times more goods and services than the average person in China and that a child born in the United States will, in the course of a lifetime, create thirteen times more environmental damage than one born in Brazil.[44]

THE SPIRAL OF OVERCONSUMPTION

Upper-East-Side lady on cell: "I know, but I was at a funeral all day…Yeah, it was sad, but I really didn't know him at all.…The saddest thing was seeing his daughters upset. They're the same ages as—*Wow!* This shirt is only $19!! You can't even buy a freaking Frappuccino for $19! I'm getting it in blue."

—Overheard at Banana Republic, 86th &
Third, New York City[45]

Over the years, some dissenters from the hyperconsumptive cult have preached "Less Is More," but that catchphrase never really got off the ground, except as a design principle relevant to coffee tables and drapes. *More Is More* is more like it—that is what we all seem to want.

Rarefied foodies may go in for nouvelle cuisine with its miniaturized offerings, but for the rest of us, it is Burger King Triple Whoppers with cheese: maximum size, minimum cost. When we are out shopping, we may *need* only the one item for $3.99, but who can pass up another one at 50 percent off, or three for the price of two? As the saying goes, "A bargain is something you can't use at a price you can't resist." Marketers are exploiting this basic human greed. And they delight in our obsessive quest for size, the way we have clamored for ever-larger SUVs, for example. The pioneering 1969 Chevy Blazer weighed 2,947 pounds; the 2010 Chevy Suburban Three-Quarter-Ton weighs 6,327—the kind of McMansion on wheels that suddenly seemed less appealing when gas prices shot up and markets slid down.[46]

In the electronics category, consumerism has increasingly taken cues from the aptly named Moore's Law, coined by Intel cofounder Gordon Moore. In its original formulation, the law said that the number of transistors on a computer chip doubles every couple of years; later this morphed into the observation that data density doubles every eighteen months. Today's gluttonous tech consumers understand it to mean that the products they crave will be twice as nifty next year and cost half as much.

No matter what the category—technology, food, automotive, retail—consumers have become spoiled and jaded, incapable of enjoying what they currently have because they are so busy looking ahead to what is next, the coming instant gratification, the next dazzler in the innovation pipeline. During the heady reign of hyperconsumption, the smart money was consistently bet on MORE and BIGGER as frenetic shoppers heaped up purchase after purchase to erect their monument to Mammon ever higher. But deep underground, seismic shifts were about to take place, and that monstrous edifice was doomed to come tumbling down.

Chapter 3

CONSUMERISM HITS THE WALL

You can't have everything...where would you put it?

—Comedian Steven Wright

Ah, the heady rush of High-Octane Consumerism. Did most of us want it to last forever? Absolutely!

For anyone with disposable income, buying what we wanted, when we wanted it, had become part of the fabric of everyday life—a habit frenetically stoked by marketers and the media and enthusiastically endorsed by governments and the culture at large. Had crucial circumstances not changed dramatically in 2007–9, hard-charging consumerism might have galloped on unabated. But change they did, in a seismic way, and that has forced us to pause and reflect, to slice up our credit cards and pare down our shopping lists. And it is not just individuals who are having second thoughts about the untethered consumer spending of recent years; fretful second-guessing is also in evidence at the highest levels of government, from Washington to London, Berlin to Tokyo.

In this chapter we examine the external factors that have thrown roadblocks into the path of carefree consumerism. But first, a quick look back at the past few years, when the High-Octane Consumerism of the 1980s and 1990s escalated into the gluttonous Age of More.

ENJOY THE RIDE: THE LAST FLING OF MORE MONEY

Until the downturn, "More Is More" had taken hold as the central paradigm of our lives as consumers. The phrase grew to be deeply embedded within our thinking about what is right and desirable. Governments and corporate leaders were under strict orders to continually deliver growth, which is just another word for More. That doom-laden term *recession* is all about "negative growth"—a euphemism for what some might consider the saddest word in the English language: *Less.*

As More took hold, countries around the globe joined the party. We watched in amazement as China and India grew at breakneck speed. China's middle class, which had stood at 15 percent of its population in 1999, swelled to 19 percent in 2003. (If the economy remains healthy, the Chinese Academy of Social Science projects that, by 2020, 40 percent of the population will be "middle class."[1]) Meanwhile, after suffering a glacial 1.25 percent annual growth rate of gross domestic product (GDP) per capita from 1950 to 1980, India exploded: By 2007, its GDP was surging 7.5 percent annually, a rate that would lead to a doubling in a decade. In no time, this once-backward market had surpassed Japan as the third-largest economy on the planet.[2] Advocates of More were profoundly impressed, and they wondered what was next. Few seemed to recall—and even fewer heeded—the warning of Mahatma Gandhi decades ago: "God forbid that India should ever take to industrialism after the manner of the West . . . If [our nation] took to similar economic exploitation, it would strip the world bare like locusts."[3]

In the hottest economies, everybody expected there to be More of More. Investment analysts grilled corporate chief executive officers (CEOs) every three months, demanding impressive growth quarter on quarter, year on year. Those CEOs who failed to deliver More were out, resulting in an average CEO tenure in North America of just 6.8 years by 2007.[4] Hungry consumers grew accustomed to a bountiful cascade of revolutionary technologies, fast-changing fashions, and shiny trifles, a deluge that filled store shelves to the bursting point with new products every month. Outputs were astonishing, even as costs fell—so low in some cases that customers wondered how anyone could stay in business with such prices: T-shirts for a dollar? A drive-through meal for a buck fifty?

Expect More formed the orthodoxy of the era, as famously summarized by Alan Greenspan, chairman of the Federal Reserve Board, when he gently cautioned us about the dangers of "irrational exuberance."[5] That was in 1996—and things were shaping up to get a whole lot more exuberant, rationality be damned. The big milestone for the Dow Industrial Average that year was hitting 6,000, which had taken one hundred years to achieve. Only one decade later, the Dow was double that. As technology fever spread, so did talk of a

New Economy in which the old rules no longer applied. Intoxicated with that heady liqueur called More, pinstriped analysts cast caution aside and predicted a Dow at 36,000, 40,000, or even 100,000—why, anything was possible![6]

As More gathered momentum, old prohibitions against greed and hyperconsumerism fell away. Way back in 1987, many were shocked when Michael Douglas's character, Gordon Gekko, praised greed in the movie *Wall Street:*

> The point is, ladies and gentleman, that greed—for lack of a better word—is good. Greed is right. Greed works. Greed clarifies, cuts through, and captures the essence of the evolutionary spirit. Greed, in all of its forms—greed for life, for money, for love, knowledge—has marked the upward surge of mankind. And greed—you mark my words—will not only save Teldar Paper, but that other malfunctioning corporation called the USA.[7]

But what had seemed outrageously satirical in 1987—a Hollywood villain's droolingly diabolical expression of lust for power and riches—quickly came to be accepted as right, normal, indeed quite ordinary. Shiny-shoed Gekkos gave way to dot-com millionaires and even billionaires, whiz kids in ratty jeans and sweatshirts who built cool business ideas fast and sold them for megabucks, making the obscure term "IPO" a household word. A 1999 *Wired* magazine story cheered on "Gen Equity. Descend into the valley of riches. Feast on the nourishment of hope. Start up a tech company and sell it."[8] Silicon Valley landlords began demanding an equity stake as a condition of rental. "Bling" became the trendy aesthetic of popular culture; monster SUVs roared down suburban lanes en route to the mall; and sales of luxury goods rose 9 percent a year with no sign of stopping.[9]

American values underwent a fundamental shift in that headstrong era, says *New York Times* columnist David Brooks. Virtually overnight, gambling went from sinful to sensational as an extraordinary forty-one out of fifty states approved it in the form of lotteries, including many in traditionally conservative and Bible-bound regions. On every level, what had been considered taboo now became commonplace. "Executives and hedge fund managers began bragging about compensation packages that would have been considered shameful a few decades before," Brooks points out. "Chain restaurants went into supersize mode, offering gigantic portions that would have been considered socially unacceptable to an earlier generation."[10]

"Nothing has defined the past decade more than the orgy of personal consumption," concludes William A. Galston of The

Brookings Institution. "From large flat-screen TVs and i-phones to furniture and foreign cars, Americans spent as though there were no tomorrow, until tomorrow came."[11] He notes that personal consumption, which had been remarkably stable in the three decades following World War II (averaging about 62 percent of U.S. GDP between 1951 and 1980), rose to 64.6 percent in the 1980s, 67.3 percent in the 1990s, and 69.8 percent between 2001 and 2008.[12] Similar growth was evident elsewhere: In the United Kingdom, for instance, consumer spending growth was 3.1 percent between 1992 and 2005, outpacing the average annual GDP growth rate of 2.8 percent.[13]

Aiding and abetting this spike in consumption was the widespread availability of credit cards and other noncash methods of payment, which have managed to reshape the old *pain-now-pleasure-later* model of purchasing into *pleasure-now-pain-later*. George Loewenstein, professor of economics and psychology at Carnegie Mellon University, explains that buyers have found ways to avoid the immediate pain of purchasing: "We developed this propensity to experience direct pain when we spend money. This explains why tightwads won't spend money even when they should. It also helps to explain why we overspend on credit cards, and why people prefer all-you-can-eat buffets instead of paying for each item they order. We like schemes that remove the immediate pain of paying."[14] Loewenstein argues that "the abstract nature of credit coupled with deferred payment may 'anaesthetize' consumers against the pain of paying."[15] High-end restaurants have long known this, having watched how customers spend more when the meal is going on a credit card. They also know that obscuring the facts of payment—say, by listing prices in fancy script without any currency symbol—makes choosing expensive food items more palatable.

CALGON, TAKE ME AWAY: THE END OF MORE

For a time, the juggernaut of consumerism seemed unstoppable. But an extraordinary combination of heavy factors, historic in their scope, managed to break its headlong rush.

The biggest causal agent by far has been the financial crisis—a meltdown that proved the chief culprit in what some have called the "Great Recession," just as bank failures touched off the Great Depression eighty years ago. But there are new factors at play too—ones of a strange, troubling sort unknown to people in the 1930s: concerns about climate change and a steadily degrading environment; the economic drag caused by soaring energy prices; the dangerous risks involved in too-easy credit; a massive excess in global production capacity; and (for some consumers across the globe) a gathering sense of unease at the sheer abundance of "stuff" and what it just might be doing to our souls.

The story of the current recession has been told endlessly, its causes minutely examined. Billions of bytes have been devoted to analyzing what went wrong, with billions more sure to follow. We will leave the bulk of that discussion to others, focusing here only on the structural factors behind the downturn that are sure to have a long-term bearing on what happens to consumerism in the future. Taken as a whole, these factors make clear that no matter how quickly the global economy recovers, no matter how soon the scars of the recession heal, we will not see the return of High-Octane Consumerism as it has existed over the past three decades. As economic theorist E. F. Schumacher once noted, "Infinite growth of material consumption in a finite world is an impossibility."[16]

The High Price of Cheap Labor

Thanks to cheap labor in developing countries, consumers in more mature markets had the opportunity to buy a lot of stuff for relatively little money—to indulge in a seemingly endless spending spree on consumer goods. Brands and corporations in developed markets could outsource manufacturing to cheap-labor countries, then sell the goods back to developed markets. For a while, everybody benefited. Developing economies built up fast by exporting goods, businesses reaped a profit, consumers bought like crazy, and the developed-world governments kept inflation in check.

But like Banquo's ghost crashing the party, there was a lurking problem: worsening trade imbalances. In 1989, the U.S. trade deficit with China was $6.2 billion; five years later, it had exploded to $29.5 billion, and in 1999, it stood at $68.7 billion. Today, that figure seems almost quaint. The deficit has continued growing every year, finally hitting a staggering $268 billion in 2008.[17] The picture has been much the same for the European Union 27; their deficit with China went from €49 billion in 2000 to €169 billion eight years later.[18] The wrinkle is that *cheap* labor doesn't mean *free* labor—despite the low costs, we have still been spending a fortune. The trade imbalances have become too big, too persistent. They are disastrously unsustainable, and they have helped end all the fun.

What's in *Your* Wallet?

Cheap money on a macro level flowed from the growing trade surpluses and savings of net exporter countries, such as China. These

markets used their trade earnings to buy government bonds, especially U.S. treasuries. This enabled the U.S. government to finance
its budget deficit with dollars owned by China rather than borrowing
from Americans. Doing this made it possible to keep interest rates
absurdly low.

Martin Wolf of the *Financial Times* has analyzed cheap money
in his book *Fixing Global Finance*. He explains that these funds
allowed banks to expand their deposits and loans to customers to an
extraordinary degree. But this did not result in higher investment in
productive capacity. Rather, corporations channeled their cash flow
away from fixed investments and into buybacks of company stock and
cash disbursed to shareholders. All in all, carefree Americans were
borrowing not to invest in new machines or other sources of future
productivity but instead to speculate on houses or gamble on mergers
and acquisitions. The resulting growth in paper wealth helped trigger
the consumption boom—but *no new resources were being created with
which to pay back either domestic or foreign borrowing.* At the end of that
high-speed-consumption racetrack lay...a big brick wall.[19]

On the street level, the cheap-money lending spree imploded
when overstretched subprime borrowers in the United States started
defaulting on their mortgages. Clobbered by massive losses, finance
houses trading mortgage-based securities had a simple solution: They
stopped lending. As home prices stalled and then began to free fall,
banks hunkered down. Expansion quickly turned to contraction.
Instead of More and More money in circulation, all of a sudden there
was Less.

Presidential candidate Barack Obama summed up the situation in
a gloomy interview with *Time* magazine's Joe Klein in October 2008:
"Basically, we turbo-charged this economy based on cheap credit.
Whatever else we think is going to happen over the next certainly
five years, one thing we know, the days of easy credit are going to
be over because there is just too much deleveraging taking place, too
much debt...at the government level, corporate level, and consumer
level."[20]

There Are Some Things Money Can't Buy;
For Everything Else, There's MasterCard

With cheap money flowing like a mighty river, consumer purchasing power underwrote the giddy buying and spending of recent
decades. But that purchasing power was increasingly based on credit
and borrowing, not on the growth of real disposable income. Major
employers, including big corporations, have undergone successive

rounds of downsizing, focusing on core competencies, restructuring, and other initiatives intended to increase productivity, profits, and shareholder value. The result is both lost jobs and restricted wages. In the United States, real weekly wages declined from an average of $302.52 in 1964 (in 1982 constant dollars) to $277.57 in 2004.[21] Europe also has seen a widespread loss of buying power as wages have remained stagnant while inflation has soared. "The problem," Spanish economist Julian Cubero told the *New York Times*, "is that if your salary rises more slowly than the cost of products you buy on a daily basis, you feel poorer every day."[22]

The dismal result has been the stagnation of disposable income. And what little lucre remains after living expenses are covered, debt rapidly swallows up. By 2006–7, household debt had risen to more than 131 percent of disposable income in the United States, and families spent 14.3 percent of that income just to service their debt.[23]

Consumers in developed countries, and in the United States in particular, could continue their hyperconsumption only so long as they had access to credit. With the economic crisis, consumer purchasing power got walloped on several fronts: As "honeymoon" periods on mortgages came to an end, payments due each month increased sharply. In a pitiable situation creating steady fodder for nightly newscasts, millions of desperate homeowners have been hit with foreclosures, losing virtually everything, while others struggle to make payments. Entire communities have been turned into ghost towns. Meanwhile, as real estate prices have fallen, home-equity credit lines are no longer available to most people. Banks and financial institutions have called in loans, tightened lending criteria, and hiked charges. Late fees for credit cards have gone way up (a trend that began well before the recession): Between 1995 and 2005, they increased more than 160 percent, from an average of $12.83 to $33.64.[24] All this has taken a big bite out of consumption.

And then, of course, there is the rampant unemployment that has accompanied the downturn. People who have lost their jobs are in no position to go on spending sprees; those still at their desks are fearful and hold ever more tightly to their purse strings. In the United States, unemployment rose from a moderate 4.9 percent in late 2007 to 10 percent just two years later, with 7.5 million people out of work.[25] In the United Kingdom, 2.49 million were unemployed (7.9 percent) by October 2009, a quarter of whom had been jobless for more than a year.[26] As of July 2009, unemployment stood at 7.7 percent in Germany and 9.8 percent in France.[27] In short, the rug has been pulled out from under consumer purchasing power in developed countries. There is no more easy money—no more low-interest, no-questions-asked credit of the kind that made supersized consumerism possible. Gone, too, is the quarter-on-quarter profit growth that flowed from all that binge buying.

As shopping sprees became a thing of the past, Paying Off Debt came to be the new focus of millions of chastened consumers. For eleven straight months through October 2009, Americans successfully reduced their credit card debt. And revolving credit card debt—the self-inflicted wound of not paying off balances in full—was dropping by an annual rate of 13.1 percent.[28] Americans had started doing the unthinkable: *actually saving money*. In September 2009, they stashed away more than 3 percent of their disposable personal incomes.[29] Compare that with four years earlier, when the rate was negative 0.5 percent, the lowest since Franklin D. Roosevelt entered the White House.[30]

It is not just consumers who have been drowning in debt. Many states and municipalities have joined them in teetering on the brink. For example, the State of California—the world's eighth-largest economy—is confronting a massive budget deficit of $20.7 billion through June 2011.[31] Among other agonizing choices, the state's controller was reduced to printing IOUs in lieu of cash to pay taxpayers, vendors, and local governments in mid-2009. Meanwhile, the U.S. federal government continues to serve as the poster child for fiscal irresponsibility. Already running a huge budget deficit even before the economic crisis, it now faces its largest deficit ever: $1.42 trillion, after all those stimulus measures and bailouts.[32]

In hindsight, it appears inevitable that High-Octane Consumerism would eventually run out of gas. Many factors conspired to kill it, including several additional ones we will examine in a moment. But the most obvious and precipitate cause was, of course, the Great Recession. Even if it does not live up to the initial media hype ("Global Economic Shock Worse than Great Depression"—*Huffington Post*, April 2009), it has proven extremely serious and historic.[33]And even if consumers wanted to resume their former ways of mindless hyperconsumption, they could not anymore—there simply is not enough cash and credit available.

Another Boom-Snuffer: High Energy Prices

Modern consumerism has long been dependent on abundant supplies of cheap oil. You have got to have petroleum for plastics, food production, logistics, travel of every sort. It is an essential ingredient in the making of acrylics, adhesives, alcohol, ammonia, anesthetics, antifreeze, antiseptics, artificial limbs, ashtrays, asphalt, aspirin, and awnings—just to start the list. Oil touches everything, so increases in oil and energy prices inexorably push up production and distribution costs, leaving less money available for consumption.

Anyone over forty can recall the paralyzing oil crisis of the 1970s, when the Organization of Petroleum Exporting Countries (OPEC) imposed an embargo on countries supporting Israel. As noted in chapter 2, the price of oil per barrel doubled, then quadrupled.[34] At decade's end, Iran's Islamic Revolution further disrupted oil supplies, and prices rose again.[35] In prices adjusted to 2008 U.S. dollars, domestic crude oil shot up from an annual average of $18.84 per barrel in 1970 to $98.07 in 1980.[36] Subsequently, oil prices zigzagged down to a low of $15.77 in 1998 before rising steadily, averaging $91.35 in 2008. In June of that year, they spiked to a new high, averaging $122.64—a frightening demonstration of what was possible.[37] In some counties in California, gas station signs read $4.79 a gallon, and soccer moms driving minivans spent almost $100 filling up the tank.[38] This was enough to sideswipe sales of thirsty SUVs, a trend that continued even after prices subsequently fell.

Today's high oil prices do not stem so much from geopolitics, as they did in the 1970s, but rather from our bottomless, guzzling demand. And today this demand is far more widespread than in the past. In 2007, ahead of the price spike, energy specialist Jad Mouawad wrote: "Unlike past oil shocks, which were caused by sudden interruptions in exports from the Middle East, this time prices have been rising steadily as demand for gasoline grows in developed countries, as hundreds of millions of Chinese and Indians climb out of poverty and as other developing economies grow at a sizzling pace."[39]

Also contributing to high prices is the growing perception that the production of oil has peaked, meaning it cannot ever get any bigger. According to the Association for the Study of Peak Oil and Gas, production of conventional oil reached an all-time high in 2005; if all other forms of fossil fuel are included—heavy oil, deep-water, polar and natural gas liquids, plus oil and gas—then production peaked in 2008.[40] Such reports give economists deep pause. In the community at large, they have spawned a fanatical fringe movement that calls itself the Peakers. "We will very soon be facing a world where chaos reigns supreme," one disciple warns. "A world of war, famine and death on a scale unknown in recorded human history [as a] consequence of the world's oil taps running dry." Better dig a bunker: "We're not talking about the distant future here, folks; we're talking about the very near future."[41] Although such doomsday scenarios are overblown, they speak to a growing recognition that the planet is being scalped of precious resources at a rate that threatens life as we know it. And that fact has caused a broad spectrum of society to sit up and take notice.

IT'S NOT NICE TO FOOL (WITH) MOTHER NATURE

Nature provides a free lunch, but only if we control our appetites.

—William Ruckelshaus, first director of the U.S. Environmental Protection Agency

For decades, energy from cheap fossil fuel made it possible to extract natural resources at prodigious rates, and in vast quantities: fish, timber, water, minerals, metals, and more. The expectation was that such vast stores would be forever available to us—and that might have been the case in the absence of an exploding global population and hyperconsumerism. Now we see shortages on all sides and are grimly facing what journalist Richard Heinberg memorably has called "Peak Everything."

"Runaway growth in consumption in the past fifty years is putting strains on the environment never before seen," warned the United Nations' *Human Development Report 1998* in the midst of the boom. Another report from that year declared that, from 1970 to 1995, the denizens of Planet Earth had exhausted *more than 30 percent of all resources that sustain life*. During that period, the world's forests declined 10 percent (each year by an area the size of England and Wales); marine ecosystems, 30 percent; freshwater ecosystems, 50 percent.[42] These shocking statistics—and others that have followed over the past decade—have woken people up, and environmental consciousness is now at an all-time high. An astonishing amount of media attention was recently devoted to the decline of just one species, the humble honeybee, the population of which fell 70 percent in 2006–7 alone—not a good thing, especially when one considers that bees pollinate a lot of the plants that become our food. All those empty beehives seemed to warn us of the accumulating damage we are doing to the planet. Are our pesticides to blame? Or genetically modified crops? What species will be next in suffering a "collapse"—perhaps us? No one can say for sure, and the uncertainty in and of itself is scary.[43]

Frightening, too, has been the avalanche of reports about climate change, starting with Al Gore's film, *An Inconvenient Truth*, in 2006 and multiplying ever since. Now barely a day goes by that we do not hear about the subject. One result of all this apocalyptic talk has been a genuine shift in consumer attitudes; many of us have embraced Going Green in a big way and, to one extent or another, have actually changed our behaviors. *National Geographic*'s 2009 Greendex survey examined consumer attitudes in fourteen countries across a two-year period. It found steady movement toward eco-friendlier habits, even (or perhaps especially) in a time of recession. In eleven of the countries, consumers are increasingly monitoring their thermostats to save energy. In nine countries, they are doing more laundry using cold water only; in seven, they have cut back on their consumption of bottled water. The study also showed an uptick in buying secondhand household items and in repairing things that were broken rather than buying new.[44]

With consumers changing their ways, businesses have responded. As we showed in our book *Good for Business: The Rise of the Conscious Corporation*, environmental concerns and the notion of sustainability are a hot topic in today's boardrooms. Everything has changed, and individuals and corporations alike are groping for the path ahead, a path that will lead us through a harsh new global landscape that promises to be—to quote the title of Thomas L. Friedman's 2008 best seller—*Hot, Flat, and Crowded*.

The circumstances that made consumerism possible in the developed world—and allowed it to ramp up every year—have now changed fundamentally. For many people, the familiar consumerist ways of thinking and living will no longer be possible—they no longer have the wealth or the credit. But for many others, the change is more conscious and directed: They have taken a cold, hard look at hyperconsumerism, and they want out. It is not so much that the recession *forced* them into a new pattern of living; instead, it provided an opportunity to stop, stand back, and ask questions. Times of turmoil and uncertainty always do that, but seldom on so vast a scale as we have witnessed since 2008.

The remainder of this book will explore these philosophical and practical responses to consumerism. Laid out in the chapters that follow are what we call the Four Paradigms of the new approach to consumption. The first paradigm, *Embracing Substance*, builds on the premise that hyperconsumerism has failed to satisfy, leaving us unhappy and feeling alienated from each other. In response, more and more people are seeking real and authentic experiences. They want to get involved with causes larger than themselves. Rapid changes in the food and travel sectors—in particular, a trend toward greater thoughtfulness and slowing down—offer a barometer of this heightened desire for substance.

The second paradigm is *Rightsizing*. The consumerist mantra "More Is Better" led to foolish habits that caused psychological harm. At last a historic reaction has set in. Hyperconsumers are now regarded as shopaholics in need of counseling and correction. A decluttering movement preaches that happiness lies in owning fewer things. Millions are embracing the culture of recycling and reusing, and frugality is chic.

A third paradigm is *Growing Up*. Recent decades saw adolescence prolonged, adulthood delayed. But today many people are reversing the trend, accepting personal responsibility and seeking to build individual competence. Increasingly they reject mindless consumption, instead embracing a more sensible and sustainable approach. Selfishness gives way to community and collaboration.

The fourth and final paradigm is *Seeking Purposeful Pleasure*. A hunger for instant gratification drove yesterday's excessive consumption. Now, burned-out consumers are seeking new sources of satisfaction and more meaningful connections with brands that share their values. For creative marketers who understand this trend, the new quest for purposeful pleasure opens up exciting opportunities.

As we explore all four paradigms, we will see how buyers are engaged in a creative search for a new way forward that docs not involve a return to the grotesque excesses of the recent past. Now that bottomless greed has been consigned to the dustbin of history, the path lies open to a more reasonable and balanced future.

PART II

THE FOUR PARADIGMS OF THE MINDFUL SHOPPER

Chapter 4

EMBRACING SUBSTANCE

There must be more to life than having everything.

—Maurice Sendak

Ever since marketing first got wise to psychology, consumerism has promised to make us feel happier, better, more fulfilled. Actress Bo Derek captured that spirit with her remark, "Whoever said money can't buy happiness simply didn't know where to go shopping."[1] But is money in fact a foolproof avenue to joyousness? "Study after study shows that money fails to buy happiness," the London *Times* recently warned. "Incomes have increased threefold in Britain since 1950 but contentment levels have barely shifted. European research indicates that lottery winners revert to their previous levels of happiness within a year of their windfall. One look at the permanently sullen face of the multi-millionairess Victoria Beckham appears to prove the point."[2]

From the 1980s through to 2007, consumption was the dominant game. Once Soviet communism collapsed and China developed its market economy, consumerism ruled as the last "ism" left standing. Certainly it kept us busy: We have been engrossed in an ongoing cycle of acquisition, endlessly trading up and seeking the next new thing—the ultimate solution until the next ultimate solution. And, for a while, the promises of consumerism—always implicit, sometimes explicit—were fulfilled. In exchange for plunking down cash for a product or service, we were rewarded with whatever golden glow we sought: social status, sex appeal, superiority, adventure, elation. All available for a low, low price! Yet increasingly, those delights have not been sufficient to keep us satisfied. They have proved both fickle and fleeting, leaving us feeling deflated and unhappy. Where can we turn now?

WHEN CONSUMPTION FAILS TO SATISFY: UNDERSTANDING THE NEW CONSUMER

In our work as global brand marketers, we spent much of the past decade tracking consumer trends and people's responses to shifting economic, social, and political realities. It is our job to understand why people are doing—and buying—certain things and how that is likely to change in the coming months and years. The most powerful current trend is a movement away from mindless consumption toward something more meaningful and sustainable. We touched on that in our book *Good for Business*, but with a focus on corporations and how they are responding to market pressures to be good and do good. Now our focus turns to the individual consumer. In 2009 we fielded The New Consumer, a survey of more than 5,700 adults in seven markets in both the developed and developing worlds: Brazil, China, France, Japan, the Netherlands, the United Kingdom, and the United States. We wanted to know to what extent this movement toward greater mindfulness truly had taken hold around the world. Here we focus primarily on the attitudes of the 1,500 respondents in the United States, although we also touch on other markets where distinctions seem meaningful. (See the appendix for multicountry results.)

Before delving into the survey findings, a few words on the respondent base: In all our studies at global communications company Euro RSCG Worldwide, we separate out from the mainstream a specific segment of leading-edge consumers we call *Prosumers*. We identify them by means of a proprietary battery of questions and have been tracking their attitudes and behaviors around the world since 2002. Who are Prosumers, and why do they matter? Simply put, they are the most influential consumers within any market. Empowered by new technologies and improved access to information, these highly knowledgeable and demanding buyers have tipped the scales of power away from manufacturers and retailers and toward themselves. Among the traits that set them apart:

- They embrace innovation and have a bottomless appetite for new challenges and experiences.
- They are early adopters of novel technologies and show a keen interest in gadgets and applications.

- They are "human media" who readily transport new attitudes, ideas, and behaviors.
- They recognize their value as consumers and expect their brand partners to do likewise through top-notch customer service, bountiful "extras," and ongoing access to information.
- They are marketing savvy, constantly plugged in to multiple media sources.
- They seek to maximize control over their lives through the smart use of information and communications.
- They are consulted by their peers for opinions and advice and go out of their way to engage others in consumer-focused conversations about products and retailers.

Prosumers typically make up 15 to 20 percent of any market. As marketers, we have made them an ongoing focus of study because, beyond their own economic impact, they powerfully influence the brand choices of others. We have found over the years that what Prosumers are doing today, mainstream consumers are likely to be doing six to eighteen months from now. As we share findings from the survey throughout this book, we will highlight Prosumer responses in order to illustrate the direction in which trends are headed. Where Prosumer scores are higher than those of mainstream consumers, it is all but certain that the bulk of consumers will soon be moving in that direction.

Owning More, Having Less: The Paradox of Modern Times

Even as buyers fill every inch of their personal space with more "stuff," they continue to feel empty inside—perhaps because the very act of consumption takes so much time and thought, leaving little room for personal relationships or activities that enlighten and inspire. Political theorist Benjamin R. Barber said as much in an interview with *U.S. News & World Report:*

> A culture that glorifies consumerism belittles other values, including all those activities that define nonmaterial life and give us our human character: play, prayer, art, love, recreation, creativity, friendship, and thought. The problem with consumerism is that it strives not just to be part of our lives—it should be that— but strives to be everything, to occupy all our time and space and

push out other things. In this sense, it is both homogenizing and totalizing.[3]

Findings from the survey highlight a culture that has grown rich in material goods yet poor in much else of significance. Most people in developed markets are satisfied neither with the state of their lives nor with the larger milieu. Two-thirds of Americans in our survey sample (and 73 percent of U.S. Prosumers) say society is moving in the wrong direction. Fifty-eight percent of the global sample agrees, including seven in ten respondents in France. A 2008 report on "social evils" released by the Joseph Rowtree Foundation in the United Kingdom confirms this sense of dissatisfaction. The researchers found that people are deeply concerned about the extent to which society has become greedy and selfish, at a cost to community ties. "Everything seems to be based around money and owning things," one respondent lamented. "The more you have, the more successful you are. There's nothing wrong with having enough, but there's pressure on people to go for more and more."[4]

New Consumer study respondents (particularly in the United States) believe that society suffers from excess ease and plenty. Three-quarters of Americans (and 84 percent of U.S. Prosumers) worry we have gotten "intellectually lazy." Global results are resounding: 60 percent believe society has become intellectually lazy; merely 13 percent disagree. That is a sweeping indictment. And it is not just our brains that have gone soft; it seems our bodies are turning to jelly too. We have grown "physically lazy," according to 67 percent of the global sample and 91 percent of U.S. Prosumers. At the same time, a majority in each of the seven markets complained that society has "become too shallow, focusing too much on things that don't really matter." Once again, U.S. Prosumers were most inclined to agree, at 91 percent.

Many of us are growing tired of disposable lifestyles and a cheap, trivial culture. Four in ten global respondents sometimes feel "uncultured" and wish they knew more about the arts, literature, and international matters. That is easy to understand when the highest-rated television programming includes the likes of *Gossip Girl* and *Keeping Up With the Kardashians* and when the media bombard us with such inanities as Balloon Boy, Tiger Woods's myriad mistresses, and the messy breakup of Jon and Kate Gosselin. Even ten years ago, writer John Seabrook saw that consumers were growing tired of bubblegum pop culture and the lowest common denominator in art and entertainment; in *Nobrow: The Culture of Marketing and The*

Marketing of Culture, he outlined the stirrings of rebellion against "a new cultural landscape where 'serious' artists show their work at Kmart, *Titanic* becomes a bestselling classical album, and Roseanne Barr guest edits *The New Yorker:* in short, a culture of nobrow."[5] He put his finger on that general feeling of something missing—of something profound and deeply resonant that has slipped from our grasp.

Reach Out and Touch...No One?

> We have found a disconcerting, precipitous decline in social interactions over the last three decades across all forms of social capital—formal and informal, high-minded and leisure, public and private.
>
> —Saguaro Seminar, John F. Kennedy School of Government

The welcome shift we are witnessing away from mindless consumption is rooted in profound discontent: It embodies a revolt against modern culture with its pervasive isolation, disconnection, and alienation. Human beings are highly social, needing intricate community and family ties to function and feel right in the world—needs that lately have gone unfulfilled. Consumerism's promises have always been focused on the greedy individual, as suggested by an advertisement for that icon of hyperconsumption, the Hummer—a military SUV targeted at rugged individualists: "Sometimes you find yourself in the middle of nowhere. And sometimes in the middle of nowhere you find yourself."[6] It is all about ME.

But being alone in the middle of nowhere can be a bummer, even in a Hummer. A study in *American Sociological Review* found that loneliness has reached an all-time high.[7] Demographics are partly to blame; nearly a quarter of homes in the United States are occupied by just one person.[8] In the United Kingdom, the number of solo households doubled from 6 percent of the population in 1971 to 12 percent in 2008.[9]

As we become more solitary, relationships dwindle: A quarter of Americans surveyed in 2004 claimed to have no friends at all—up from 10 percent in 1985.[10] Euro RSCG's survey found that around half of Americans suffer from a dearth of close friendships. Their feelings are echoed by significant percentages in other markets surveyed, ranging from 29 percent in France to 51 percent in Brazil. In the United States, only a quarter of our sample claimed to have close relationships with most of their neighbors, and 57 percent (70 percent of Prosumers) stay in touch with people primarily through the faceless media of e-mail and social networking. Not surprisingly, a majority of the global sample (51 percent) worries that such digital communication is weakening human-to-human bonds.

Against this sorry backdrop of disconnectedness, we are finally starting to see individuals reach out to each other, deliberately rees-tablishing bonds that were torn apart in the age of hyperconsumer-ism and creeping demographic isolation. Harvard sociologist Nicholas Christakis has made headlines with his experiments that show that happiness can spread like a contagion through networks of friends—provided they live nearby and see each other in person. "When a person who lives within a mile of a good friend becomes happier," *Time* magazine reports of Christakis's research, "the probability that this person's good friend will also become happier increases 15 percent. More surprising is that the effect can transcend direct links and reach a third degree of separation: when a friend of a friend becomes hap-pier, we become happier, even when we don't know that third person directly."[11]

In our increasingly isolated, computer-mediated society, some-times it takes a special effort to beat down the barriers we have erected around us. In 2004, an Australian who goes by the pseudonym "Juan Mann" started the Free Hugs movement, hoping to rehumanize the population by offering friendly embraces to passersby. Appropriately, he began his efforts at a shopping mall, giving consumers a different kind of fulfillment than they had perhaps expected to find. Mann's ideas caught on, and there is now an International Free Hugs Day annually. In the United States, Reid Mihalko helped found "Cuddle Parties," in which adults don pajamas and cozy up in a group for three hours, enjoying the unfamiliar pleasures of nonsexual human touch (under the watchful eye of a "lifeguard" who breaks up any too-ardent cuddles) and ending with an exuberant "puppy pile." Mihalko explains that we are "touch-and-snuggle deprived. Our need for touch has gotten so packed down and warped and pressurized that we fear its release."[12] Cuddle Parties are intended to change that, he says, "in a way that's conscious, healthy, and nutritious."[13]

Not ready to cuddle up with complete strangers? A puppy might be the answer. Writing in the *Boston Globe*, journalist Michael Schaffer ties the current boom in pet ownership to our "less connected, lonelier society."[14] A 2001 survey by the American Animal Hospital Association found that 83 percent of pet owners refer to themselves as their pets' "mommy" or "daddy."[15] Over the years, the emotional relationship of pet and owner has intensified, leading 67 percent of owners to take their pets on vacation and 37 percent to take them to work.[16] Pet stores (with their crassly consumerist overtone) are renamed Companion Animal Education Centers; doting "mommies" hire live-in pet sitters; trained experts offer therapeutic massage for dogs and cats and even parrots and iguanas (hey, it's not easy being green).[17] Such pampering has been accompanied by a huge increase in spending: The American Pet Products Association estimates 2009 U.S. sales at $45 billion, up from $17 billion fifteen years prior.[18]

Can't We All Just Get Along?

Perhaps we increasingly turn to pets because human interactions have grown so sour. A Rasmussen study found that 75 percent of adults believe Americans are becoming ruder and less civilized.[19] In a blog post on "The Collapse of Civility," Kentucky pastor David Head points to hyperconsumerism as a root cause:

> Civility is collapsing because we have fed the monster of me and starved the soul of consideration for others. We have fed the monster of selfishness by raising our children to preen their self-esteem more than accept genuine discipline; by building larger houses and buying a television for each room so we don't have to share space or the remote; by applauding ostentatious possessions, laughing at outrageous rudeness, and redefining simply bizarre behavior as merely interesting; by resisting forgiveness and by constructing individualized platforms from our computers and web site preferences, cell phones, and cars that enable us to shout to the world, "I am somebody worth adjusting to—right now!"[20]

Our consumerist society has helped spawn what some have termed a "gladiator culture" in which we have become inured to people "telling it like it is" (no matter how strong their bias or offensive their delivery). Politics grows uglier and more polarized. The 2009 incident in which Representative Joe Wilson disrupted President Obama's healthcare address to a joint session of Congress with a cry of "You lie!" was perhaps most notable for the outrage it unleashed. Given the routine bellicosity and incivility spewed over our airwaves and streets, it is almost quaint that we still expect some level of decorum in the halls of government. It is in this context that 57 percent of Euro RSCG's global sample and 62 percent of Americans (72 percent of U.S. Prosumers) report being concerned that we are losing our ability to engage in civil debate and becoming less willing to consider the views of others.

A desire for a return to civility is broadly apparent. Polls from *U.S. News & World Report, Good Housekeeping,* and ABC News show that at least eight in ten Americans are deeply concerned about the dearth of simple courtesy.[21] A survey by Public Agenda found that 79 percent of Americans consider lack of respect a "serious national problem."[22] Business leaders have grown so concerned that they have begun to enroll their employees in "protocol" and etiquette classes. Loews Hotels has instituted a corporate training program ("Living Loews") that includes instruction on how to shake hands the "Loews way" and the importance of penning handwritten notes.[23]

Getting Back to "Real"

So, let us recap: Many of us now feel disconnected and alone. And we miss the simple courtesies and social graces that used to be taken for granted. There is more behind our feelings of emptiness, however, and it has to do with something that runs much deeper: the unpleasant sensation of being somehow inauthentic, not truly *real*. In an increasingly artificial world, many of us have lost our sense of being grounded in the tangible and genuine. At home, we watch fake "reality" programming flickering across an LCD screen, listen to computer-generated music that comes through wires, walk on vinyl flooring meant to resemble wood, breathe the fruity aromas of room deodorizers, snack on foods filled with artificial flavors and dyes. There seems almost no limit to how artificial we can go: changing the color of our hair and eyes, Botoxing our brows, enhancing our busts...or going online and inventing a younger, more beautiful "avatar." There is even "cosmetic psychopharmacology," as described by psychiatrist Peter D. Kramer (author of *Listening to Prozac*): the disturbing trend in which healthy people pop pills in order to make themselves more outgoing, more confident, more energetic. Some observers fear that employers will soon pressure workers to take medicines that make them artificially smart and hardworking, or that parents will order "designer children" from genetic labs—10 percent of one thousand Americans who recently sought genetic counseling expressed an interest in paying for embryonic tests that would give them a better chance of having taller, more athletic offspring.[24] In a world of hyperconsumerism, the individual person becomes a product to be forever tweaked and enhanced, made better and better (and less and less authentic)— ceaselessly boosting "Brand Me."

All of these strange excesses marked the gilded age of consumerism. Most of us cruised along with it, blissfully shuttling goods from store to home to landfill, then heading back to the store for more. Perhaps, we imagined, the very next purchase would make us the person we wanted to be—or at least lead others to mistake us for that person. In a society that rewards artificiality and evinces little interest in depth, it has been all too easy to glide through life without seriously considering a better alternative...but finally we did.

Can we pinpoint the tipping point that began to spell the end of High-Octane Consumerism and the mindlessness that underlay it? Perhaps not—but certainly there were many warnings, most of which went unheeded. Already in the nineteenth century, homespun philosopher Henry David Thoreau chided his fellow citizens in *Walden*, "Do not trouble yourself much to get new things, whether clothes or friends.... Sell your clothes and keep your thoughts."[25] And British advocate of handicraft John Ruskin cautioned, "Every increased possession loads us with a new weariness."[26] Such warnings—and many subsequent to them—might have forever fallen on deaf ears had our More Is More culture made us truly happy, but it did not. If anything, the more material possessions we accumulated, the more we found things about which to complain. Surely Socrates had it right, centuries ago: "He who is not contented with what he has would not be contented with what he would like to have."[27]

Just how dissatisfied are people with the way they have been living their lives? Strikingly, the New Consumer survey found that nearly half the global sample (44 percent) and more than a third of Americans wish they could "start fresh with an entirely different lifestyle." Six in ten respondents around the globe worry about humankind having become disconnected from the natural world. And one-third frets about the state of their own mental health and/or that of their spouse or partner.

Possessions piled high are clearly not enough to bring joy. Nearly four in ten Americans express a desire to feel more connected to a religion or life philosophy; half wish they were leading more spiritual lives. We long to experience life more fully, feel part of some sort of harmonious web of interconnectedness—hence the developed world's heightened interest in the mysticism of the East, in spirituality-focused religions such as Buddhism and Kabbalah, and in colorful ancient practices such as sweat lodges and labyrinth walking. The blockbuster movie *Avatar*—which grossed more than $1 billion in its first seventeen days and eclipsed *Titanic* as the highest-grossing film of all time—was centered on an alien culture that embraces the notion that all life is intertwined. The message of a symbiotic relationship between people and planet struck a deep chord.

When the Great Recession hit, it brought anxiety and hardship—yet it also brought a paradoxical sense of relief and opportunity. Having been jolted at long last from the consumerist merry-go-round, buyers dusted themselves off and began to reflect. By pulling back from robotic shopping—as an activity and as a mind-set—they had a chance to reconsider the role that money and commerce play in their lives. Provided that the financial hardship is not too great, having one breadwinner laid off or having burdensome work hours reduced gave some of us a long-overdue glimpse of what it is like to take a break from a frenetic, always-on-the-go pace.

It is the view of the authors that we are witnessing a historic turning point. Nearly three-quarters of the global sample (72 percent) and an astonishing 92 percent of U.S. Prosumers say they are making a definite effort to improve the way they live. Seventy-one percent of the global sample and 91 percent of U.S. Prosumers agree with this statement: "I making an effort to improve the person I am." And half the global sample and six in ten Prosumers agree: "I am actively trying to figure out what makes me happy." For marketers and manufacturers—and even for governments—this hunger for improvement forms the crux of a big question: *What can we offer people in terms of merchandise, services, and communications that will satisfy them and, ultimately, increase their happiness?*

LOOKING FOR SOMETHING
"BIGGER THAN SELF"

> It is preoccupation with possessions, more than anything else, that prevents us from living freely and nobly.
>
> —British philosopher Bertrand Russell

One hundred Canadians were brought together by Vancouver-based communications firm James Hoggan & Associates. Their assignment: Write a story about a phrase related to the concept of *sustainability*. The tales that emerged were tinged with discontent, an uneasy feeling that things are not quite right. Many betrayed a yearning for *meaning and fulfillment*, featuring flashes of realization and "waking up" when the protagonist sees how his or her life fits into a bigger here, a longer now. Another theme was a desire for *being in it together*, giving and receiving emotional support, sharing and working together—especially when the going gets tough. Also evident was a need to *make things right*. All in all, the Hoggan project uncovered a deep sense of malaise: Society is dysfunctional, individuals are conflicted. Increasing numbers of us want to fix what is broken, embarking down a path of healing and reconciliation, ending in transformation and responsibility.[28]

That thought-provoking study was undertaken in 2005, well before the recession, but it already pointed toward today's more mindful consumption. The real hardships that have befallen many during the downturn have only intensified the general yearning for communal experience. People want to be united in common cause, to invest time and effort in something more substantive and significant than can fit inside a Macy's bag. Half of Euro RSCG's global sample, including 57 percent of Americans and 72 percent of U.S. Prosumers, say they would like to be part of a "truly important cause." They seek a more important reason to "be"—beyond paychecks, beyond outings to the mall. More than a third of the global and U.S. samples sometimes feel they are actually *wasting their lives*.

In recessionary times, the heart turns back to the past, and nostalgia has never been what it used to be. Owens Lee Pomeroy, a preservationist of old-time radio shows, put it this way: "Nostalgia is like a grammar lesson: You find the present tense, but the past perfect!"[29] For those born after World War II, the recession has tapped into a latent yearning for communal sacrifice of the kind that effectively pulled people together during that era of hardship and privation. Citizens are sick of partisan politics, corporate infighting, and personal pettiness; they seek a common cause toward which to work, and they want to take pride in something more substantive than the electronics they own or the car they drive. The stringencies of World War II produced "the Greatest Generation"; later generations feel shallow by comparison and defined by greed, not bravery or stoicism. Can you imagine President Franklin Roosevelt in December 1941 suggesting that Americans should support their country by going shopping, as recent political leaders have done in times of crisis?

As marketers consider these deep sociological undercurrents, this longing for serious purpose and common cause, they might look at Hollywood and the way the *Star Wars* movie franchise was conceived. Director George Lucas borrowed heavily from Joseph Campbell, the American mythologist and expert on comparative religion, whose book *The Hero with a Thousand Faces* offers a rich lode of thoughtful ideas about human longing and the quest for fulfillment. And they might look at current politics, too, where we have witnessed a surge in grassroots involvement and enthusiasm. The Obama campaign mobilized supporters through technology: Joining forces with the founders

of Facebook, they created a social-networking tool, MyBO, which at
its peak numbered half a million members spread out over eight thousand affinity groups.[30] The campaign scrapped the long-established
top-down structure, instead building its base from the bottom up,
allowing individuals tremendous autonomy.[31] Herein lies a lesson for
marketers: In its inverted organization, the campaign exploited the
anti-consumerist mood of the times, not merely begging for money
but instead turning over responsibility to the local campaigner, who
was expected to pitch in with effort and time. The campaign gave
eager activists a role to play and plenty of room to improvise and be
creative.

Obama understood the psychology behind the movement, telling
a reporter for *Time* magazine:

> I think our campaign was an expression of people wanting to be
> engaged and involved in different ways. They didn't want to just
> be passive consumers of political television ads. They wanted
> to have their voices heard. They wanted to interact with their
> membership—or with their neighbor and their friends. They
> wanted to be part of something larger than themselves. And
> we I think tapped into it in technological terms. But it wasn't
> really the technology that was the story. It was that there was this
> underlying impulse for people to get involved, especially among
> younger people.[32]

The campaign's novel approach continued even after the election
victory, when Obama issued a "call to service" online, to which millions
responded on Martin Luther King Day and other occasions.[33] Young
people have been especially enthusiastic—for example, joining the
75,000-strong ranks of AmeriCorps in record numbers. Signups nearly
doubled between 2008 and 2009.[34] In their lives, the members of Gen Y
have seen firsthand the importance of pitching in, from the rubble of
the Twin Towers to the aftermath of Katrina and the Haiti earthquake;
they have no expectation that government can handle it alone, and they
want to get involved and make a difference. Volunteering among college-age youth has doubled since the 1980s, and two-thirds of college
freshmen say it is an essential or very important duty of any human
being to help others.[35] This attitude helps explain why increasing numbers of college students are opting to forgo the traditional spring break
debauchery for something more meaningful. Already by 2006, some
35,000 American students were participating in "alternative spring
breaks," which might include tutoring migrant farm workers, building

homes for families in need, or registering voters.[36] Minnesota-based Students Today Leaders Forever has begun organizing community service projects for kids as young as middle school. We are witnessing a historic change as millions look beyond the consumerist frenzy and seek to participate in something larger than themselves.

THE NEW MINDFULNESS UNFOLDS:
RETHINKING FOOD AND TRAVEL

In examining the growing quest for real experiences and a more sociable, interconnected life, there is no better symbol than the Slow Food movement, which takes the new mindfulness and applies it to one of the most basic aspects of our lives: what we eat. In the age of hyperconsumerism, eating became just one more materialist category in which we devoured goods at a frenzied pace, always with an eye to the next new thing. But what a category: Food products and brands multiplied exponentially in the era of excess, with the average grocery store coming to offer, for example, more than 150 kinds of cereal and even thirty kinds and sizes of oatmeal.[37] Fast food in particular has exploded: U.S. sales escalated from $6 billion in 1970 to more than $110 billion in 2000—more than is spent on movies, books, magazines, newspapers, videos, and recorded music combined. In the same period, McDonald's worldwide grew from about one thousand restaurants to twenty-eight times that many.[38] Simultaneously, the much-publicized "obesity epidemic" has unfolded, with more than a third of U.S. adults currently considered obese.[39]

Enter Slow Food International, a nonprofit, eco-gastronomic organization founded in 1989 to combat fast food and unthinking attitudes toward eating. More than twenty years later, the organization has grown to include 100,000 members in 132 countries.[40] In September 2009, 20,000 Americans participated in rallies organized by Slow Food USA that demanded healthier lunchroom choices for children.[41] More significantly, *slow food*, with its pleasing connotations, has become a household term. Slow Food's mission is a simple one: to promote enjoyment of eating through an improved understanding of where food comes from and by encouraging traditional methods of preparation and serving. As its adherents have been known to say: "If we are what we eat, who wants to be fast, cheap and easy!"

Slow food dovetails with the localism that many thoughtful consumers now favor. Slow Food USA sponsors the "Ark of Taste," a listing of regional foods that are vanishing, owing to "market standardization, industrial agriculture, and environmental damage."[42] Foods added to the list in 2009 include "Turkey" hard red winter wheat from Kansas (almost extinct due to the modern push for high-yield varieties), Lake Michigan whitefish (replaced by farmed salmon), and the Hauer pippin apple (a California variety now found in three commercial nurseries only). Slow food invites us to participate in a larger dialogue about consumption—to learn food's rich folkways, its heritage, its implications—and asks that we reflect before we dine. It draws us into a world that is complex and interesting and communal.

Similar to slow food is the slow travel movement, which proposes a more leisurely approach to vacationing: "Slow down, immerse yourself in the local culture and avoid the fast pace of rushing from one guide-book 'must-see' to the next."[43] It stresses an immersive personal con-nection with the destination visited—getting to know the community, its history, and its culture at a pace sufficiently languid to allow for unexpected discoveries and simple pleasures. A recent market research report analyzed the phenomenon:

> As modern life gets faster and the population of the Western world becomes both more urbanized and "cash rich but time poor," it becomes evident that other things are lacking, such as spiritual-ity and community. It's these factors—along with greater health awareness, uptake of alternative therapies, and more environmen-tal and psychological awareness—that drive demand for holidays addressing the need for time out and rejuvenation, along with a deeper experience of ourselves.[44]

The colorful new vocabulary of travel and tourism reflects a far broader social movement. A host of new approaches is emerging right now, including *geotourism* (aiming to sustain a place's culture or envi-ronment), *flashpacking* (trekking made more accessible by adding some creature comforts), *Rough Luxe* (luxury that incorporates authentic personal encounters with people, cultures, and food), *agritourism* (waking up to the mooing of cows), *staycations* (finding adventure near home), *voluntourism* (a service trip). All are linked by a desire for a more ethical and sustainable approach to consumption—and life.

The recession hit us hard, but it has brought with it an opportu-nity to stop and think. For many observers, our intellectual laziness and consumerist greed are appalling patterns that need reassessing. Slow food and slow travel both demand greater thought and more conscious decision making than their fast-paced alternatives; both require awareness of contexts larger than ourselves. Along with the other trends we have examined in this chapter, they imply a marked increase in the desire for intangibles, such as having control over one's life and health, striking a balance between work and personal life, discovering spiritual fulfillment, and giving generously of our time to help others in need. In chapters to come, we will investigate more deeply the needs of the mindful shopper in this new age of conscious consumerism: knowing just how much is enough, growing up and developing self-control, and seeking more purposeful pleasure.

Chapter 5

RIGHTSIZING

There are two ways to get enough: One is to continue to accumulate more and more. The other is to desire less.

—British writer and philosopher G. K. Chesterton

As people have come to realize mindless excess does not bring happiness, they have begun to seek a more substantive and mindful way to live. Rejecting the over-the-top excesses of the past, they are looking for an approach that offers greater emotional and practical benefits. In their role as consumers, they are attempting to "rightsize," aiming to consume neither too much nor too little, but to find a harmonious balance.

A clear component of this trend is *intelligent simplification*. A strikingly high percentage of U.S. respondents to Euro RSCG's New Consumer survey (77 percent in all, and 84 percent of Prosumers) agree that "most of us would be better off if we lived more simply." Moreover, about a quarter of the global sample and a third of Americans agree they would be happier if they "owned less stuff." And about half the global and U.S. samples (46 and 47 percent, respectively) said they wish their homes were less cluttered. Clearly, people are growing tired of being surfeited with commercial goods, overwhelmed by consumer choices, and drowned in clutter and waste. A historic reaction has begun to set in.

COULD CONSUMERISM BE KILLING US?

Owning too much yields not happiness but misery—or so the great poets have long told us. "The world is too much with us," William Wordsworth warned two centuries ago. "Late and soon, getting and

spending, we lay waste our powers."[1] His American follower Ralph
Waldo Emerson agreed: "Things are in the saddle, and ride mankind."[2]
In today's world, the poets' message is being repeated more widely
and with greatly increased urgency, for we have never had more material things—and they are not making us joyful the way advertisers
promised they would.

Diminishing Returns from the Pleasure Treadmill

In spite of the superabundant production of consumer goods in the
last half century—or perhaps because of it—stress has inexorably
grown. "Increasing Stress Making Millions Ill," the *Guardian* reports
with alarm in Britain.[3] The American Psychological Association's
2009 Stress in America survey showed that 24 percent of adults experience high levels of stress, and half complain of moderate stress.[4]
Our harried lives are fueling a boom in antidepressant drugs, which
were dispensed across U.S. pharmacy counters 232.7 million times
in 2007 alone.[5] Use of such drugs has doubled in less than a decade,
now involving one in ten Americans (half of whom are not clinically
depressed but, rather, suffering fatigue or other issues).[6] Everyone is
affected; the fastest-growing population using antidepressants is said
to be preschoolers.[7]

    Could consumerism itself be a major source of this stress epidemic?
An increasing number of researchers feel it contributes, and they keep
issuing studies showing that an ever-bigger gross domestic product
(GDP) does not translate into higher levels of individual satisfaction.
Ronald Inglehart of the University of Michigan has tracked changes
through time using the World Values Survey (WVS). By tapping into
a global network of social scientists who have carried out representative national surveys, the WVS captures data from more than eighty
societies on all six inhabited continents, representing 85 percent of the
world's population.[8]

    In a recent paper on happiness trends around the world, Inglehart
and his colleagues Roberto Foa, Christopher Peterson, and Christian
Welzel reported there is strong evidence that the citizens of rich
societies are happier than those of poor societies—yet beyond a certain
point, the curve levels off. Once the threshold of $10,000 is reached,
Inglehart says, there is practically no relationship between income and
subjective well-being. Using figures for 1999, he noted that the Irish
were happier than the Germans, although the Germans were twice
as wealthy; the Taiwanese were as happy as the Japanese, although
the Japanese were three times as wealthy.[9] Inglehart has gone on to
say that "beyond a certain level, more wealth doesn't do anything, it

does less."[10] This is another way of saying *diminishing returns;* beyond a certain threshold, More becomes Less.

Several other investigations have confirmed Inglehart's assertion that more goods may equate to less joy. People are, in many ways, less satisfied with their lives today than their ancestors were. "Compared with their grandparents, today's young adults have grown up with much more affluence, slightly less happiness and much greater risk of depression and assorted social pathology," says Hope College psychologist David G. Myers. "Our becoming much better off over the last four decades has not been accompanied by one iota of increased subjective well-being."[11]

Being better off might just be the problem, says psychologist Tim Kasser, author of *The High Price of Materialism.* Kasser's research shows that when extrinsic goals such as product acquisition become the organizing principle in an individual's life, he or she may experience more psychological ills, such as greater unhappiness in relationships, and more depressed moods.[12] Psychotherapist Allen Kanner goes further: "Corporate-driven consumerism is having massive psychological effects, not just on people, but on our planet as well." He faults "the huge corporate culture that's invading so much of our lives."[13]

Maybe Wordsworth and Emerson had it right.

Paralyzed by Choices

No wonder we are stressed by consumer choices: We are standing beneath a veritable Niagara Falls—with our mouths open. Take just one example: In 2006, more than 100,000 new packaged food and drink products were launched globally, at a rate of nearly 300 per day.[14] It is exhausting to be faced with so many decisions and depressing to constantly be reminded of alternatives we chose not to pursue. "There's no question that we have more choices than ever before," says Scott Plous, a psychology professor at Wesleyan University and author of *The Psychology of Judgment and Decision Making.* "And decisions are generally harder and more time-consuming when there are lots of alternatives."[15] We have strayed just about as far as we can get from the nineteenth-century wisdom of Thoreau, who wrote, "Simplicity, simplicity, simplicity. I say, let your affairs be as two or three, and not a hundred or a thousand; instead of a million count half a dozen, and keep your accounts on your thumb nail."[16] Once he refused the gift of a doormat for his cabin at Walden Pond because he did not want to have to dust it.

Every year brings more product innovations, more "must have" items. Pew Research Center surveys in 1996 and 2006 asked Americans to rate a series of products as "luxuries" or "necessities." The number of so-called necessities jumped as computers, cell phones, microwave ovens, dishwashers, air conditioning, and clothes dryers all came to be considered indispensable by millions.[17] These gadgets relentlessly press us to make complex choices in their selection and to tend to their upkeep and repair. Not to mention the sheer difficulty of trying to learn how to operate them, with their ever-multiplying capabilities and options! One British purchaser of a digital camera laments, "Frankly cameras are getting so complicated that you'll need a university degree to be able to operate one soon."[18] A researcher in the Netherlands found that half of all "malfunctioning" products returned to stores actually work fine—it is just that consumers cannot figure them out. She called in product developers to have them witness ordinary people struggling with newly purchased gadgets, and they were "astounded by the havoc" their products wreaked.[19] It is little wonder, then, that seven in ten respondents to the New Consumer study agree: "I no longer want lots of 'bells and whistles' on products I buy; I'd rather just have the functions I really need."

Everywhere we turn, more and more consumer choices demand our attention and energy—and not just in the fast-burgeoning world of cameras, computers, and cell phones. The exhausted customer surveys as many as 300 produce varieties (and 30,000 items in all) in a single Ralph's supermarket, sorts through 1,500 different drawer pulls at The Great Indoors, chooses from among 15,000 songs on an iPod or 35,000 movies on Netflix. Tropicana Pure Premium Orange Juice now comes in *16* varieties, including Low Acid, Antioxidant Advantage, and Calcium + Vitamin D—and this does not include several additional offerings in the new Trop50 low-sugar line. No wonder we find ourselves suffering from what one expert calls "consumer vertigo."[20]

Unable to decide among the countless treats on display at a local Dunkin' Donuts (its stores offer nearly fifty types of doughnuts, munchkins, rolls, and sticks), writer T. M. Shine came to realize that he gets hopelessly paralyzed by consumer options: "These days, there are so many choices to labor through, from the most basic, such as paper or plastic at the grocery checkout counter, to the nearly suicide-inducing, such as the friends-and-family plan or unlimited texting. And don't even get me started on undercoating or extended warranties."

As a humorous experiment, Shine decided on the spot to henceforth make no life decisions whatsoever, instead turning to strangers for their advice and doing whatever they told him. The man who chose his doughnuts had a penchant for sprinkles, and his selection "fell into the box with the majesty of a fireworks grand finale.... Later in the day, when I asked a sandy-haired woman at Old Navy to pick out a shirt for me, she quickly devoted herself to the cause. 'I want you to have a crisper, cleaner look,' she exclaimed." Shine considers his experiment a great success, achieving his consumerist dream of "not having to be the one to make the tough decisions."[21]

Why More Is Less

Swarthmore psychologist Barry Schwartz visited his local consumer electronics store and shook his head in disbelief: There were 45 kinds of car stereo systems, 110 kinds of TVs, and enough components to create 6.5 million different stereo systems. His book *The Paradox of Choice: Why More Is Less* argues that Americans are being made miserable by this bewildering array of alternatives. A reviewer has praised the way Schwartz highlights the problem of shoppers "driven bonkers by the staggering array of consumer goods from which we must choose. Choosing something as (seemingly) simple as shampoo can force us to wade through dozens, even hundreds, of brands. We are, the author suggests, overwhelmed by choice."[22]

"We do better and we feel worse," Schwartz told us in an interview in which we asked for his perspective on the 2008–9 recession and changing consumer attitudes.[23] Over the past several years, he says, shoppers and producers have engaged in "a symbiotic pursuit of an absurd number of options. People want more rather than less, even though they suffer. And producers are catering to customer demand." Now the economy has tanked—but marketers, he predicts, will be extremely hesitant to evolve and adopt new ways. "All the evidence shows that if you limit options, you will sell more. Yet the orthodoxy of marketing is that you want there to be something for everybody. It's very hard to change that thinking."[24] Difficult though it may be, marketers urgently need to learn to think differently if they are going to respond to the new, more conscious consumer, who is intolerant of excessive options, skeptical of finding happiness in material things, and concerned, as we shall see, about overconsumption and waste.

TODAY'S CAUTIONARY TALE: CONSUMERS GO WILD

As runaway consumerism becomes less acceptable, attention is being drawn to the shopaholic as a stark example of how destructive binge buying can be. The 2009 movie *Confessions of a Shopaholic* treated the subject humorously. (Perversely, the heroine takes a job at a thrift magazine.) In the media lately, actor Nicolas Cage has emerged as a poster child for excess: Foundering in debt, he has been forced to pare down his more than a dozen homes, more than twenty cars, four yachts, two Bahamian islands, and a prized collection of shrunken heads. Carole Lieberman, a psychiatrist and compulsive-shopping expert, weighs in: "By being unable to resist the impulses to spend, Nicolas Cage fits the profile of an out-of-control shopaholic."[25]

Cage is not alone in his malady. A 2002 study showed that half of Americans were "money abusers," struggling to control excessive spending and debt, trying repeatedly to cut back and yet unable to.[26] In the New Consumer survey, more than six in ten Americans reported having trouble saving as much money as they would like and nearly half admitted to sometimes feeling bad about themselves when they buy too much. Forty-seven percent agreed: "I have wasted lots of money on things I don't need." Another study suggests that more than one in twenty Americans fit the shopaholic mold. "Do you buy new makeup weekly or compact discs by the fistful?" asks an MSN report. "You might be a shopaholic.... Compulsive shopping [is] tacitly condoned by our materialistic society."[27]

Books about the shopping habit are almost too numerous to list, with such titles as *Born to Spend*, *In the Red*, *Digging Out*, *Consuming Passions*, *Stop Me Because I Can't Stop Myself*, and *Hooked!*. In her 2008 book, *To Buy or Not to Buy: Why We Overshop and How to Stop*, New York psychologist April Lane Benson joined the bandwagon of those fretting about the burgeoning problem of America's 18 million shopaholics. Benson's Web site, Stopping Overshopping, reports a surge of hits from seventy countries as "compulsive buying becomes a bigger and more global problem." Espousing the mantra "You can never get enough of what you don't really need," Benson advises her clients to carry a card in their pockets that they can pull out before ever swiping their Visa. It reads like an existential chant: "Why am I here? How do I feel? Do I need this?"[28]

The ultimate villains, Benson and many others believe, are advertisers. "Above all," she cautions, "don't fall prey to the myth of product transformation. Though marketers have taught us to think otherwise, things don't transform us: not the shampoo, or the clothes, or the jewelry; not the fountain pens, the cars, or the houses. We are who we are—and if we want to change ourselves, we need to move from mindless buying to mindful being."[29]

One of Benson's clients thanks her rapturously for curing her hyperconsumerism and leading her to rightsizing. "Life feels so much richer and more meaningful; I am rarely feeling empty or lonely these days. I have no personal debts and money in the bank. I haven't used a store credit card since 2005." But she confesses, "Yesterday, I almost slipped and put a cashmere sweater on layaway."[30]

Hyperconsumers Just Might Be Nuts

As negative attention mounts against those who consume too much, experts argue over whether excessive shopping is a psychiatric disorder and whether it should be added to the official *Diagnostic and Statistical Manual of Mental Disorders* when that bible of the mental health professional is next revised. In other words, are superconsumers basically insane, victims of inner psychological demons and outside marketing manipulators?

At clinics across the country, problem shoppers are injected with antidepressants and the antialcohol drug naltrexone, to little effect. What else can be done for them? "Sadness may spur excess spending" was the conclusion of a psychological study in 2008 in which subjects were divided into two groups, one that listened to a weepy story and one that did not. Members of both groups were then offered the chance to buy a nice-looking water bottle. Researchers were astonished to find that the subjects who heard the sob story were prepared to pay almost four times as much as the others.[31] Apparently shopping fills some deep emotional void. People find themselves in a Catch-22: Modern, materialistic life makes them unhappy; they shop as a result; then they find themselves trapped by their materialistic things and even more unhappy. Back to the mall.

"It's really hard to imagine how sad these cases are," says Karen Finlay, a marketing and consumer behavior professor at the University of Guelph in Canada who studies shopaholics. Her research looks at "how retail environments contribute to the disorder by causing anxiety," especially "big-box stores with oversized shopping carts, oversized stores and multiple shelving."[32] Meanwhile the Department of Applied Health Science at Indiana University lists suggestions for anyone caught in the tragic cycle of consumerism: turn off TV shopping channels, cut up your credit cards, leave home without your wallet, only window-shop after hours, and avoid discount warehouses. Finally, "If you feel out of control, you probably are. Seek counseling."[33]

Personal Fulfillment Equals Fewer "Things"

By buying too much, shopaholics are seeking catharsis—to feel better about themselves amid the troubles of daily life. But as we have seen, many argue that consumerism itself is making us miserable by focusing us on selfish pleasures and at the same time dissolving our sense of connectedness to others. That is what Yale professor Robert E. Lane argued in *The Loss of Happiness in Market Democracies:* Beyond a point, increased income contributes almost nothing to happiness, and, in fact, we experience erosion of what we really value: family and community ties.

Recently, reporter Dick Meyer of CBS News went back to his hometown of Glencoe, Illinois, to investigate the ravages of conspicuous consumption, or what he calls "aggressive ostentation." The changes in Glencoe were appalling, he found, and he contrasted them with the modest way his mother had lived—always within five miles of where she was born:

> Most of her friends were friends from childhood. She rarely needed to do business with people she didn't personally know. You bought appliances from Charlie at Skokie Electric, who also fixed them. Arthur Weinecke owned the hardware and toy store, Wally King owned the record store and you bought sports stuff from Ray. Johnny, a tallish midget who once threw a snow shovel at my dog, delivered prescriptions. There were no chains in Glencoe, no spas, no luxury stores.

Many of us can relate to this story, with its theme of a bygone world of close-knit communities, few luxuries, and consumerism kept in reasonable check.

Meyer blasts the shop-till-you-drop culture that has taken the place of this happier world. "I would argue that the decline of those communitarian ties is alienating and contributes to consumption—to public signaling—that is not just conspicuous but passively antisocial." He puts his finger on one of the key arguments behind the rightsizing movement: that material things rob us of interpersonal connections, and it is only those connections that can really bring us joy.[34]

RECONSIDERING CONSUMERISM, REPRIORITIZING LIVES

Meyer's attitude is catching on: There is a pervasive sense that consumerism needs to be tempered by a thoughtful awareness of its negative social and personal implications. All across America, one sees evidence of this new concern. Residents of Boulder, Colorado, have convened a discussion group to consider, among other things, the thorny issue of "Owning things—How does owning things (beyond those things that aren't necessary for survival) increase the joy you feel in life? Is there a point beyond which owning fewer things could improve your life? Do you think of yourself as owning a lot of stuff? Have you ever reduced the amount of stuff you own strictly in order to improve your life, or accidentally found that your life improved when you got rid of stuff?"[35]

And one sees similar discussions taking place across the globe, as the recession gives people an opportunity to reevaluate their priorities and finally consider rightsizing their lives. An office worker in Kenya quit her job in order to become a writer, fulfilling a longtime goal. "In all my years as a career woman, I can honestly say that I never felt immense joy in an office job," Rasna Warah says. "I am now wondering whether I wasted several years sending meaningless emails and editing pointless documents instead of doing the many things I love." The economic downturn helped propel her decision: Kenyans are now "more aware of the fragility of life and the need to maintain and nurture relationships in times of crisis....Many are finding that the relationship between money and happiness is illusory." As in other parts of the world, "an increasing number of people are 'downsizing' by either taking up part-time employment or escaping the rat-race by seeking employment in less stressful professions. Some are eschewing consumerism in favor of simplicity."[36] Four in ten global respondents—and nearly half of U.S. Prosumers—say they have adopted or thought about adopting a "slower" lifestyle in recent years.

"Simple pleasures don't fuel the marketing machine so they don't get a great deal of air time," says a pastor in Brisbane, Australia. "But they can be just the antidote for our modern melancholy. Imagine incorporating a 'living simply day' once a week, or even a month, when we unplug, de-clutter, slow down and take a moment to savor the things that make life rich—things such as friends, family, ideas, dreams, love and laughter. A game of cricket in the park, lazy afternoons with a book, a bowl of homemade soup served with great conversation—simple pleasures that so often get crowded out by the 'stuff' of busy lives."[37]

These are international examples, but the same holds true in America: 67 percent of New Consumer survey respondents (and 73 percent of Prosumers) feel that "the recession has served to remind people of what's really important in life—and that's a good thing." The downturn has shocked us out of our old, mindless-consumer ways, and we are ready to think about rightsizing at last.

The Global War on Clutter

> Eliminate physical clutter. More importantly, eliminate spiritual clutter.
>
> —Minimalist advocate D. H. Mondfleur

There are said to be four paths to Nirvana but only two lead to rightsizing: (1) shop less and (2) haul your excess out to the curb. Respondents to the New Consumer survey are doing both: Just less than half the U.S. sample and 58 percent of U.S. Prosumers agreed: "I'm getting a sense of satisfaction from reducing my purchases during the economic downturn," and nearly six in ten Americans (and seven in ten Prosumers) said that, in recent years, they have thrown out (or thought about throwing out) lots of stuff in order to declutter their lives and homes.

A decluttering movement is rapidly gathering momentum, sweeping all before it. Marketing expert John Quelch has identified a new type of citizen, whom he calls the "middle-aged Simplifier. She finds herself surrounded by too much stuff acquired. She is increasingly skeptical in the face of a financial meltdown that it was all worth the effort. Out will go luxury purchases, conspicuous consumption, and a trophy culture."[38]

Among declutterers, Gail Blanke is emerging as a leading guru. Her 2009 book, *Throw Out Fifty Things: Clear the Clutter, Find Your Life*, argues that the wastebasket can be profoundly transformative. In an interview with Wisconsin Public Radio, she sounded a sharply antimaterialistic note—one would never have guessed that she is a former senior vice president at Avon Products, a company whose bountiful offerings clutter many a drawer across the planet. Like many increasingly mindful Americans, Blanke now views consumerism more negatively, as an almost pathological drain on one's life force. Owning too many things, she says in language recalling the advocates of colonic irrigation, "makes you feel heavy," "saps your energy," "dulls you down." As a lifestyle coach, she urges her clients to go home and immediately discard fifty useless or annoying items, asking themselves, "Is this me? Is this what I am about?" (One fired-up client went home and immediately threw out her boyfriend.) Purging clutter, Blanke implies, is a way of starting life anew. "We have just entered the age of reinvention," she says. "We are repurposing ourselves. There's a freedom that comes from letting go of things."[39]

Turning to the Downsizing Specialist

As a new generation of spartans strides onto the scene, dustbins in hand, a communications agency predicts the rise of "new bragging rights among the citizenry. 'It's not how much you have; it's how little you need.'"[40] But sometimes the clutter is just too much, and the would-be rightsizer feels he or she must call in the cavalry. The *New York Times* has reported on the growth in "downsizing specialists" whose job "combines organizing, psychology and plain old handholding. People with backgrounds in gerontology, social work, health care and psychology are entering the field...[and] often catering to the boomer clientele." "It was 9/11 that got people thinking that they wanted to simplify and get their affairs in order," says Standolyn Robertson, president of the 4,200-strong National Organization of Professional Organizers, whose ranks include an increasing number of downsizing specialists.[41]

In Lakeway, Texas, Gwen and Eugene Prewit felt suffocated by the accumulation of possessions in their four-bedroom home: "Some days we could barely get in the door." They hired downsizing specialist Barry Izsak to help. "What we're trying to do is arrive at the right amount of stuff for the right amount of space," Izsak explains. He pushed the Prewits to ask themselves mercilessly "Do we really need this? Do we really love that?" Only the material goods that genuinely bring happiness were allowed to stay.[42]

Curious about this trend, we spoke with a U.S.-based downsizing specialist who, citing privacy concerns, asked to remain anonymous. She hears much talk nowadays about the advantages of the simple life. "I'm seeing people respond to the idea. They've seen those TV shows about uncluttering, and even *Hoarders* [on A&E]. They read *Real Simple* magazine. I think they have heightened awareness." But actually achieving one's rightsizing goals can be difficult, this woman cautions. Americans love their possessions, even when the clutter piles high. "It's surprising what you see when you visit people in their homes, and you say, Oh my gosh! But they are comforted by their things. If you took their stuff and got rid of it, it would panic them"— especially, of course, the compulsive hoarders, a condition she finds surprisingly common.

And it's not enough to declutter your life just once. She sees clients whose new, smaller homes quickly overflow. "Personally I think QVC buying leads to people owning a lot of stuff. I think there ought to be a support group—like the bartender says, 'I'm not going to serve you, you've had too much'—there ought to be a limit to buying."

Revolt against Waste

A downside to decluttering is that it heaps our landfills even higher. Every year, the United States generates 230 million tons of trash, equivalent to the weight of 2,421 Nimitz-class aircraft carriers.[43] The average person discards 4.6 pounds of it every day. In a year, that adds up to 1,679 pounds of garbage, more than the weight of a Smart Car. In spite of the recent growth in recycling awareness, less than one-quarter of U.S. waste avoids the landfill. [44]

But Americans are becoming concerned about the trash problem, even outraged. A recent Yankelovich survey asked consumers what they value about grocery store products. "Tastes good" was most important, followed by concerns about waste. Price was a distant number six. Respondents singled out as wasteful, for example, the Costco multipack of chips, which contains many flavors that no one in the family wants to eat.[45] Without question, we are seeing a growing revulsion against wasting resources. In the New Consumer survey, 73 percent of U.S. respondents (and 82 percent of Prosumers) said, "I feel good about reducing the amount of waste I create."

The mindful consumer wants to add as little as possible to landfills. Businesses have helped by "lightweighting"—for example, shrinking the thickness of aluminum drink cans by half since the 1960s. And government can do its part by collecting curbside trash less often (which has been shown to stimulate recycling) and adopting pay-as-you-throw schemes (as a quarter of Americans are already experiencing in their communities). To make manufacturers face up to the true cost of waste disposal, the European Union has embraced "extended producer responsibility," requiring makers of cars and computers to take back their products after customers wear them out, then recycle the parts. Out of self-interest, companies are responding to these new regulations by finding ways of making recycling more affordable. After a decade of experimenting, Hewlett-Packard now makes its laptops 90 percent recyclable, using screws instead of glue and only five kinds of plastics, not two hundred as before.[46]

Although we still have far to go, recycling efforts have made great strides in the United States: There are nearly nine thousand curbside recycling programs nationwide, container and package recycling has risen to 40 percent, half of all paper products are recycled, and 62 percent of yard waste gets composted.[47] San Francisco is aiming for zero waste by 2020, and in 2009 it reached a 72 percent recycling rate, the highest in the nation. This includes all waste generated on construction sites, which by local ordinance must now be kept out of landfills.[48] A whole generation of young people is growing up with this more eco-conscious mentality.

Rethinking "New"

As people work toward rightsizing their consumption, they are thinking twice before buying new from a retailer. Some are participating in clothing swaps ("Be good. Be green. Be glam!") or turning to Web sites like Craigslist and ReUseIt to find (or sell) a gently used toaster or bedroom set.

"Repurposing" has become a mania, especially for a hardcore cadre who have learned to crochet with used cassette tape or plastic grocery bags, make quilts out of old bras, turn house keys into wind chimes, or make scouring pads out of fingernail clippings. A new book reveals 120 ways just to reuse T-shirts.[49] And the National Crayon Recycling Program—yes, there is such a thing—has kept more than 47,000 pounds of petroleum-based crayons from going into landfills (although 120,000 pounds of additional crayons are manufactured every day, evidence of the uphill struggle devoted recyclers face).[50]

These are offbeat examples but behind them lies an enormous "recycled economy" inexorably emerging before our eyes. Of the one thousand adults polled by *Time* magazine in summer 2009, nearly half said protecting the environment should take priority over economic growth—and this in the midst of a recession![51] For these concerned consumers, stemming the flow of trash has become a subject of paramount concern. "Perhaps more than any other single element, not being wasteful will define overall value in the recovery consumer marketplace," one trends report predicts. "This doesn't portend a retreat from luxuriousness and style so much as a renunciation of wastefulness, particularly in light of heightened social concerns over resource scarcity."[52]

Thrift Stores Redux

Recycling and rightsizing are about more than just reducing expenses and waste; they are components of what is becoming a popular lifestyle. Twenty-five-year-old Welsh pop singer Duffy speaks for many in her generation in downplaying the gaudy trappings of wealth and fame and talking up a more mindful approach to consumption: "I don't get too caught up in it. I do [have] nice things, but, to be honest, they're not important. I'm not after a big house in the city, or anything like that....I like to wear vintage designer clothes, you can never go wrong with that....I love wearing things that have been around longer than I have, and seen more than me."[53]

Not just celebrities are visiting those vintage clothing emporiums. The recession has proved a boon to thrift stores everywhere: The National Association of Resale & Thrift Shops reported a 35 percent increase in business in late 2008 at a time when traditional retailers were experiencing a sharp decline.[54] But even before the downturn, more and more people were shopping in secondhand stores. A decade ago, there were just nine Salvation Army thrift shops in Detroit, with sales of $2.7 million; today there are twenty-five, collectively raking in $30 million.[55]

Old stigmas against shopping at Goodwill and similar venues are quickly fading. "Cultural mores are shifting," *Daily Finance* reports. "Shopping at thrift shops now gets you admiration, not pity."[56] In Tampa, Dot Murphy recently enlarged her store, Dot's Thrift Shop, after only three months, so popular has it proved with shoppers. A self-described "thrift store junkie," she happily hands out a map to customers showing fourteen competing stores nearby. "Thrifting is really about recycling and not throwing things away," she says. "You can't get any greener than that."[57]

Amy Hardin Turosak, a close observer of the thrift store phenomenon, sees a new paradigm emerging. "The new product retail market has conditioned us for years to believe 'if it's not new, it's eww!' We bought this notion hook, line, and sinker; and now we're caught in a net of product surplus and waste on top of a mountain of debt."[58] As noted in the *Christian Science Monitor*:

> Turosak sees the repurposing market as the wave of the future: Change is brewing down below where retail executives dare not go. People are turning to the old ways of bartering not just items but services. A new family-style economy is growing roots in neighborhoods and communities from complete necessity. Proud "frugalistas" are ready to strut. And, in come the "environistas," who shop with the intention of lowering their carbon footprint. Consumers are changing because we have no choice. We are out of jobs, out of money, and we see our environment in disrepair. We realize we can no longer demand "More!" from factories on the other side of the world. Besides, how could any other country take our demands for environmental progress seriously when we're steeped in piles of our own junk?[59]

The Crusade against Nondisposables

As Americans recoil from the culture of wastefulness, they seek alternatives to disposable products. Forty-eight percent of U.S. respondents to the New Consumer survey (and 61 percent of Prosumers) say "I am making an effort to buy fewer disposable goods (e.g., paper plates, paper towels, disposable razors)." Here are but a few examples of the products they worry about:

- Eighteen billion *disposable diapers* are used in America every year, enough to stretch to the moon and back nine times. The average baby eventually will go through one ton of them.[60] In reaction, sales of cloth diapers are on the rise.
- *Paper towels.* "Chuck works on motorcycles, and I'm a kitchen clean freak," one married Cornell University employee confesses. "We used to go through a shameful amount of paper towels. Like buy in bulk, hate-the-earth, bulldoze-Costa Rica amounts." But now she uses rags instead, made of old T-shirts.[61]
- Americans consume 34 million rolls of *toilet paper* daily. "In truth we should all be using water sprays," says the *Guardian.* "If everyone in the world used as much toilet paper as people in the U.K., let alone Americans, there would not be a single tree left."[62] Some people are installing bidets, as in Europe.
- More than 2 billion *disposable razors* end up in landfills every year in the United States.[63] Although old-fashioned straight razors have serious disadvantages, consumers are starting to consider them again.

Skeptics point out that these unpleasant although eco-friendly alternatives are in fact a cautionary reminder of why disposables were invented in the first place. But in today's transformed consumer environment, the anti-waste crusade continues to gather steam, and disposable products are sure to come in for increasing contempt.

THE NEW THRIFT

At the heart of rightsizing, reusing, and recycling lies a concern for thrift. It is an old virtue, of course, stretching back through history. The American strain of it got going with Benjamin Franklin's aphoristic proselytizing. In the 1950s, millions laughed at entertainer Jack Benny when he flaunted his cheapskate ways. In England, Queen Elizabeth is a famously frugal soul, in spite of being one of the wealthiest women on the planet. She wears her dresses repeatedly and stores cornflakes in Tupperware. In 2009, a *Daily Telegraph* columnist was aghast at the revelation that "Her Majesty eats breakfast off a tatty tray bearing mismatched china that would shame a Blackpool B&B

[bed and breakfast]. It's all rather admirable, but I wonder if she's overdoing the thrift."[64]

During the years of hyperconsumerism, the queen and her ilk had few followers in their habit of sensible moderation. In developed countries everywhere, observers charted a steady decline in thriftiness. "It became old fashioned, sadly," says Laurie Campbell, executive director of Credit Canada. For young people, "it's not cool to be thrifty. To be honest, I don't think they know the meaning of the word *thrift*."[65]

But all that has begun to change with the recent economic crisis. Out of nowhere in 2009, the buzzword *frugalista* became so popular that consternation erupted when a blogger in Miami trademarked the term and had her lawyer warn other bloggers to stop calling themselves that.[66] Everybody, it seems, wants a piece of the new thriftiness.

Thrift advocates are happy to report that a sharp increase in savings has been one of the striking results of the downturn. In June 2009, the *Wall Street Journal* noted that U.S. consumers were saving more of their incomes than at any time since 1993, "a major shift toward frugality that's expected to be one of the lasting effects of this deep and lengthy recession."[67] Many consumers said they intended to permanently increase saving. "We have gone in a radically short time from conspicuous consumption to conspicuous saving," a Chicago-based retail consultant told *Daily Finance* two months later. "Everybody, retailers included, recognizes this is a major change—lasting change."[68]

Frugal Means the Good Life

Steering clear of the "frugalista" flap, blogger Sarah Gilbert calls herself a "frugalite." Thriftiness will be the new norm, she predicts. "Frugality has shifted from survival mechanism to art form, making this Recession-era practice a thing that will stick long after our GDP recovers and jobs are once again plentiful. Frugality is smart, green, and beautiful, and I'm proud to think of myself as one of the new frugalite."[69]

There is more to thriftiness than merely pinching pennies and scrimping, its devotees agree. In an interview with *Newsweek*, David Blankenhorn, president of the Institute for American Values, expresses hope that the idea of thrift is changing, its connotation as Scroogish penny-pinching slowly being replaced by a more positive conception. "The goal of thrift is not to cut back or scrimp and save, but rather to enjoy the good things in life."[70]

Gilbert similarly notes that, for many young people and mindful consumers, thrift forms part of a vibrant, innovative lifestyle:

> You see, frugality is not just what you go without, but what you do instead of buying things. When they're not growing food, they're joining food buying clubs, becoming members of community-supported agriculture (CSAs), buying in-season, frequenting U-pick farms, or simply going freegan and gleaning or Dumpster-diving [more on this in chapter 6]. Most frugal foodies I know (like me) combine many of these strategies, growing what they can; finding or swapping unpicked fruits, vegetables and nuts; sticking religiously to local, seasonal food; and never turning down marked-off produce.[71]

In other words, thriftiness need not imply hardship or a pinched and crabbed attitude. Gilbert and others make it sound like fun—a way to live that is at once more meaningful and more pleasurable.

SIGNS OF RIGHTSIZING: WEDDINGS AND BIRTHDAYS

Observers of today's economy can point to many signs that rightsizing is taking hold. Here we take a close look at a couple of them, weddings and birthdays—festive occasions that had, in recent years of consumerist frenzy, gotten seriously out of hand.

Blowing Homemade Bubbles

Along with "Bridezilla," lavish weddings have gotten a bad rap lately—further evidence that the rightsizing mentality is taking hold. "When Wedding Is a Big Show, Marriage Often Doesn't Last," one newspaper grimly warns us.[72] But perhaps the divorce rate is about to fall: Sifting for trends among the more than two million weddings in the United States in 2009, wedding planners noted a growing preference for simplicity and intimacy—smaller ceremonies with fewer guests, choosing off-peak times (mornings, afternoons, Fridays and Sundays, with October "the new June"). As couples found new ways to economize, spending slumped 10 percent compared with 2008, which itself had seen a decline of around 20 to 30 percent from the year prior.[73]

Bridal registries have shown a definite shift toward simplification, the casual, and the practical. "Five-piece place settings are for my mother's generation," says recent bride Julie Mathers of North

Carolina. "We wanted gifts that would work with our lifestyle and help make our home more inviting and luxurious—and luxury for me is a home where my husband and I can escape from the world. Silver is fine for some people, but we wanted gifts we knew we would use." Absent from their registry were fine china, sterling flatware, and silver serving dishes; in their place were handmade pottery and sturdy patio furniture.[74]

Today's more mindful bride mails invitations on recycled paper processed without chlorine and that have garden seeds embedded in them. Only a Neanderthal would throw rice anymore, of course, but it turns out birdseed is bad too: Throwing it "in a nature preserve or state park can cause havoc to that ecosystem," one Green Wedding Web site cautions in all seriousness. Far preferable is "throwing native wildflower seeds" or "blowing homemade bubbles from recyclable containers."[75] Fringe-granola as all this sounds, it may be common-place in decades to come, when people look back on today's weddings as the height of profligacy and eco-irresponsibility.

When Present Opening Turns to Chaos

Like weddings, children's birthday parties provide an intriguing index of changing attitudes about waste and the shift to rightsizing. Years ago, most everyone recalls, they were modest affairs, with few invited guests (*Emily Post's Etiquette* advised that five-year-olds should have no more than six guests, six-year-olds no more than seven, and so on) and token presents of little monetary value.[76] If a clown showed up, it was truly memorable. But in the recent age of bloated excess, parties got out of hand. In Orange County, California, Over the Top Productions spends six weeks planning children's tea parties with fine china or military-themed parties led by former Marines at a cost of up to $10,000.[77] In November 2008, it threw a gala for a girl named Bailey (daughter of actor Scott Baio), a 1950s-themed Sock Hop extravaganza complete with poodle skirts, hula hoops, ice-cream float bar, and a birthday cake in the form of a sculpted pink Cadillac with work-ing taillights. Bailey's outfit was custom designed in satin and tulle, adorned with 1950s-era appliqués. Bailey had just turned one.[78]

There will always be such parties, but the average American parent is beginning to doubt the wisdom of the over-the-top approach. They are starting to complain about having to attend too many parties (including those for "half birthdays"), being expected to invite numerous guests and hand out overflowing gift bags, engage in frenzied competitions to throw the most memorable fêtes, and pay for expensive presents that are met with petulant scorn by spoiled children. A worried mother writes Dear Abby about the consumerist mayhem that routinely breaks out: "Present-opening turns into chaos [as] children crowd closer and closer to the present-opener to get a better look, and some children cry about the gifts the birthday child has received while their parents promise to buy them a 'better one.' "[79]

Enter Birthdays Without Pressure, a Minnesota-based parent action group devoted to "studying the phenomenon of out-of-control birthday parties." "It's a trend that has evolved that didn't exist 20 to 25 years ago," says Linda Zwicky, who founded the group in 2007. "We have more expendable income in our consumer culture and parents have this different parenting philosophy that everything's got to be special.... There may be consequences for throwing these lavish parties year after year. The expectations are greater as kids get older, they feel more of a sense of entitlement and then there's the long-term concern about the materialistic values we're sending our kids."[80]

According to Zwicky, at the very heart of the party problem lies—what else?—our culture of rampant consumerism. Lavish galas lead children to "develop materialistic values that equate personal celebrations with accumulating things." And parents are victims too: "They feel overloaded with TOO MUCH STUFF, which they have to manage, organize, and clean up." The conclusion: "Out of control birthday parties contribute to [a] too much stuff culture, a me first culture, a trash and waste culture." Children beware: Proposed solutions include replacing gifts with canned food donations or seed packages for the garden.[81]

Not surprisingly, there is an ecological dimension to the anti-big-party crusade. In a conversation in April 2009 on the National Public Radio program *Tell Me More*, mothers expressed angst about the carbon impact of runaway birthday parties: "This big old footprint left on the earth," one called it. "I'll just be honest about this," another said. "I was cleaning up from my last kid party, and I am looking at the balloon leftovers, the plastic eggs, and I'm thinking OK, that was fun, but is there a way to do this that doesn't leave us with two bags of trash?" Various solutions were proposed: asking guests to bring their own picnic settings; using plates made out of recycled yogurt cups; buying plates and cups at Goodwill and, yes, donating them back again. A girl's party could consist merely of frolicking in the meadows, weaving crowns of wildflowers, and dyeing silk with beets. (A far cry from Miss Bailey's Sock Hop.) Little hope was voiced for reforming boys' parties, however, with their barbaric obsession with "cars and trucks and trains...all of which use fossil fuels."[82]

As part of the recent rebellion against disposables, some consumers have begun buying party plates made from biodegradable sugarcane or bamboo. Michael Dwok founded a company called VerTerra to manufacture disposable dinnerware from fallen palm leaves in South Asia. The idea came from a trip to India, where he saw rural women soaking leaves and then pressing them in a crude waffle iron to make plates for that evening's supper. Using squished palm leaves for plates requires 90 percent less energy than recycling paper, he says, and the production process creates only one bag of garbage per week. The soiled plates can go right into the compost bin, where they disappear in 62 days.[83] VerTerra plates have caught on lately, and they are even being used at concession stands at the Statue of Liberty.[84] But at more than fifty cents per plate, they are far more expensive than the usual paper or plastic ones party givers are accustomed to. Still, their popularity suggests that the mindful consumer is willing to pay more to waste less.

Rightsizing is a new way of life, part of the mindful consumption now taking hold. Rightsizers seek a better balance in their lives; they look to communities and relationships for their happiness instead of to material things, which they know cannot fulfill them in the long run. They have learned lessons from the years of excess and, now, from the inevitable downturn. Going forward, they will apply those lessons to their consumer choices permanently. They are putting aside their old, childish ways of buying and spending and are ready, as the next chapter's theme has it, to start Growing Up.

Chapter 6

GROWING UP

Growing up can be hard to do in a land of plenty. "Even though I'm an adult, I don't always feel like a real 'grownup,'" said fully half of U.S. respondents (and 58 percent of Prosumers) to the New Consumer survey. But as rightsizing becomes the norm, a cultural shift is taking place among the young—and the not so young. We are witnessing the reembrace of personal responsibility, an eagerness to grow up and be more mature and accountable to the larger community. This paradigm reverses the trend of recent years in which childishness was prolonged, consumerism ran rampant, individual needs were shamelessly gratified, and the "here and now" was about as far ahead as anybody cared to look. Growing Up promises to be a development with sweeping implications.

A LENGTHENED ADOLESCENCE

Pre-recession, many social commentators remarked on how young people were managing to put off "adulthood" far longer than previous generations. Popular culture usually was blamed, with its unrelenting stress on youth, beauty, and fun and the way it caricatures marriage and jobs as forms of soul-numbing imprisonment.

Canadian journalist Robert Fulford has traced the emergence of the "teenager" in the mid-twentieth century. "Millions were delighted to embrace their new role, with its simple-minded culture," he says. "They liked it so much they clung to it long past age twenty. And as the first teens became parents and then grandparents, the media steadily lowered the quality of culture in the direction of childishness."[1] Soon everyone was acting like a teenager.

We pause here to note that our own research at Euro RSCG refutes the notion that members of Generation Y are any less serious-minded than their boomer parents or grandparents. If anything, we have found them to be even more focused on achieving their goals and attaining their dreams. However, there are other factors at work here: According to a study by the University of Pennsylvania, the transition to adulthood has been delayed by societal changes, including the fact that it now takes more years of schooling to prepare for technical and information-based careers. With baby boomers retiring later and later, young workers can expect less responsibility and a much longer climb to positions of authority.[2] They have little incentive to knuckle down when the rewards are likely to be slight.

In some ways, younger generations have been victimized by new freedoms. The runaway consumer culture, unprecedented access to information, a general trend toward permissiveness, and the habit of constant mobility have brought a bewildering panoply of possible life choices to millions. So many choices, in fact, that many of us are overwhelmed and anxious. Men especially have suffered from confusion and lack of direction, writes Fulford. They put off growing up and establishing independence. "Something about maturity arouses in young men a combination of apathy and fear," he says. "It's hard to remember that, in previous eras, young people longed to escape their parents and set up on their own."[3]

Staving Off Adulthood: Twixters and Twits

In 2005, *Time* magazine featured a cover story on "twixters," people who are "not kids anymore, but [are] not adults either."[4] These young men and women flit from job to job, live in apartments with a succession of partners, party all night. In the world of the twixter, no one thinks of their twenties as a time to "settle down." And turning thirty does not necessarily push one into a new phase: The British media have taken to examining a cohort labeled "twits": "teenage women in their thirties."[5] For some, responsibility is to be avoided as long as possible.

The proof is in the data: In 1960, 30 percent of all twenty-five-year-old women and 77 percent of thirty-year-old women had completed the five major transitions to adulthood: finishing school, leaving home, achieving financial independence, getting married, having a child. By 2000, only 6 percent of twenty-year-olds and 46 percent of thirty-year-olds had done so.[6] The median age of first marriage is now twenty-eight for men and twenty-six for women, up from twenty-three and twenty-one, respectively, in 1974.[7]

In 2006, *New York* magazine reported the demise of "the long-held idea that in some fundamental way, you cross through a portal when you become an adult, a portal inscribed with the biblical imperative 'When I was a child, I spake as a child, I understood as a child, I thought as a child: But when I became a man, I put away childish things.' This cohort is not interested in putting away childish things." In fact, these "forty-year-old men and women who look, talk, act, and dress like people who are twenty-two years old" are very much focused on their things: The whole phenomenon springs from "abundant money" and "*stuff*." Here are "a generation or two of affluent, urban adults who are now happily sailing through their thirties and forties, and even *fifties*, clad in beat-up sneakers and cashmere hoodies."[8]

Hope for Peter Pan

Even before the recession, however, there were signs of impatience with the twixter lifestyle and mind-set. Much derision has been aimed at the "boomerang generation" with its "failure to launch." "Peter Pan syndrome," many have called it. An undergraduate at Texas Tech University identifies such childishness as "the pandemic of our generation....Symptoms include a refusal to go on dates, spending hours upon end playing video games and eating pizza every meal of the day. In short, it is a refusal to take responsibility for life." But "taking responsibility is a good thing," he believes. "It makes us more capable individuals."[9]

In a 2008 *Newsweek* magazine essay, "Why I Am Leaving Guyland," a recently married twenty-something confessed to having found serious drawbacks to playing Peter Pan, including the self-loathing that so often comes from binge drinking and one-night stands. "A raft of recent studies suggest that married men are happier, more sexually satisfied and less likely to end up in the emergency room than their unmarried counterparts," he says. "They also earn more, are promoted ahead of their single counterparts and are more likely to own a home."[10] But of course the fact of being married does not necessarily mean that young men (or women) are truly grown up, embracing their duties to spouse and children.

Encouragingly, there are definite signs of change now. The undergraduate who proclaimed that "taking responsibility is a good thing" is part of a new generation, many of whom do not fit the threadbare stereotype of slacker youth. Gen Y has been caricatured as a slouchy collection of me-firsters accustomed to being lavishly rewarded for even mediocre performance—those "everybody's a winner" awards ceremonies in elementary school, for example. One hears increasing complaints about how adults have cosseted children in recent years, insulating them from difficulties and at the same time robbing them of valuable chances to learn life skills in the school of hard knocks. It is a phenomenon that Michael Chabon lambastes in his 2009 book, *Manhood for Amateurs*, what he calls the "helmeting and monitoring, the corralling of children into certified zones of safety."[11]

But for all the trophies and corralling, evidence shows that these emerging young workers and consumers are more resourceful, responsible, and disciplined than many imagined they would be. A 2009 survey in Canada by Kelly Global Workforce Index shows that Gen Yers closely resemble the so-called Greatest Generation in their attitudes: Far from being "footloose and impatient…their levels of commitment and pride in their work were consistent with those of older workers, and they were less likely than Gen X and baby boomers to want to change jobs." According to a director of the survey, Gen Yers "place value on work which is personally satisfying, which builds competence and self-belief." They want to grow up, not remain adolescents forever.[12]

PROOF OF ADULTHOOD: THE NEW COMPETENCY

That striving for "competence and self-belief"—what forms does it take? One index of the trend toward growing up is the recent explosion in do-it-yourself (DIY) endeavors, as consumers turn away from prepackaged sources of fulfillment and seek inner happiness through genuine self-worth and self-competence.

Growing up, taking charge, DIY: They are all parts of the larger revolt against mindless buying and spending. An "Overcoming Consumerism" Web site warns against "societal suicide" as Americans buy more and more things, ignoring genuine sources of fulfillment. Advertisers are excoriated for their pernicious role. And suggestions are offered for DIY as a means of breaking free from a supposed capitalist stranglehold. Why not, for example, DIY a fort for your child by poking holes in a big cardboard box? "Toys 'R' Us keeps slaves in China busy making pastel plastic play structures that cost a fortune and pollute the environment because people haven't thought of this."[13]

OK, perhaps that cardboard box does not do justice to the DIY Revolution. Millions of consumers are starting to make interesting things instead of buy them, partly for the sense of self-competence they gain, partly to be less wasteful, partly to simplify and essentialize their lives. Thirty-seven percent of Americans who responded to the New Consumer survey affirmed that "in recent years, I have started or thought about starting a 'quiet' hobby such as gardening, knitting, or pottery," all of which involve DIY and a return to basic, useful skills.

Proponents find deep, transformative meaning in DIY. As the jacket cover of Matthew B. Crawford's 2009 book, *Shop Class as Soulcraft: An Inquiry into the Value of Work*, describes it, it is "an experience that was once quite common, but now seems to be receding from society: making and fixing things. Those of us who sit in an office often feel a lack of connection to the material world, a sense of loss, and find it difficult to say exactly what we do all day." By contrast, the book promotes "the intrinsic satisfactions and cognitive challenges of manual work. The work of builders and mechanics is secure; it cannot be outsourced, and it cannot be made obsolete." Crawford earned a Ph.D. in political philosophy but then quit his cubicle job and opened a motorcycle repair shop, reorienting his whole life toward the DIY ethos.[14]

GROWING UP, RIGHTSIZING THE HOME

A house is perhaps the most powerful symbol of growing up. Home ownership implies responsibility, personal integrity, stability. But for the new generation of mindful consumers, the 1990s mega-home will not do as a model. Today, growing up means rightsizing: The house should fit one's budget; it should avoid excessive show and a massive carbon footprint. This new attitude marks a dramatic shift from recent habits.

We have just lived, goggle-eyed, through the age of the Starter Mansion and the Garage Mahal. When neighbors of a 10,000-square-foot behemoth under construction in Lake Placid, New York, complained about its size, the owner could not understand what all the fuss was about. His home was "only 6,500 square feet," he said, "unless you count the basement."[15]

As conscientious consumerism takes hold, however, we are seeing signs of a revolt against huge houses. Even before the recession, the breakneck growth in square footage had slowed—but mostly because owners wanted to have enough money left over to buy fancy Sub-Zero refrigerators and stainless-steel countertops.[16] In today's economic climate, rightsizing is more urgent. Mindful consumers are asking hard questions about what size of house is really right for them. And in the New Consumer survey, more than one-third of U.S. Prosumers reported that "in recent years, I have moved or thought about moving to a smaller or more affordable home."

The year 2008 brought a decline in the size of new homes, reversing the long-standing trend toward the Herculean.[17] At the same time, many people began voicing their interest in "tiny houses"—perhaps to live in full time, or as a weekend getaway, or just to tuck into a corner of their garden as a symbol of how they are determined to essentialize their lives. As a deliberate alternative to the over-the-top houses in most "shelter" magazines, the upstart *Dwell* has taken to illustrating modernist homes as small as 1,200 square feet.[18] And a flood of books have lately appeared, enough to overwhelm the microbookcase in any microhouse: *Tiny Home to Call Your Own*; *The Very Small Home: Japanese Ideas for Living Well in Limited Space*; *Portable Houses*; *Little House on a Small Planet: Simple Homes, Cozy Retreats, and Energy Efficient Possibilities*, to name a few.

Rightsizing one's home—paring it down to the size that is perfect for one's needs, and no larger—can have enormous financial and psychological benefits, proponents say. Erin Doland, who runs the Web site Unclutterer, went from being a packrat to "having a fanatical commitment to a more minimalist and simple lifestyle." Her new attitude as a consumer can be summed up as "buying quality over quantity." And she relates this approach to her conviction that "a clean, uncluttered home is an essential component of a less stressful life." Doland's Web site features testimonials from happy people who have moved into smaller homes and who, in spite of occasionally bumping against the furniture, are emphatic about the spiritual and psychological benefits of rightsizing:

- "My partner and I recently downsized from a (by today's standards) modestly sized house to a slightly smaller apartment. We jettisoned enough stuff to fill a single-car garage, and now we have less stuff to take care of, plus a smaller space to clean. Which all adds to more time spent doing things we enjoy."

- "Many people in my demographic (yuppie thirty-somethings with or without kids) are stressed to the limit by their possessions and households. So many of us were brought up to think that a big yard, big house, multiple cars, a boat, and tons of sports equipment are the markers of happiness. But in reality, these things can quickly become drags and sinkholes of money. My suburban friends are victims of this."

- "Enjoy the downsizing, it's fun and very satisfying! My wife and I had worked our way up through increasingly larger houses because that's just what you do. [We downsized] and couldn't be happier. Plenty of room to live and have guests even, and less time and money spent maintaining and fiddling with our physical possessions. They had started to own us! Getting rid of eighty-plus percent of our junk really lightened our mental burden as well as physical."[19]

For these homeowners and many others like them, the quest for bigger and better has been replaced by a more mature attitude. They have made the commitment to rightsizing and are enjoying the benefits.

Can Someone Steal My House?

Some have gone to extremes and now inhabit truly tiny houses. If you do so, expect a local TV crew to show up—because viewers are fascinated by these experiments. It is another bellwether of rising interest in sustainable living and minimizing one's personal impact on the planet.

Take these examples from the media recently:

- California entrepreneur Jay Shafer proudly occupies a house "smaller than some people's closets." Limiting himself to 89 square feet allows him "a simple, slower lifestyle," he explains. His Tumbleweed Tiny House Company sells plans for a whole range of such homes, and he has appeared on *Oprah.* Shafer gently talks potential buyers through their worries, including "Can someone steal my house?"[20]
- In Iowa, Gregory Johnson directs the Small House Society. He abandoned a conventional home for a ten-by-seven-foot cabin, leaving behind electric bills and homeowners' insurance forever. Lacking a kitchen, he eats his food raw and has lost 100 pounds. "There's something about living simply that transforms everything about you," he says. His heating costs are less than $100 a year, but the absence of a bathroom might discourage the fainthearted. Johnson rejoices in his newfound freedom. "Technology," he says, "has really helped shrink down our lives."[21]
- "I am not a man of means," a construction worker named Tyson confesses to *Small Living Journal.* Rightsizing his home was a way of critiquing "a society built so heavily on self-aggrandizement and the display of material status symbols," which, he says, "leaves me in a state of virtually perpetual disgust." He likes how tiny houses invite a hands-on approach: "Participation in the design and construction of one's own home is not only deeply fulfilling, but also an unsurpassed opportunity for practical education and confidence building."[22]

- Prominent medical doctor Matthew Sleeth first turned "Christian environmentalist" when he noticed a rash of cancer cases in his hospital. Opening the Bible, he discovered lessons of how "personal responsibility, simplicity, and stewardship could be applied to modern life." Concluding that the planet is dying from our excessive consumerism, he moved his family out of their luxurious home and into a dwelling the size of their previous garage. Thanks to the rightsizing, he says, "Spiritual concerns have filled the void left by material ones. Owning fewer things has resulted in things no longer owning us."[23]

- Nor is the phenomenon confined to America. In a much-publicized experiment in England, Mark Boyle, thirty, spent much of 2008–9 living in a trailer in a field, rejecting his "life of materialism." The former businessman, a self-described "freeconomist," did not spend a penny. "It has been the best year of my life and there is no way I want to return to a money-orientated world," he says. "I've given up bank statements, utility bills, traffic jams and now I can honestly say there is nothing I miss about my old lifestyle. The social aspect of not having any money and living hand-to-mouth did take some adjusting to at first but I think it has made me more complete."[24]

These uber-rightsizers are, in a sense, the new Thoreaus—and in fact a whole series of replicas of Thoreau's tiny house at Walden Pond have been erected nationwide in recent years, including one by undergraduates at Furman University, South Carolina, in 2009. That last example may be the most telling of all, for it involves group effort, not the solitary endeavors of an isolated individual. As consumers strive to buy responsibly and achieve sustainability, they are increasingly seeking ways to collaborate.

THE NEW COLLABORATIVE COMMITMENTS

If American culture has long been mired in wasteful consumption, other world traditions point to ways of achieving moderation and balance. Buddhism preaches a "middle way" that avoids sensuality on one hand and self-abnegation on the other. And the Swedish have a word, *lagom*, that means "just enough, just the right amount," to suggest a deep-rooted societal commitment to finding happiness through moderation. Now Americans are beginning to embrace what other peoples have long known: Satisfaction can come from simplicity. As the New Consumer survey shows, 78 percent of Americans (and 84 percent of Prosumers) agree with this comment: "I respect/admire people who live simply (minimal purchases, debt free, etc.)." This is in stark contrast to the mere 15 percent of Americans who agree that "I respect/admire people who live a high-luxury lifestyle (lots of indulgences, expensive possessions, etc.)."

Admiring the "simple life" does not mean, of course, that everyone is ready to pack up and move somewhere like Sieben Linden in Germany, an "eco-village" where 120 diehards live in houses of wood, straw, and mud. They burn mountains of cordwood for heating, use only solar for power, and compost their human waste. A chief focus there is to own fewer possessions; items are handed around from person to person, and appliances and cars are shared. The founder of the village explains that consumption of things is less important to them than communal life; for example, sharing the pleasures of ice-skating or tai chi.[25]

This may seem extreme—but, in fact, many of the Sieben Linden principles are rapidly gaining acceptance in mainstream circles in the United States and elsewhere. Among them is the collaborative aspect, the idea that individuals cannot save the planet themselves but must band together to do so. The new Growing Up paradigm argues that mature, responsible consumers are not satisfied with merely living and consuming for themselves; instead, they think in terms of moderation and are mindful of their impact on others.

Finding Common Cause in the Reverse Boycott

"Proud 'frugalistas' are ready to strut," Amy Hardin Turosak told us in chapter 5. "And in come the 'environistas,' who shop with the intention of lowering their carbon footprint." Without question, there will be many more environistas in years to come, consumers who withhold their American Express from firms that are not protecting the planet or are otherwise acting unethically. According to the New Consumer survey, 67 percent of U.S. respondents (and 79 percent of Prosumers) say that "As a consumer, I have a responsibility to censure unethical companies by avoiding their products." How very grown up of them.

The flip side of this attitude is an eagerness to *reward* ethical companies by deliberately choosing to buy their offerings. Charting the "Responsibility Revolution" among U.S. consumers, *Time* magazine emphasizes the new power of the reverse boycott: Companies have begun to realize "that just as some consumers boycotted products they considered unethical, others would purchase products in part because their manufacturers were responsible."[26]

As consumers who formerly thought only of satisfying their personal predilections now find power in community collaborations, we are seeing the rise of highly creative organized efforts. Since 2008, a California-based activist group called Carrotmob has rewarded small businesses that promise to install energy-efficient lighting or otherwise help the planet. Young founder Brent Schulkin calls it a new kind of activism, one based on rewards (giving a "carrot") rather than punishments. "Boycotting, protesting, lawsuits—[those are] about going into attack mode," he says. "What's unique about a Carrotmob is that there are no enemies." [27]

As his movement spreads nationwide (and to Europe and Asia), student volunteers hand out carrots on college campuses to attract new recruits. Businesses compete to win a visit from a hoard of Carrotmob members, who boisterously make purchases in their store. A portion of the proceeds goes toward paying for the promised environmental upgrades.

By embracing capitalism and working within the system, Schulkin sounds a very different note from the radicals of past generations. He acknowledges that Carrotmob is too consumerist for diehard, off-the-grid ecofreaks.

> If you're really hardcore, and you grow all of your own organic food and weave your own clothes out of hemp, you're probably not going to start buying Carrotmob's preferred brand of pork rinds just because we got the pork rind factory to start using solar panels. Let's be honest: You are just a way better person than the rest of us. Keep doing what you're doing. We know that Carrotmob is doing nothing to reduce our global consumption habit. We know that "people buying stuff they don't need" is a huge problem. But we're not fighting that fight right now.[28]

In fact, Carrotmob illustrates the maturing and mainstreaming of eco-consciousness as cranky individual Thoreaus are replaced by everyday intelligent consumers. They will continue to buy things, but they are determined to buy more responsibly now and are fully aware of the creative power of the mob.

GREEN WAYS TO GROW UP

As the "Responsibility Revolution" takes hold, one key definition of acting responsibly is to do something to save the planet. Accordingly, the new trend toward growing up and being mature sounds a strongly ecological note. For many people, going green is the first truly adult commitment they have ever made, the first cause larger than themselves that they have embraced.

Doing good is a powerful motivator, but there is an added impetus: As noted earlier, about six in ten adults we surveyed around the globe are worried about our loss of connectedness to the natural world. As many commentators have lamented in recent years, modern life has brought detachment from the land. Over the past century, the number of Americans engaged in full-time farming has gone from nearly 50 percent to less than 2 percent.[29] Amazingly, only 17 percent of us even live in a rural area anymore.[30] Whereas previous generations at least had a relative who was a farmer, to millions of current citizens, the profession seems as remote as something from the Middle Ages—although we depend on farmers every day to feed us. Much has been written on the troubling consequences of this sense of alienation.

With the current crisis surrounding consumerism, many people are finding an opportunity to reconnect. A growing number of homeowners are learning the skills of gardening or animal husbandry, for example, and applying them to suburban and even urban milieus. This is not merely a hobby but a means of growing up by learning a new, self-empowering trade that is, at the same time, deeply ecological. "Could a new generation of Americans, raised in a wealthy, consumerist society, be ready to rediscover the gift of agrarian self-sufficiency?" asks an editorial in the *Dallas Morning News*. "If you have skills in gardening and animal husbandry, however rudimentary, you don't feel helpless in the face of growing uncertainty."[31]

Gardening Provides Self-Sufficiency

"In recent years, I have started or thought about starting a home vegetable or fruit garden" say 43 percent of U.S. respondents to the New Consumer survey (and 48 percent of Prosumers). They are participating in a worldwide trend toward being more self-contained and resourceful, one that responds to the recessionary crisis but also fills that back-to-nature craving. These straw-hatted enthusiasts blog about their "sustainable backyards" in which they plow under the dahlias to plant heirloom tomatoes, grow bountiful "container vegetables" in recycled buckets, and set up workstations where they (to neighbors' amazement) produce their own jam, soy milk, tofu, and even soap. The recession added fire to the trend: Some seed companies are reporting that sales of seeds for home gardens spiked as much as 80 percent in 2009.[32]

In an increasing number of communities, the vegetable garden doubles as a barnyard as urban animal husbandry comes into vogue.

Would-be back-to-the-landers ignore the cramped confines of city lots (and, sometimes, local ordinances and regulations) as they experience the thrill of self-sufficiency by raising and culling animals for food and profit. Devotees attest to a sense of taking control of their lives as they engage in manual tasks very different from their rarified cubicle jobs. Some need basic training: In Oakland, California, the Institute of Urban Homesteading obliges by teaching city dwellers the fine arts of feeding goats, wrangling chickens, and slaughtering rabbits for their fur.[33]

These new hobbies grade into what the *New York Times* calls "The New Survivalism." Barton M. Biggs, former chief global strategist at Morgan Stanley, warns that we should all "assume the possibility of a breakdown of the civilized infrastructure. Your safe haven must be self-sufficient and capable of growing some kind of food. It should be well-stocked with seed [and] fertilizer." In Washington State, Joyce Jimerson, coordinator for a recycling-composting program affiliated with Washington State University, has replaced her grassy yard with an "edible garden" full of fruit trees and vegetables, in case the pumps run dry, the economy collapses, or the oceans rise: "It's all the same ball of wax, as far as I'm concerned." As she weeds among her brussels sprouts, she is ready for any contingency.[34]

"Somewhere at the intersection of New Urbanism, DIY culture, and the resurgence of gardening for self-sustenance," writes Sarah Rich of *Dwell* magazine, "an active and growing community of artist-maker-activists is redefining urban survivalism. While their work addresses our tenuous food security and the threats of catastrophic climate change, it's not a fear-driven movement. Rather, the best of these 'new survivalists' are embracing radical self-sufficiency because it fuels their creativity, arms them with a sense of personal empowerment, and strengthens their communities."[35]

Examples of these urban, self-sustenance gardens can be drawn from everywhere, but let us look at London. If such green endeavors can be undertaken there, in one of the most crowded places in the western world, they can be done anywhere. And in fact, London has become a center of ecological consciousness and small-site gardening. In December 2009, the *Evening Standard* hailed the city's "eco heroes," including a restaurateur who sources food only from inside the city beltway; gardeners who get together to help troubled youth or the elderly and disabled; a woman who created a program through which children cook their own healthful, fresh-veggie meals at school. Mark Shearer's "Project Dirt" fills large, heavy-duty builders bags with topsoil and places them on paved surfaces in a blighted area, renting the bags to local gardeners for a pittance. The bags become the containers in which the crops grow. A nearby housing project, "once the haunt of knife gangs, is now safe. The police [say the program has] been worth three bobbies on the beat."[36]

A chorus of voices attests to the benefits of gardening for self-sufficiency and personal pride, not to mention the societal plusses. But are you ready to experience the ultimate in gardening commitment—to recycle your own biological waste as compost? This may be the next craze. Joseph Jenkins wrote the *Humanure Handbook: A Guide to Composting Human Manure* years ago, but it has lately become a sensation, with one reviewer calling it "one of those life-changing books."[37] Jenkins wants us to follow the example of his Pennsylvania home and replace our toilets with a simple bucket. The contents are topped off with sawdust after each use and emptied once a week into a compost bin in the yard. He shows off pictures of his garden, and his sunflowers are enormous.

Silence of the Leaf Blowers

As we looked into these green trends, we noticed one culprit was singled out again and again for its eco-unfriendliness: the leaf blower, that poster child of the hyperconsumerist approach to lawn and garden. Introduced in the 1970s, the energy-sucking noisemaker took the place of that ancient and mercifully quiet implement, the rake. Recent years have seen growing rebellion against this bane, however. They are criticized for emitting fumes equivalent to a parade of automobiles, filling the air with dust and nasty spores, desiccating the soil with hot 180-miles-per-hour winds, and shattering the quiet of suburban neighborhoods (which were, ironically, first marketed in the 1920s as places to escape the noisy, fumy engines of trucks, then filling city streets). Detractors call them the antithesis of conscious consumerism and the desire to achieve a less impactful, more ecological lifestyle through lawn-and-garden work.

By 2006, leaf blower sales had reached 2.5 million in the United States, and in many communities the whine of these devices proved inescapable during the warmer months.[38] But an increasing number of towns have banned the backyard menace, especially on the West Coast and around New York, and 2009 saw sales plummet.[39] Much attention has been brought to bear on their pernicious effects, with some arguments waxing philosophical: Leaf blowers benefit the selfish individual but harm his neighbors; raking, by contrast, has a Zen-like rhythm and offers an excellent cardio workout. Three cheers for the classic rake: silent, inexpensive, planet-saving, heart healthy. As the Swedes would say, it is very *lagom*.

The Locavores

Of the 1,000 adults polled by *Time* magazine in summer 2009, 82 percent had deliberately supported local or neighborhood businesses that year.[40] The grown-up consumer shows heightened awareness of his or her place in the local community, as "a piece of the continent, a part of the main." Such consumers desire to support local producers, artisans, and manufacturers: 69 percent of U.S. respondents to the New Consumer study (and 76 percent of U.S. Prosumers) say it makes them "feel good" to do so. Part of the allure of local comes down to size: About two-thirds of U.S. respondents and seven in ten Prosumers prefer that their money go to small businesses rather than large corporations. With the exception of the United Kingdom, this anti-Big Business sentiment was far more evident in the United States than in any of the other markets surveyed.

In Australia, Sustainable Living Groups are springing up, preaching the mantra of "living locally." One organizer explains, "There are many simple ways to leave a smaller carbon footprint. Just by eating local food, supporting local entertainment and making friends in the neighborhood. It's also a great way of building community and feeling more connected to people and the place we live in." Members attend lectures on raising chickens, growing vegetables, and using biodegradable "nappies."[41]

Not everyone agrees that local is best, however. *Forbes* published an essay in August 2009, "The Locavore Myth," that showed that buying local may not have the benefits many claim. What if local lamb is raised in factorylike conditions, whereas a distant lamb is raised more naturally? In this case, the carbon footprint is less for the distant lamb, in spite of greater transportation costs. And transportation amounts to only 11 percent of the carbon footprint of food, anyway; fully one-quarter of the energy required to produce food is expended in your home kitchen. Thanks to economies of scale, distant farmers who ship their produce in bulk actually may save fuel, compared with local farmers who transport extremely small quantities: Trucking two thousand apples a distance of two thousand miles consumes the same amount of fuel per apple as trucking fifty apples fifty miles by pickup to a market stall. Buying local means helping local farmers, but at the same time it hurts distant agriculture; a recent campaign in the United Kingdom to discourage the consumption of green beans flown in by airplane from afar has resulted in substantial harm to the livelihood of sub-Saharan farmers.[42]

Despite such expressions of skepticism, 55 percent of U.S. respondents to the New Consumer survey (and 67 percent of Prosumers) maintain that "buying locally produced goods is easier on the environment (e.g., reduces transportation/'food miles')." And most U.S. respondents agree that "locally produced foods tend to be more healthful (e.g., fresher, fewer preservatives)." Four in ten Prosumers report they have "more confidence in the safety of locally produced goods." Clearly the newfound enthusiasm for the locavore lifestyle is not going away.

HYPER-SELF SUFFICIENCY: FREEGANS AND GLEANERS

As we explore emerging trends in our work, always seeking to catch a glimpse of the future for clients, we pay attention even to the most offbeat extensions. They just might offer clues of what is to come.

As millions adopt a new attitude toward consumerism—more grown-up, less irresponsible—there are a few among them who go the extra mile. Freegans, in particular, embrace a colorful lifestyle of anti-consumerism. In December 2009, the *Boston Globe* described their ways, which range from searching curbs for old sofas and bicycles to subsisting almost entirely on throwaway food. It profiled a young woman who "started eating food out of dumpsters shortly after she graduated from Harvard University.... She does it to make a statement [against] profligate waste."[43]

In these strange habits, one perceives an emerging mind-set. If it catches on, the implications are enormous for our consumer culture. The web resource *Freegan Info: Strategies for Sustainable Living Beyond Capitalism* explains the impetus to minimize consumption and live more independently from the "profit-driven economy":

> Freegans are dismayed by the social and ecological costs of an economic model where only profit is valued, at the expense of the environment and human and animal rights. We view our participation in this economy as workers or as consumers as a form of complicity in practices like sweatshop labor, rainforest destruction, and factory farming, practices used to create everyday consumer goods, but never mentioned in the corporate advertisements that assault us every time we look at a billboard, turn on a radio, or open a newspaper.[44]

Freeganism, in other words, is a holistic lifestyle aimed at radical self-sufficiency and opposition to the consumerist mainstream. Like so many movements that aim to rightsize, there is a back-to-community ethos. Freegans value authentic communal experiences:

> In a society that worships competition and self-interest, freegans believe in living ethical, free, and happy lives centered around community and the notion that a healthy society must function on interdependence....Freegans resist manipulative advertisements that tell us we can find happiness and self-worth on retail store shelves. By buying less "stuff" and taking care of vital needs without paying money, freegans are able to work less or not at all. This is motivated not by "laziness," but by a desire to devote their time to community service, activism, caring for family, appreciating nature, and enjoying life.[45]

Lately freegans have become famous, or infamous, for Dumpster diving. Practicing "urban foraging," they sneak behind grocery stores at night, wading into slimy containers to find perfectly edible packages of food. Once a private, even furtive activity, Dumpster diving has lately grown popular among a surprising number of college-educated youth and has come out into the open. In 2009, freegans in New York invited the public to join them in a pre-Thanksgiving excursion through the city's Dumpsters, as if nothing could be more ordinary or delightful. Freegans run "trash tours" in several cities, showing neophytes which alleyways to frequent and how to avoid getting pricked by a hypodermic needle or trapped by a slamming Dumpster lid. The subtext is anti-consumerist: An "Overcoming Consumerism" Web site sees the purpose of Dumpster diving as creating "a reduction of demand" that takes power away from the corporations.[46]

THE NEW/OLD VIRTUE OF RESPONSIBILITY

All these trends toward growing up and achieving self-sufficiency seem very new, but at the same time they mark a return to traditional ways—with a fresh, contemporary spin. "Old is the new new," says U.K. financial blogger Harvey Jones. After an orgy of consumerism, "Now it's all gone horribly wrong, we're finding ourselves flying back in time," with a cathartic "return to traditional ways."[47] One communications agency terms this the "New Pragmatism: a more common sense, even old-fashioned approach to everyday lifestyle choices."[48]

For all its novelty, mindful consumerism actually dovetails with the traditional values of the past. "It's funny, being green to me was ingrained because my parents were always trying to save money, save water, turn off the lights, or arrange a carpool," says SuChin Pak, cohost of *G Word* on Planet Green network. "Some of the most green people in our lives are our parents and grandparents, who always bought locally and carefully. I remember my grandmother would buy a jar of cream and make it last for a long time. To me, that is just as green as something with an expensive, eco-savvy label on it."[49]

Writing in *Newsweek* in March 2009, social critic Joseph Epstein called for a return to the time-honored virtues of prudence and thrift:

> Those of us old enough to have had parents who lived through the Depression had the habits of thrift imbued in us along with an ingrained disbelief in life as limitless progress. We were instructed that life, like Greek plays, features *peripeteia*, or reversals of fortune. Prepare for it. Turn off the lights when you leave a room, finish the food on your plate, thoroughly squeeze the toothpaste tube, forget about the stretch limo.

Today's young people, Epstein observes, have had little experience with thrift—until now. "With our recent penchant for McMansions, Hummers, $6,000 wristwatches, gourmet dog food and other items of opulent squalor, Americans could do worse than relearn, in fact memorize, the useful platitudes of thrift."[50]

For blogger Sarah Gilbert, whom we met in chapter 5, today's "frugalites" are part of a long tradition:

> It's clear that frugality has had a resurgence of the sort not seen since the Great Depression. And really: This looks so much like the time when my grandmother was a young bride, I often look to her generation for guidance. After all, that was the time when everything was patched, and patched again; when old sheets and curtains were made into dish towels and aprons and clothes for little girls; when nothing was thrown away until it was used up, beyond all recognition.[51]

One might add that today's sustainable backyards resemble the Victory Gardens of World War II. In England, Patricia Nicol's 2009 book *Sucking Eggs: What Your Wartime Granny Could Teach You about Diet, Thrift and Going Green* highlights such connections between now and the 1940s. "We do not have to look far back in our own history for a timely lesson in making seismic lifestyle changes," she says. "The grandparents at whom we may once have scoffed for hanging onto leftovers and hoarding pieces of string were, by contrast to us, model global citizens. Their carbon footprints barely left a mark." They were, she concludes, "pioneering anticonsumerists."[52]

"It's time for us to be more like our grandparents and less like our neighbors," says writer W. Hodding Carter, who has embarked his family on an "Extreme Frugality" experiment to spend no more than $41,000 annually. "Like 70 percent of our fellow Americans, we were living off our VISA cards with no means of paying them off any time soon. As a result, we had $75,000 in credit-card debt and owed $245,000 on a $289,000 house. What had I been thinking?" He is not alone, he points out: "Ninety percent of us buy something we don't need every month, and Americans in all walks of life—except the very rich—carry $961 billion of credit-card debt at any given moment, paying $1.22 for every $1 they spend."

But Carter is changing his ways now, determined to rightsize and really grow up. "For the first time ever, my family is going to do the unthinkable. We're going to live within our means."[53]

We spoke with Rebecca Saeger, executive vice president and chief marketing officer at Charles Schwab Corporation, who says the Carters are not alone in rethinking their approach to spending:

> For years, we saw a relative lack of attention to a gap that existed between what people were going to need as they retired and what they were actually going to have based on their savings and spending habits—very little money saved, no pension, and Social Security a big unknown. Now, what we're seeing—and it started even before the recession—is an emerging understanding that people are responsible for their own money and their own futures. They cannot count on anyone else. I've been really encouraged by how people are taking charge of their financial lives, being more engaged with their investments and paying down debt. These people know that achieving their financial goals will take time, but they are focused on it, and they are absolutely determined to make it work. And they will.[54]

And, indeed, we see that more than one-third of Americans and 43 percent of U.S. Prosumers are putting more money into savings than they used to.

In chapter 5, we looked at wedding trends as an index of rightsizing. And weddings, too, show a conscious return to traditional values, including thrift. In 2009 *The Knot*, a wedding magazine, lauded "the crafty bride" who adopts a DIY approach to favors, bouquets, programs, seating charts, and anything else that can be made rather than purchased (in case she didn't have enough to do already). It is OK to seek out antiques instead of the latest items, *The Knot* assures young couples: "Looking for a wedding cake topper on a dime? Find one on eBay or borrow your grandparents'." Inexpensive honeymoons are acceptable, too, with permission found in the past: "Make like JFK and Jackie O who honeymooned in Santa Barbara's exclusive San Ysidro Ranch. Skip the far-flung destinations and sequester yourselves in a honeymoon-worthy domestic locale."[55]

Everywhere we look, the New Pragmatism is finding inspiration in what's old.

REPLACING CASUAL, A GROWN-UP FORMALITY

As Growing Up becomes the goal, many are questioning their slouchy, adolescent attire—the "beat-up sneakers and cashmere hoodies" we met earlier. Maybe our grandparents had the right idea by dressing for success and favoring the formal over the casual. "In tough economic times, the ethic of achievement is more important," says media consultant Alex Castellanos. "Crew cuts will come back—symbolizing value, discipline, security. We'll see the return of the white shirt. Discipline will be the new style."[56]

We have just lived through the age of the ultra-casual, of course, when the very word *suit* came to mean a faceless corporate drudge. As *New York* magazine put it, the workplace trend in recent years was toward "using a messenger bag instead of a briefcase, and staying out too late too often, and owning more pairs of sneakers (eleven) than suits (one)."[57] Casual Fridays became the norm, erasing the traditional distinction between the professional and the blue-collar employee. The *New York Times* first noticed such Fridays in 1993: "Blue jeans, T-shirts, even—horrors—thonged sandals are replacing pinstripes, oxford cloth, silks and Italian leather."[58] By a gradual erosion of standards, soon it was "business casual" every day: By 2008, only 12 percent of men and 6 percent of women reported still wearing formal attire to work.[59]

But signs of a backlash are evident lately, and stuffiness may be on the rebound. "A lot of companies have found that with Casual Fridays the dress has gotten sloppier and so has their work," says Dallas-based business etiquette expert Colleen Rickenbacher. "A lot of companies have gotten back to a business dress. Some have created an office casual dress code."[60] And that code is getting stricter. "I think it's important to understand that business casual is still a professional look, not T-shirts and jeans," says a menswear-store owner in Bellingham, Washington. "The khaki pants and a polo shirt isn't really business casual anymore. That's for Saturday. That's for the golf course. Business casual is dressier than that."[61]

Image consultant Sandy Dumont goes further when she proclaims, "Business Casual Is Dead." "Most large companies are finally beginning to recognize that 'corporate casual' or 'business casual' dress has many shortcomings. For one, it is difficult to define. Secondly, it is sorely abused. And last, but not least, recent studies indicate that we are less productive in casual attire."[62]

Suddenly we are sounding a lot like our grandparents, whose sartorial advice even extended to wearing clean underwear "in case you get hit by a bus." On the HBO comedy *Curb Your Enthusiasm*, a character fires his lawyer for being dressed casually, saying his legal affairs are far too important to entrust to someone who looks like that.[63] And a commentator on the "Women on Business" Web site warns:

> Women who aspire to get ahead in their organizations should dress a notch higher than their peers. This sets an example for employees and makes an impression on those higher up. Wear casual pants, not jeans or capris, and keep a neutral suit jacket, scarf or fancy sweater in your office to dress up your outfit. Even on dress down days, it is wise to look professional enough to attend an impromptu meeting if the need arises.[64]

In other words, casual is full of pitfalls for the ambitious and industrious—just as conventional wisdom once had it.

New Life for an Old Symbol: The Necktie

The revived interest in wearing dressy clothes to work is part of a broader commitment to greater seriousness and maturity. But how far are we willing to go? For men, what about the necktie, that hated symbol of responsibility and enforced adulthood?

When he was a boy, comedian Ben Stein remembers, "Ties were a symbol of white-collar status, although even some workmen wore them under their leather aprons. If you had on a necktie, it showed you had some sense of organization, some sense of dignity about yourself."[65] But lately neckties have been going the way of the Edsel. Sales peaked at $1.3 billion in 1995 and fell steadily thereafter, to $677.7 million in

2007, by which time only 6 percent of American men wore ties to work every day.[66] Facing the inevitable, the tie makers' trade group, Men's Dress Furnishings Association, shut its doors in 2008.[67]

As casual became a cult in recent years, everybody had their own reason for taking off the tie. Presidents of the United States wanted to connect with the people, or to seem more vigorous, or more commander in chief-like. Lawyers wanted to avoid intimidating clients who were themselves wearing knit shirts. Doctors left their ties at home when scientific studies showed them to harbor swarms of bacteria. And dot-commers, of course, wouldn't even know how to tie one. In a fascinating inversion, wearing a tie became a symbol not of authority but of underling status. "Historically, the guy wearing the navy suit, the white shirt and the burgundy tie would be the CEO," says Marty Staff, chief executive of JA Apparel Corp. "Now he's the accountant. Power is being able to dress the way you want."[68]

But now that casual is beginning to fizzle, there are signs of renewed interest in wearing ties. They were everywhere on men's fashion runways in fall 2009—along with old-timey metal tie clips. "It is not dead," rejoices tie enthusiast Chris Lambert, who owns a menswear store in Fort Wayne, Indiana. "It's still an important part of the wardrobe. There's still a market for fine neckwear, I don't see it ever going away." Some Fort Wayne companies, he notes, have dropped their liberal "business casual" policies and again require serious dress. And he has customers who are relieved to be picking out suits and ties instead of guessing what constitutes an acceptable business-casual wardrobe. He sells fewer ties nowadays, but nicer ones, and sales are strong for specialty, custom, and limited edition neckwear. "We've decided we'll keep stocking the better ties because there's always a market for quality. There are some tie connoisseurs out there."[69]

Lee Terrill, president of the neckwear division of Phillips-Van Heusen, the nation's largest tie maker, laments that sales have fallen from nearly 250 million in the early 1970s to 50 million today. But he believes the decline has now leveled off. As dress codes grew lax in the 1990s, men who had always been required to buy ties "were making a statement. I'm not going to wear a tie because I don't have to wear a tie. But now so many people don't wear a tie, that it's a statement to wear one."[70]

Already in late 2007, CBS talk show *The Early Show* reported the "comeback of the necktie," with tie sales down among older populations but up more than 13 percent in one year among eighteen- to thirty-four-year-olds. "We're seeing a lot of younger customers coming into our store," says Robert Dundon, president of luxury shirtmaker Thomas Pink USA, who adds, "There has been a backlash to the whole casual dress thing."[71] On its Web site, Thomas Pink empowers young shoppers to "customize your tie." No longer a suffocating symbol of corporate blandness, the tie becomes another opportunity for authentic Gen-Y self-expression. "Put yourself in the design seat and customize your own Personally Pink tie. First, select your design: stripes or flowers, then select your background color followed by your 'highlight' color."[72]

In that one Personally Pink tie, many threads of the Growing Up paradigm blend together. Increasingly, young people are bucking the trend of prolonged adolescence and responsibility avoidance; instead, they are dressing up for success on the job and in life. They are looking back to the past, to their grandparents' values and sense of style, but with a strikingly modern twist. Their partiality for flowers suggests an interest in the ecological, among their most deeply held beliefs. And they want to have the opportunity to DIY their own tie—to take a little power away from the corporations, to make a dazzling personal statement—even as they accept one of society's most conventional fashion norms. It is a complex and fascinating new culture that is emerging before our eyes.

Chapter 7

SEEKING PURPOSEFUL PLEASURE

The pleasure principle plays a vital role in how we make choices. Here we examine how the quest for pleasure shapes our decisions as consumers, telling us how to spend our time and money—and how that is likely to change in the future, as a promising new regime of "purposeful pleasure" takes hold.

The decision to buy something and the making of choices among competing products are never purely rational. They always involve a combination of thinking and feeling, the cognitive and the emotional. We choose a particular product or service because it promises to deliver the most positive feelings. We enjoy the tingle of excitement as we make our selection, the satisfaction in having made the "perfect" choice, and the pleasure of owning and using it. In the recently departed era of High-Octane Consumerism, one of our most constant sources of pleasure was the *instant gratification* that came with most of the things we bought. Following the mind-set of "see-buy-consume-discard—what's next?" we rarely if ever paused to consider the more substantial, long-term, and purposeful pleasures that might be available if only we took the time to cultivate them.

Now, given the recession and other shocks, we have had to reassess, to take more care in deciding what—and whether—to buy and to think harder about the value we will receive for our money. Impulse shopping has given way to a more considered—and conscientious—form of consumption. But what lies ahead? With the economic skies beginning to clear, will instant gratification resume its giddy reign? Or will other pleasures—perhaps deeper and truer ones—take its place, bringing with them new and more grounded ways of consuming and behaving?

THE MARSHMALLOW TEST:
ONE NOW OR TWO LATER?

I can resist everything but temptation.

—Oscar Wilde

At the TED (Technology, Entertainment, Design) conference in California in February 2009, motivational speaker Joachim de Posada delivered an entertaining talk called "Don't Eat the Marshmallow Yet." Coming as it did right after the financial meltdown, it held the audience rapt. De Posada showed a filmed set of experiments at Stanford University involving four-year-olds. Each was given a marshmallow. A researcher patiently explained that he would come back in fifteen minutes. If—and only if—the marshmallow were still there, the child would receive a second marshmallow and would be allowed to eat both.

What do you think happened? Did the tug of instant gratification win out? Or did the children resist that urge in order to experience double the pleasure in the end?

The audience laughed to see the expressions on the children's faces as they struggled with the agonizing choice. But as industry professionals, many of them also recognized the extraordinary relevance of that experiment to today's consumer landscape, with the tough choices it presents and the constant dilemma of whether to spend or save, splurge or hoard.[1]

The marshmallow experiment was carried out years ago, but it has garnered much attention of late. In a widely cited article in the *New Yorker*, Walter Mischel, the Stanford professor of psychology who conducted the study, reported that only about 30 percent of the 653 children were able to withstand the temptation of the marshmallow until the researcher returned.[2] The story continues further: Mischel continued to track his young subjects into adulthood, and he discovered a correlation between those few who had forsworn the marshmallow and, remarkably enough, high academic achievement—specifically, scoring well on the Scholastic Achievement Test (SAT). In fact, those who had been able to delay gratification for fifteen minutes scored an average of 210 points higher than those who could not control themselves.

Nor did Mischel's investigation end there. He pursued his subjects into their thirties and found that the marshmallow-gobblers ended up with a higher incidence of weight problems and substance abuse than was found among their more disciplined peers.

Mischel concludes that every human being starts off in life unable to wait for anything. Only gradually do we learn how to delay. The crucial skill, he believes, is "strategic allocation of attention." That is, the ability to distract yourself, to focus on some other task instead of that terribly seductive temptation that is driving you half mad. In the experiment, some of the four year olds covered their eyes in order to withstand the temptation, some turned away, some kicked their desk leg or hummed a tune. Strategic allocation of attention empowered them to resist the marshmallow now in order to eat two later—and, further on in life, it enabled them to handle "hot emotional states" when cravings and passionate urges threatened to overwhelm. These children were blessed with the valuable ability to think long-term: to study for the SATs instead of playing Grand Theft Auto, to save for retirement instead of blowing their paychecks on big-screen TVs and Land Rovers.

So there are two key points here: (1) It is often better to defer pleasure—the rewards being much bigger later on. And (2) seeking instant gratification is a wormy little habit with pernicious consequences. Both of these points are salient as we consider how consumers are going to respond to a new world with reduced opportunities to Buy Now.

ENJOYING LIFE COLD

Human society has not always operated according to the principle that soonest is best. The cultural concept of deferred gratification goes back a long way. On the dark side, it is the basis of the old Italian saying "*La vendetta è un piatto che va servito freddo*" (vengeance is a dish best served cold). Those able to resist the allure of instant gratification—whether it takes the form of a decked-out home theater or a stab in the back—learn that the rewards to be had *later* can be especially big and gratifying. It is a lesson that applies not just to individuals but to entire economic systems. Deferred gratification and its promise of enhanced return have formed the bedrock of modern capitalism, with its farsighted investment in industry and research and its gradual piling up of wealth. By learning to act cold-bloodedly (with patience and pragmatism) rather than warm-bloodedly (with impulsivity and unrestrained passion), modern western societies have amassed fantastic amounts of capital, to the benefit of most.

More than two hundred years ago in *The Wealth of Nations*, pioneering Scottish economist Adam Smith spoke of the importance of impulse control: "If the prodigality of some was not compensated by the frugality of others"—that is, if society did not have those few virtuous types who can delay eating a marshmallow—then "the conduct of every prodigal, by feeding the idle with the bread of the industrious, tends not only to beggar himself, but to impoverish his country."[3] In other words, nations would collapse and civilization perish if everyone lunged for the marshmallow as soon as the researcher turned his back. Smith understood that deferred gratification was profoundly necessary for the accumulation of investment capital and building a sound future for a nation's citizenry.[4]

In an influential paper delivered in 1961 to the American Sociological Association, Murray A. Straus (then at the University of Minnesota) reviewed various historical philosophies concerning impulse control. One was that of nineteenth-century sociologist Max Weber, author of *The Protestant Ethic and the Spirit of Capitalism*, who contended that Protestantism decisively shaped the development of modern capitalism by emphasizing the ultimate in delayed gratification: *life after death*. "Expect nothing on this earth," Calvinist Christians were essentially told, "because your reward lies only in heaven." The Protestant work ethic sprang out of this tough philosophy of enjoy-it-much-much-much-later. Sigmund Freud and his school of psychoanalysis equated impulse control among toddlers (learning to master their sphincter muscles and use the toilet, for example) with the self-control and "acquisitive character structure" necessary for the growth of market economies.

So impulse control has cultural roots in both biology and religion. A third factor is purely sociological: Delaying gratification traditionally has been the mark of "respectable" people who lead orderly, disciplined lives. It has long been aspirational, viewed as evidence of probity and high character. In a landmark 1953 paper, Louis Schneider and Sverre Lysgaard firmly established the notion in "The Deferred Gratification Pattern: A Preliminary Study." "Impulse-renunciation" is characteristic of middle and upper social classes, they found, whereas "impulse-following" is more characteristic of the lower class.[5]

Investigations into instant versus delayed gratification continue today. One recent study examined the behavioral differences between "tightwads" and "spendthrifts," seeking to understand how they respond differently to the "pain of paying."[6] If delaying gratification came easily, everyone would do it naturally, as a default option. But it is not easy, and it comes with real costs. At one extreme, being a tightwad can lead to the joyless miserliness of Scrooge in *A Christmas Carol*, whom modern researchers probably would enjoy analyzing as someone who suffers from acute psychic agony every time he parts with a nickel. For true tightwads, all material pleasure feels sinful, with gratification permanently delayed.

Don't Care How, I Want It Now

But in recent decades, we have not met many tightwads. Instead, the emphasis has shifted toward speedy gratification. Schneider and Lysgaard's "impulse-renunciation" was scarcely in evidence among the upper classes during the economic boom of recent decades. The ability *not* to wait, *not* to carefully consider one's purchases, *not* to edit one's shopping list came to be seen as the mark of true wealth (class be damned). Being cautious and prudent, in contrast, came to be associated with buttoned-down conformity, the company man and his dreary bourgeois values. Starting in the 1960s, it was not cool to worry about the future or to tiptoe cautiously; these were suffocating, grown-up behaviors that squelched creativity, frustrated the id, bummed us out, killed the soul.

Popular music referred constantly to fiery desires, gratified immediately. Appetites were gargantuan. And while rock stars have earned a reputation for being all about sex and drugs, their lyrics sound remarkably like anthems to our consumerist culture—as witnessed by the hundreds of tunes that have been made into commercials for products of all kinds, now that the taboo against such profiteering has faded. *I want, I need, I've gotta have*—these constant refrains might refer to a girlfriend or, just as easily, to a brand of dishwashing detergent. One recalls the song that gluttonous Veruca Salt sang in the movie *Willy Wonka and the Chocolate Factory*: "I want the works, I want the whole works—presents and prizes and sweets and surprises of all shapes and sizes! And now, don't care how, I want it now!" We may not meet many Scrooges nowadays, but Veruca Salts are a dime a dozen.

"I don't believe that old cliché that good things come to those who wait," says American actor Ashton Kutcher, speaking for many in our pell-mell culture. "I think good things come to those who want something so bad they can't sit still."[7] Delayed gratification might have spurred capitalism in the time of Adam Smith, but modern businesses much prefer the theories of Mr. Kutcher. The last thing marketers want is for us to put off a purchase, to think too much about it, to fret about the "pain of paying." They make buying sound like pure, delicious pleasure—"Yes! Yes! Yes!" to quote the suggestive TV commercial for one of Procter & Gamble's shampoos, which guarantees purchasers a "Totally Organic Experience." We are so accustomed to cheery pitches about *quicker, easier, more fun, get it now;* just imagine if advertisers were to promise us, for a change, *slower, more difficult, less fun, you're gonna have to wait for that.* Utterly inconceivable.

All We Ever Wanted Was Everything reads the title of Janelle Brown's novel, a satire on Silicon Valley that depicts the ruinous effects of credit card debt, among other modern woes.[8] Such warnings aside, during the last few decades, one could almost have imagined that everyone was winning from accelerated consumption, from the Pursuit of Everything. Shoppers found just exactly what they wanted and bought it on the spot with the swipe of a little plastic card. Retailers "moved product" and cleared shelves fast to make room for the deposits of the belching sixteen-wheelers pulled up to the loading docks out back. The spiraling upward trajectory was irresistible: Corporations and brands competed by upping the ante to offer purchasers still more of what they desired, and even more quickly; consumers became spoiled by myriad choices, expecting to always call the shots—*No more anguishing about* either/or. *Let me have* both*!* They did not quite perceive it at the time, but both businesses and consumers were caught in a vicious cycle that eventually would come to a crashing end.

INSTANT GRATIFICATION GIVES WAY TO PURPOSEFUL PLEASURE

The economy collapsed. In a historic shift, consumers began saving instead of buying—imagine! And all of a sudden, the people who try to sell things were asking themselves in a panic "Is this the end of the old paradigm? Has 'I Want It Now' lost its shine?" They had raised, of course, a multibillion-dollar question.

We can say without hesitation that the quest for pleasure is not dead. Society may be split on whether *Everybody Loves Raymond*, but there is no doubt at all that everybody loves pleasure. Even a hairshirted Calvinist derived pleasure from his righteous self-deprivation: Sacrifice can be its own reward and source of perverse joy. "I can't get no satisfaction," Mick Jagger famously sang, offering a succinct statement about the ever-expanding limits of basic human desire. That 1965 song, you might recall, aimed a couple of zingers at the new marketing culture. Yet even as Jagger twitted consumerism, he showed perfect comprehension of its central shibboleth: *satisfaction.*

But what if the source of that satisfaction is changing? What if modern consumers are discovering new and different forms of pleasure as part of their consumption choices? We are seeing signs of just such a shift taking place.

Tastes Great, More Filling: Toward New Sources of Satisfaction

That hunger for satisfaction is fundamental to the human condition. It is even woven into our neurons, as U.K. cognitive neuroscientist Neal Hinvest told us when we spoke with him recently about the psychology of consumerism. "The brain is hard-wired," he says, "to motivate us to continually seek out pleasurable experiences while avoiding aversive ones."[9]

So people are not going to quit seeking pleasure—no way. But what has changed, probably forever, is their attitude toward mindless consumption as a reliable generator of pleasure. On one hand, it has gotten a lot harder for most of us to buy things—so we are forced to rethink what we value and how and where we are going to find joy. Premium-price disposables may not be an option anymore. On the other hand, and more intriguingly, many of us are using the recession as an opportunity to seriously rethink our priorities and to reassess how the items we purchase—or pass up—make us feel. As we have already seen, there has been a growing sense of diminishing returns when it comes to purchasing: The gap between *what advertisers promised we would feel* and *what we actually feel* seems vast right now. As our expectations steadily rose throughout the 1990s and beyond, we had to purchase more and more to get any kind of kick out of shopping. We were stuck on a "hedonic treadmill," in the words of Professor John D. Sterman of the MIT Sloan School of Management, and facing "a no-win situation in which no level of income or consumption remains satisfying for long."[10]

In this context of diminishing returns, one can see how there might be a sort of pleasure to be gained from hopping off the treadmill. This pleasure might be all the more potent if it were to offer a sense of *control* at a time when communal and individual worlds were crumbling into chaos. And that is precisely what has been happening: As noted earlier, Euro RSCG's New Consumer study found that a near majority of Americans and 58 percent of U.S. Prosumers reported getting a sense of satisfaction from reducing their purchases during the downturn. Not a sense of frustration or deprivation but of *satisfaction*. Making do with less is making them feel better, not worse—as is evidenced by the 87 percent of Americans and 91 percent of U.S. Prosumers who agreed: "Saving money makes me feel good about myself." This change promises to be permanent: Four in ten global consumers and six in ten Americans are committed to reducing their use of credit cards, long term. And most Americans (52 percent, and 58 percent of Prosumers) say they will not go back to their old shopping habits even when the economy rebounds. This is not a reaction limited to the United States: 48 percent of the global sample (54 percent of Prosumers) agreed.

Why are so many consumers finding pleasure in downsizing? Professor Scott Rick, of the University of Michigan's Ross School of Business, told us the reaction is an adaptive response: "The more anxious people are about the economy, the more pleasure they are reporting from saving. If you're worried about losing money, finding ways to make saving pleasurable can be quite beneficial, both psychologically and financially."[11]

Evidence of the anxiety Professor Rick cites can be found in abundance around the world—and especially in the Buy Now, Pay Later United States. People are worried about their ability to earn as much as they need now and in an uncertain future. Fifty-six percent of the global sample and 61 percent of Americans worry about money often. A majority of U.S. consumers have become more anxious about keeping up with the cost of living (56 percent) and having sufficient funds with which to retire (51 percent). And four in ten Americans are increasingly anxious about their ability to crawl out from under a pile of debt. More generally, 55 percent of the global sample and 57 percent of Americans worry more than they used to about their own and their families' futures. More than a third of the global sample and four in ten Americans (five in ten Prosumers) are concerned about the stress the downturn has placed on their loved ones.

And fretfulness is not confined to finances. A majority of both the global and U.S. samples (54 percent of each) say they are generally more anxious today than they were a few years ago. Just under half the global sample (49 percent) and 55 percent of Americans worry about health issues, and, as we saw earlier, more than one-third of the global sample worry about their *mental* health. By taking control of their spending and boosting savings, consumers worldwide are working to temper these anxieties. They cannot control the world economy, nor can they guarantee that they will keep their jobs—but they can effectively control their cash flow, and they can take pleasure and pride in making smarter choices.

Saying "No" Requires a Bigger "Yes"

So what are the prospects for millions of consumers who have grown up on immediate gratification and become accustomed to the all-pervasive ethos of scarfing it down now rather than savoring it later? Are they facing a dreary future of diminished pleasure and infinitely deferred gratification? On the contrary. The movement we are seeing points to an emerging set of pleasures that are not tied into "instant everything," pleasures that promise real delights without the instability and insubstantiality of the old ways. They are rooted in three basic trends we have already explored: Embracing Substance, Rightsizing, and Growing Up.

As we consider these shifts, it is important to understand the underlying psychology of the purchase process. There are many complex elements in play, but these three aspects are most relevant to our discussion:

1. On balance, if they have the option, people prefer to make choices that make them feel good rather than bad. Pretty obvious. Exactly what triggers positive or negative (aversive) feelings is subjective, however, and depends on the context. For example, standing in a line is typically a negative, but it can turn to a positive if a second line opens and one is suddenly moved to the front.
2. It is difficult for consumers to make good decisions when one element of the decision delivers in the here and now and the other one, far in the future. For example, consider the tantalizing choice between a Friendly's Giant Crowd Pleaser sundae now or the possibility of a slimmer waistline tomorrow.
3. Our sense of well-being is relative and in constant flux. We measure how happy we are, how wealthy we are, and what a good (or bad) deal we have gotten against our past experiences and those of our friends and neighbors. Our smugness at having gotten a new car on the cheap will be soured as soon as we learn that Susie was offered the same price...plus a year's free service.

In the same way, a product or brand message that resonates brightly in one moment of our lives—under a specific set of circumstances—may produce a discordant clang later. A 2003 article in *Brandweek* described ads for the Hummer H2 that "deliberately show only parts of the vehicle, as if it were too large to fit a frame.... Another ad features a bulldog shot of the truck's toothy grill and front wheels from the perspective of a small car, or someone about to get squashed."[12] That was 2003, when grotesquely scaled mega-vehicles still had cachet; the same ads today would likely be met with eye-rolling and revulsion.

MEET THE NEW CONSUMER

In our recent studies, Euro RSCG has identified emerging consumer traits and behaviors that show consumption becoming much more mindful and considered. Thanks in part to the Internet (which was in just 18 percent of U.S. homes in 1997 but in 62 percent ten years later[13]), consumers have become smarter shoppers, have grown more mindful about what they consume, and are eager to establish meaningful relationships with each other and with brands.

Consumers are smarter. As we first pointed out in *Good for Business,* improved access to communication and information has played a dramatic role in equipping us to be savvier, more empowered shoppers. Euro RSCG's Future of Shopping study in 2008 reported that 76 percent of global respondents agreed with the statement: "For major purchase decisions, my first step is usually the Internet." Percentages were even higher in the United States, where 78 percent of the total sample and more than nine in ten Prosumers agreed. The New Consumer survey similarly shows an increase in consumer "smarts":

- "I do lots of consumer research online (e.g., seeking out product information, reviews and ratings, price comparisons)": global, 62 percent; United States, 61 percent (U.S. Prosumers, 82 percent)
- "I am a more demanding shopper than I was a few years ago": global, 63 percent; United States, 64 percent (U.S. Prosumers, 82 percent)
- "I am a smarter shopper than I was a few years ago": global, 69 percent; United States, 77 percent (U.S. Prosumers, 87 percent)

Sixty percent of global respondents in The Future of Shopping study agreed: "I would like to be part of an online community of customers who share opinions and information about companies and brands." Among U.S. Prosumers, the total was a striking 74 percent, evidence of how the Internet is transforming the experience of being a thoughtful consumer. Underlying this interest in banding together with other consumers is the sense that fellow shoppers are more truthful than corporations and even the media when it comes to evaluating products and companies. Fifty-seven percent of Americans and 69 percent of U.S. Prosumers agreed: "I trust customer reviews more than I trust 'expert' reviews."

Consumers are more mindful. In myriad ways, people are demonstrating a new level of mental alertness (and skepticism) in their choice of brands. The New Consumer study bears this out:

- "I am shopping more carefully and mindfully than I used to": global, 72 percent; United States, 80 percent (U.S. Prosumers, 86 percent)
- "I am more interested today in how and where products are made": global, 51 percent; United States, 54 percent (U.S. Prosumers, 66 percent)
- "I am paying more attention to the quality and freshness of the food I buy": global, 76 percent; United States, 78 percent (U.S. Prosumers, 88 percent)
- "I pay more attention to the color, feel, and overall design of products than I used to": global, 43 percent; United States, 47 percent (U.S. Prosumers, 63 percent)
- "I research the safety of the products I buy more than I used to": global, 47 percent; United States, 41 percent (U.S. Prosumers, 60 percent)

As has been amply evident in the media of late, and as we have discussed elsewhere in this book, consumers have also become more mindful about the environment and their impact on it, with increasingly more people being cognizant of their own personal carbon footprints. Fifty-four percent of the global sample and 63 percent of Prosumers said, "I am paying more attention than in the past to the environmental and/or social impact of the products I buy." Moreover, 45 percent (54 percent of Prosumers) are willing to pay a slightly higher price for products that are environmentally or socially responsible.

In keeping with what we saw with regard to their reduced spending, consumers are deriving a sense of satisfaction from their efforts to be green. "Making environmentally friendly choices makes me feel good" is the sentiment of 64 percent of global respondents and 65 percent of Americans (U.S. Prosumers, 73 percent). Eco-consciousness is especially strong in emerging economies: In both Brazil and China, 80 percent feel good about making environmentally friendly choices, including an extraordinary 91 percent of Prosumers in each market. This stands in contrast with the just three in ten global consumers who agree: "Buying luxury items makes me feel good about myself."

At the same time, consumers are abandoning their old obsession with instant gratification, as seen in their responses to this set of statements: "In the past year, I have been asking myself more often...":

- "Do I really need this?": global, 51 percent; United States, 63 percent (U.S. Prosumers, 67 percent)
- "Is it of solid, good quality? Will it last a long time?": global, 47 percent; United States, 51 percent (U.S. Prosumers, 65 percent)
- "Can I afford it?": global, 45 percent; United States, 59 percent (U.S. Prosumers, 63 percent)
- "Will I really get pleasure from buying this brand/spending this money?": global, 35 percent; United States, 39 percent (U.S. Prosumers, 49 percent)
- "Can I wait until it's on sale?": global, 43 percent; United States, 56 percent (U.S. Prosumers, 63 percent)

Again and again, U.S. Prosumers are leading the way. And their resounding responses make it clear in which direction we are trending: toward mindfulness and responsibility, and away from frivolity and mindless excess.

Consumers seek relationships. As *Good for Business* showed, the more consumers have gotten to know about brands, the more interested and engaged they have become. They are looking to partner with companies with which they feel good about doing business, seeking a more involved, deeper relationship—as brand ambassadors, content creators, contributors to corporate social responsibility efforts, and much more. Consider these results from Euro RSCG's 2008 study, The Future of the Corporate Brand:

- "It is important that companies stand for something other than profitability": global, 85 percent; United States, 86 percent (U.S. Prosumers, 96 percent)
- "As a consumer, I have a responsibility to censure unethical companies by avoiding their products": global, 76 percent; United States, 80 percent (U.S. Prosumers, 87 percent)

And from the New Consumer:

- "I prefer to buy from companies that share my personal values": global, 57 percent (global Prosumers, 70 percent); United States, 59 percent (U.S. Prosumers, 77 percent)
- "I prefer to buy from companies that have a reputation for having a purpose other than just profits": global, 49 percent (global Prosumers, 60 percent); United States, 56 percent (U.S. Prosumers, 69 percent)
- "I avoid shopping at stores that don't treat their employees fairly": global, 51 percent; United States, 52 percent (U.S. Prosumers, 65 percent)

As noted earlier, a resounding 70 percent of U.S. Prosumers agree: "Compared with a few years ago, it is more important for me to feel good about the companies with which I do business." Clearly, consumerism has evolved into a new phase; shopping is no longer just about the product or service being acquired. Instead, the purchase is viewed in light of a wide range of other considerations, including: Who makes it? Is the company admirable and trustworthy? Does it share my values and support the causes that are meaningful to me? Is it having a positive impact on the lives of all the people its business touches?

If companies and brands are to grow and thrive in the new millennium, they must understand this remarkable new environment. The pleasure principle has evolved into something more sophisticated and nuanced, with consumers taking pleasure from new and surprising sources. Instant gratification is beginning to give way to intelligent analysis and longer-term thinking. This quest for more purposeful pleasure opens up exciting opportunities for smart brands, assuming they are willing to discard the old ways of thinking. To connect, they will need to create products and services that offer longer-lasting and more fundamental satisfactions. They must provide consumption choices that minimize the negatives (e.g., *eco-toxic, antisocial, stress-inducing, unhealthy*) and maximize the positives (e.g., *contributing to society, allowing more time with family, rightsizing*). Customer service must make an evolutionary leap into holistic relationships based on trust and mutual support. And, critically, brands must rethink the way they communicate with customers, who are hungry for positive and helpful messages, skeptical of inflated claims, and disgusted with bogusness and deceit. The Four Paradigms we have outlined ought to be at the forefront of the minds of manufacturers as they conceive new products and of marketers as they develop improved strategies for engagement.

The future is full of risks and pitfalls—along with bright opportunities. In the following chapters, we explore brands that are doing things right.

Part III

MARKETING TO THE NEW CONSUMER

Chapter 8

TRIGGERS FOR CHANGE

As we have seen, the new paradigms of the mindful consumer represent a big break with the long-held assumption that *owning more* means *having more*. Has mindfulness moved beyond the leading edge and overtaken the consuming masses? Not by a long shot, but there is clear evidence that it is moving in that direction.

Things can change fast nowadays—witness the meteoric growth of the Internet with its far-reaching ramifications—and already a broad spectrum of consumers is showing greater concern and involvement. These shoppers read labels to check ingredients, for example; they care about nutritional values and country of origin. And many are now factoring "big picture" considerations into their consumption, including Fair Trade, local production, corporate reputation, and sustainability. In Euro RSCG's New Consumer survey, 65 percent of the mainstream and 75 percent of Prosumers in the seven countries surveyed said the most successful and profitable businesses in the future will be those that practice sustainability (in the United States, those figures jumped to 67 and 81 percent, respectively).

Even before the recent economic crisis, the cultures, symbols, and language of mindful consumption were becoming noticeably more familiar and less "alternative." Suddenly organic goods and compact fluorescent light bulbs were readily available at mass merchandisers. Reusable bags became a fixture at supermarkets and discount stores. McDonald's began selling Fair Trade coffee, and Wal-Mart introduced a sustainably packaged line of gold and silver jewelry whose origins could be traced from mine to market. The downturn has stimulated such innovations by calling into question the premises underlying mindless consumerism. How fast mindfulness grows from here on in will depend on three main variables: governmental policies and regulations, the will of consumers, and the involvement and support of business.

WHY GOVERNMENTS DO NOT WANT MINDFUL CONSUMPTION

"The engine of economic growth for the past twenty years is not going to be there for the next twenty," presidential candidate Barack Obama told *Time* magazine's Joe Klein.[1] The "engine" to which he referred is consumer spending, which had just hit a wall. But if President Obama foresees big changes in the future, most politicians do not; there is little indication that governments in general regard hyperconsumerism as a problem that needs to be addressed. On the contrary, it buoys gross domestic product and tax receipts even as it keeps unemployment down—all of which help politicians stay in power. Much political thinking is short term, anyway. Health agencies are among the few that think far ahead; it is notable that they are now promoting mindful consumption to address obesity and its costly public health consequences. But most arms of government are not interested in radical change or simply are unwilling to endure the political fallout. As Canadian auto industry commentator Jeremy Cato observed recently, "Governments, if they were being honest and courageous, would propose a fuel tax floor with a sliding tax rate. If done properly, this would slowly, steadily, and predictably move new vehicle buyers away from higher-emitting, fuel-consuming vehicles, into vehicles that use less fuel and emit less pollution." But he says that governments in North America lack the political will to undertake so daring a policy.[2]

With government asleep at the wheel, there remain two other potential sources of change: consumers and corporations.

CONSUMERS DRIVING CHANGE

Mindful consumption will flourish if consumers embrace it en masse. If enough of us change the way we buy, businesses will have no choice but to adapt. As the Internet has taught us, when tens of thousands of people band together to work toward a common end, it quickly gets the attention of corporations. Christian McMahan, chief marketing officer of Heineken USA, spoke with us about these ever-more-empowered consumers and their intensified interest in correcting and rewarding brand behavior:

> This is not a passing fad at all; it is part of the new reality of doing business. Information is available to consumers like never before on the companies that interest them, and this will only increase as technologies improve. Step out of line or fail to hold yourself to the values you put forward, and consumers will be there ready to challenge you. On the flip side, if consumers not only engage with your brands but also like who you are as a company, they will embrace you enthusiastically.[3]

As we saw, this embrace of select businesses and brands is the principle behind Carrotmob, which describes itself as harnessing "consumer power to make the most socially responsible business practices also the most profitable choices."[4] Carrotmobs exemplify a growing kind of quiet activism in which, according to Jim Fielding, president of Disney Stores Worldwide, "People seek to make the world better through their consumption choices."[5]

But the shift toward mindfulness may be gradual. For most of us—including those who aspire toward mindful consumption—there is a wide gap between how we would *like* to consume and how we actually *do* consume. Such is human nature. One indication of the potentially slow pace of consumer change comes from Scott Rick of the University of Michigan's Ross School of Business. In our interview, he said his research reveals very little change in American consumers' attitudes toward spending and saving, even in the midst of the economic downturn. He believes we form our attitudes toward money by early adulthood and that they are largely set for life. According to his reasoning, real growth in mindfulness may have to wait until a new generation of consumers comes of age.[6]

But consumer habits, however ingrained, can be influenced by various means—a fact of which marketers are increasingly aware. Richard Thaler of the Graduate School of Business at the University of Chicago and Cass R. Sunstein of Harvard Law School devised the concept of "Nudge" (introduced in the book of the same name) to describe how positive outcomes can be achieved simply by structuring choices differently. A "nudge" may be as straightforward as putting unhealthful foods on a high shelf where they are less likely to catch the eye or placing a mirror behind a breakfast buffet counter so that we see our corpulent selves before making the choice of whether to load up on danishes. Tax authorities in Minnesota tried in vain to get citizens to complete their returns on time until they hit on a "social norm" nudge: Instead of threatening or cajoling, they simply publicized the fact that most Minnesotans had already filed their returns. The number of people submitting tax forms shot up overnight.[7]

Research from Euro RSCG consistently shows that consumers are tired of mindless excess and aspire to "do the right thing"; they crave a different approach to consumption as part of a more mindful way of living. But few of them are capable of heeding the first stirrings of mindfulness and making full-blown change. After all, decade upon decade of marketing and consumer culture have encouraged them to take the low road, to surrender to temptation, to consume without thinking. Perhaps all they need is a nudge—one coming not from disengaged and shortsighted governments but from forward-thinking, consumer-facing businesses and brands.

WILL CORPORATIONS CHAMPION
A NEW WAY OF CONSUMING?

As we have seen, farsighted companies have already led the way in promoting mindful consumption. With its sustainability-focused "Nutrition Labels," Timberland has gotten shoe and apparel buyers to reconsider their personal carbon footprints. TOMs Shoes turns every customer into a philanthropist by donating one pair of shoes to charity for every pair sold. Ben & Jerry's has recruited ice cream lovers to help "Lick Global Warming."

But surely these are isolated exceptions, you might say. For corporations as a whole, what possible sense does it make to further the cause of mindfulness? It would be like turkeys voting to keep Thanksgiving on the calendar, right? Not at all. Our research shows that the smartest brands and corporations are adopting a longer view of consumerism. They know that the pipelines feeding the explosive growth of previous decades have been cut off. There will be no more easy credit, no more cheap and widely available supplies of nonrenewable resources, no more getting away with shady business and environmental practices that might have been overlooked in the pre-Internet days. As they look forward, they see a rapidly expanding cohort of consumers who realize that what they desired and aspired to yesterday has little relevance for them today. And they foresee a new climate in which *reputation* becomes one of their most valuable assets—and drivers of growth. Following the examples of such innovators as Whole Foods,

Google, Nike, and eBay, they recognize that cultivating and satisfying evolving consumer desires—rather than continuing to follow the unsustainable and discredited route of disposable everything—is the path to future profitability.

The business school case for embracing mindfulness is persuasive. Brands grow by figuring out better ways to meet existing needs or by identifying needs that are emerging. Under the dying regime of hyperconsumerism, we have reached a point at which most brands have nailed our obvious needs and fully burnished their ways of meeting them. With thousands of products being frenziedly upgraded, updated, reformulated, and innovated every month, there is little scope for most brands to gain competitive advantage. Apple is one of very few companies to have mastered the art of making products that did not exist one day and seem indispensable the next. The vast majority of brands are having to make do with merely incremental progress.

But embracing mindfulness offers a way out of this dead end. Brands that recognize the growth potential in mindful consumption will seek to find and develop triggers that will activate the wants and needs of consumers inclined toward mindfulness. By doing so, they will foster greater engagement with these valuable customers. These triggers are not the same hot buttons that have been firing up hyperconsumers all these years. Rather than promising instant gratification and More, More, More, they will be grounded in the four paradigms: Embracing Substance, Rightsizing, Growing Up, and Seeking Purposeful Pleasure. In the next two chapters, we will see how companies are already taking advantage of the paradigms, both in terms of the products and services they provide and the ways in which they communicate with an increasingly concerned and sophisticated public.

Chapter 9

SATISFYING THE SUBSTANCE SHOPPER

If the world is cold, make it your business to build fires.

—Horace Traubel, American reform writer

In our changed economic world, companies must move quickly to meet the fast-evolving needs and desires of the New Consumer. As the Four Paradigms of consumer behavior take hold, leading brands across categories are already developing innovative approaches and offerings in response.

EMBRACING SUBSTANCE: LET'S GET REAL

Fed up with the modern world's empty feelings of artificiality and disconnectedness, people are looking to get grounded and engaged. Today's smart brands are addressing this need in four ways: (1) by providing a welcome taste of authenticity, often by emphasizing an appealing provenance; (2) by offering opportunities for community and interpersonal connections; (3) by linking consumers with causes that inspire and motivate them; and (4) by continuously seeking new ways to forge vital, substantive partnerships with customers—to everyone's advantage.

When we spoke with Carlos Abrams-Rivera, vice president of marketing for Nabisco Snacks, about what brands must do to win the loyalty of the New Consumer, he stressed the importance of authentic values—from product ingredients all the way through to packaging and marketing communication:

> Today's consumers are more empowered than ever to make smart, informed choices. They are not looking for reformulations or surface changes; they want real value and real *values*. Who you are, what you believe in as a company will have an intrinsic value to the new consumers. Social responsibility and ethical practices now sit next to quality and price in the value equation.

It is essential, Abrams-Rivera adds, for companies to think long term and both have and communicate a clear vision:

> Brands cannot just sell the value of today; they must also offer the value of tomorrow. Why buy a brand of computer system unless you believe in the value the brand will add to your life in the future? Besides electronics, you can see it in other industries—Why buy from a specific auto company unless I know there is a vision of the future I want to invest in? Even in our brands like Triscuit we are living a clear vision with cleaner ingredient lines and the authentic goodness of real whole grains.[1]

"Authenticity is the benchmark against which all brands are now judged," confirmed John Grant in *The New Marketing Manifesto*.[2] Name a consumer industry, and you can readily find examples of brand offerings that emphasize the sense of authenticity, substance, and interconnectedness that so many consumers crave. Consider the travel sector, for instance: We are seeing all sorts of fresh approaches to tourism that emphasize more substantive, less invasive ways to explore the globe. Rather than focusing solely on the traveler's physical needs—comforts and indulgences—forward-thinking brands are taking steps to make the travel experience more meaningful and more emotionally, even spiritually, fulfilling. WHL Travel has helped refine the notion of sustainable tourism with its Stay Another Day in the Mekong (a six-nation region bordering one of southeast Asia's largest rivers). The program incorporates a panoply of cultural, social, and environmental experiences into the itinerary in order to create a more authentic plunge for the traveler that includes an exploration of the rich diversity of the local cultures. With its Caring for the Destination project, the company identifies local hostelries willing to participate in community-friendly and sustainable activities, such as employing orphaned children or restoring historic buildings. These activities become brand differentiators that attract today's thoughtful travelers, offering them "either a unique experience or, at least, an opportunity to feel that by staying with this accommodation provider they [are] doing some good."[3]

Authenticity and *connectedness* are key watchwords in the food and dining sectors as well. Innovative brands are concocting all sorts of ways to slow down the experience and make it count for more than the calories consumed:

- In a witty approach to connectedness, Café Emunah in Fort Lauderdale (founded by a rabbi and a psychologist) offers "the first-ever Kabbalistic lifestyle lounge and tea bar."[4] Tired of your dining companions' banal chitchat? Then order up a serving of "Table Talk"; the psychologist will sit with you and chat about "spirituality, parenting, health…whatever [you] want."[5]
- Marketers for Glenmorangie Scotch Whiskey offer customers a richer, deeper experience by effectively summoning an archaeological back-story for their product: "Our ancient ancestors drank the pure, mineral-rich waters of the Tarlogie Springs, where the fallen rain seeps and filters through lime and sandstone over a period of 100 years."[6] The brand narrative places the drinker in a historical timeline, offering the feeling of being connected to something larger and more compelling than the here and now.
- McCormick & Schmick's restaurant chain injects a sense of history and authenticity into its drinks menu by offering a Celebration of the American Cocktail program that resurrects fifty classics. The list is arranged by historical era, and each drink comes with information about its origins and the provenance of the ingredients.

Feeling the winds of consumer desire shift, makers of apparel are turning toward authenticity too. Athletic garb has undergone a particularly evocative transformation of late: It has become noticeably simpler and more old-fashioned, hearkening back to a less complicated era in sports—before multimillion-dollar contracts, commercialism, and steroid scandals. The University of Iowa wrestling program has just redesigned its uniforms, or "singlets," in the direction of authenticity, "reverting the nation's toughest singlet back to its original form."[7] In Canada, the Hudson's Bay Company (HBC) reconceptualized the clothing of the nation's Olympic team in time for the 2010 Vancouver

Games, making it, the *Toronto Star* reports, "pared down and simple, with a slight vintage feel." The designs are a "far cry from the wildly graphic prints of Canadian and Chinese patterns the company used—to much criticism—for the Beijing Olympics," which proved a merchandising flop. HBC says the "clean, spare look was inspired by the great Canadian graphic artists of the '60s and '70s."[8]

Adidas is revitalizing sales of its shoes by emphasizing the brand's cultural history. The triple-stripe pattern created by company founder Adi Dassler turned sixty in 2009. "Sixty Years of Soles and Stripes," a product line with a variety of styles, revisits memorable moments in the brand's history. And special "Era Packs" include sneakers from each decade, starting with the 1950s.[9]

Real People, Real Places

Modern consumers feel disconnected because they are. Most of us have no ties whatsoever to the people who design and assemble the products we use, sew our clothes, and grow our food. We may not even know where in the world these workers reside. As customers worldwide begin to push back against this anonymity and divide, they are turning to brands that do away with myriad layers of commerce and reconnect buyer and seller in a more direct way. One such business, the online site Etsy—where artisans personally sell their handcrafted wares—has enjoyed phenomenal growth as a consequence of this hunger for connectedness. Some 2.4 million people in 150 countries have registered on the site, and more than 155,000 vendors sold $58 million in goods in the first five months of 2009, doubling Etsy's sales over the same period the year prior.[10] Etsy has become the go-to place for conscious consumers looking for "real" products created and sold by "real" people.[11]

The purchase process need not be direct, however. A colorful provenance can provide an authentic, more personal experience as well. The store A Vida Portuguesa in Lisbon, housed in a former soap factory, only offers brands that are unique to Portugal, are handmade, have stayed true to their original packaging, and represent the best of indigenous craftsmanship. Even within these tight parameters, the store stocks more than a thousand products, ranging from toiletries to stationery and homewares. Part of the attraction is that the items offer an alternative to mainstream brands and strike a blow against modern artifice.[12] "Taking a firm stand in the face of globalization," one visitor says, "A Vida Portuguesa has tracked down Portugal's unique brands and opened a store dedicated to products that have resisted the urge to keep up with changing times."[13]

Absolut Vodka is a worldwide brand, but lately it has honed a local touch with its Cities Series: for New Orleans, a special mango and black pepper blend inspired by indigenous traditions;[14] for Boston, a black tea and elderflower flavor, marketed with a green backdrop suggesting the "Green Monster," Fenway Park baseball field's high rear wall.[15] Such linkages have the ability to evoke a particular time and/or place and the values connected to them.

Getting Together

Interconnectedness need not be limited to building links between companies and their customers. It is also important to facilitate interaction *among* customers. There is no better example of this than the Harley Owners Group (H.O.G.), sponsored by Harley-Davidson. H.O.G. assures prospective members that it is "much more than just a motorcycle organization. It's one million people around the world united by a common passion: making the Harley-Davidson dream a way of life." State-level events offer "live bands, parades, bike shows, great riding opportunities, fun and games....No two state rallies are ever alike because so much local flavor goes into each event." The tough-looking biker who dons chaps and "brain bucket" before catching flies in his teeth may epitomize the freewheeling individualist, but H.O.G. offers him a heartwarmingly communal experience: "Meet the thousands of brothers and sisters you've always wanted."[16]

Duracell has come up with a smart way to bring people together in common cause while highlighting the company's brand promises. Each New Year's Eve, it sets up a Smart Power Lab in New York City's Times Square. Passersby are encouraged to jump on a pedaling machine and contribute their muscle power to light up the iconic crystal ball, which drops at midnight. No fewer than 300,000 participants enthusiastically pedaled during New Year's 2009. "We're trying to encourage the world to think about power and how important it is to capture it," explained Craig Bida, brand manager for Duracell North America, adding that the project is part of an ongoing Smart Power initiative: "Every little bit counts."[17] "Our guests will be able to say they truly powered the start of a new decade," said Rick June, Duracell vice president and general manager, North America, of the 2010 event. "The Smart Power Lab is just one example of how Duracell delivers innovative, efficient and reliable ways to power important moments."[18]

RIGHTSIZING: REDUCE, REUSE . . . DECOMPRESS

Burned-out consumers eager to follow the Thoreauvian dictum of "Simplify, Simplify" appreciate brands that help them meet their rightsizing goals. There are a number of ways to do this, including offering environments aimed at reducing stress, providing products and systems that simplify life, and making it easier to make smart choices.

Slowing It Down

Moderation in how much we consume goes hand in hand with a more moderate pace to our lives. Millions are seeking to hop off the tread-mill and take the time to truly savor experiences—a huge audience for intelligent brands to capture. In response, retailers are fashioning simpler, more soothing environments that serve as an oasis away from the hubbub of daily life. Single-focus retailers such as Apple Store and Jacques Torres Chocolate encourage connoisseurship and a deeper brand experience. At the Jacques Torres Hudson Square location in New York City, visitors can watch the entire process of cocoa beans being turned into chocolate bars on restored vintage equipment. Small café tables and comfy leather chairs invite people "to sit, sip hot choco-late and enjoy a freshly baked pain au chocolat."[19] Quite a different experience from stirring a powered cocoa drink in a Styrofoam cup in the company break room.

Bob Evans Farms goes by the folksiest of names but is in fact a $1.75 billion company that owns and operates 713 restaurants across the United States. Lately it has found retro inspiration in its modest 1948 origins as a single, twelve-stool truck-stop diner. A design and development firm, WD Partners, has been hired to revamp scores of Bob Evans restaurants with a "Homestyle Restyle." The "re-imaged look...draws upon the homestead feel of the original family home in Rio Grande, Ohio, where Bob Evans and his wife Jewel raised their family." The move is intended to make the chain "more relevant in today's marketplace," where customers want to slow down, relax, and reconnect. Among the innovations: the ambiance of an eat-in kitchen, including a Big Red Round table that allows families and friends to gather comfortably for cheerful socializing. Not that retro means historical stringencies, however: Jewel Evans would have been flabber-gasted by the restaurants' Wi-Fi connections and flat-screen TVs.[20]

Those who are charmed by the "Homestyle Restyle" may find themselves drawn to the Bob Evans Farm Festival, an annual crafts-and-music extravaganza on the original family homestead in Ohio. Loyal fans travel for hours to be a part of what feels like a local hoedown, notwithstanding its decidedly corporate origins. "I love the festival, the sorghum, the apple butter," one participant gushed in 2009. "I love the food. We love Bob Evans. We have them in South Carolina."[21] Clearly this brand has found creative ways to forge positive connections with its customers while also helping them "step out" of the modern world for a spell and enjoy a retreat into simpler times.

Retailers outside the food and beverage industries are also creating sense-satisfying oases that offer a break from the impersonal grind of modern life. Consider the difference between picking up a bar of packaged soap at a discount store and purchasing a freshly made and cut Figs and Leaves handmade soap at Lush. Everything about the experience is different, from the sights and scents to the level of pleasure derived. The former is an errand, while the latter is an indulgence. As a reviewer from Dublin posted on Yelp.com:

> Lush smells just like a massive sweet and tangy soap bubble just exploded inside the store. It's full of creative and curiously named bath bombs, soaps and creams. The products are handmade and the shop's interior emphasises the natural homemade aspect with worn wood and "handwritten" tags. Crate-like boxes filled with straw store the colourful soap bombs and other treats.... This is... "girlie luxury" at a decent price.[22]

Keeping It Simple

The New Consumer is also responding positively to products that carry the comfort of simplicity. Euro RSCG asked respondents to its New Consumer survey to indicate which of a list of twenty-five product descriptors were most appealing to them. The top five selected: *durable, useful, practical, trustworthy, simple.* The bottom five: *elite, prestigious, sophisticated, luxurious, personalized.* For many, notions of value have been turned upside down. As simplicity takes hold, basic single-color T-shirts have been flying off the shelves at Old Navy, Target, H&M, and American Apparel. But simplicity doesn't have to mean cheapness: Donna Karan's "Cozy" cashmere wrap ($245) is marketed as basic and endlessly versatile, able to be worn a dozen ways to create entirely different looks: "One sweater. Every color. Endless ways to wear it."

The food industry is particularly well positioned to speak to the "simplification" aspect of rightsizing. Euro RSCG's Prosumer

Pulse® survey in 2004 found that 70 percent of Americans were reading nutritional labels on food packaging, and the 2009 New Consumer study found that 71 percent (and 81 percent of Prosumers) are more aware of the nutritional/health value of the foods they eat than they used to be. More and more, consumers are reading ingredient labels with an eye to what is *not* there—the fewer ingredients, the better. This has motivated some brands to boast of their minimalist ingredient counts. Lärabars, for example, contain no more than eight ingredients ("Pure and simple, just as nature intended").

In 2009, ice cream maker Häagen-Dazs launched a product line called "Five," with each flavor made up of exactly five simple ingredients "for incredibly pure, balanced flavor...and surprisingly less fat."[23] Selections are limited to mint, ginger, coffee, vanilla bean, passion fruit, brown sugar, and milk chocolate—a back-to-basics approach in a category that has seen mind-numbing proliferation lately. (Ben & Jerry's currently carries sixty-two flavors!)

Inexpensive, highly versatile products are particularly well positioned to enjoy growth in the age of rightsizing. Duck Brand stresses the usefulness of its duct tape for almost everything—since mindful consumers know it is smarter to repair things than to replace them. Customers are encouraged to get involved and use their imaginations: "1% Inspiration, 99% Duck Tape" is the motto for a product that can patch a jogger's shoe, a traveler's suitcase, or a panicked bride's ripped hem ("When the Wedding Bells Are Ringing, Don't Forget Duck Tape"). No longer always an industrial-looking silver, Duck Tape now comes in twenty colors, including camouflage, fluorescent green, and pink—something for every mood. In a time when homeowners are eager to save money and go green, Duck Tape posts diagrams on its Web site showing exactly where energy loss occurs in our homes. Tape can effectively stop those leaks.[24] To emphasize its versatility, the brand sponsors a Duct Tape Saves the Day Promotion, awarding the person with the most compelling story with $5,000 and a year's supply of product.[25] In 2007, Dan Gardner of Gladstone, Virginia, was chosen out of 2,650 applicants. Rather than euthanize an injured horse, he healed it by wrapping its damaged hoof in swaths of duct tape.[26]

Other companies are simplifying life by "editing" our choices, relieving us of stress while introducing us to new pleasures. Trader Joe's, which bills itself as "a store of stories," has buyers travel the globe in order to present a constantly changing—and enticing—selection of foods and beverages chosen for their uniqueness, high quality, and value. *National Geographic*'s Novica.com does much the same with art—showcasing the works of handpicked artists from Latin America,

Asia, and Africa. Right on their desktops, busy consumers can pull up art and learn a bit more about the cultures of developing nations. In the United Kingdom, Topshop prides itself on being an arbiter of "mass cool," partnering with some of today's leading designers to offer fashion and accessories that meet its criteria for cutting-edge style. At the premium end, Priscilla Carluccio (sister of design icon Terence Conran) has opened Few and Far, a shop of vintage and new merchandise that reflects the owner's style and taste. She has been quoted in *Vogue* as saying nothing is sold at the shop "unless I think it's really lovely and would have it myself—that's my only benchmark." Shoppers in any of these retail spaces can be confident the products on offer have been selected with a discerning eye.

Across the board, companies are trying to make things easier for thinking consumers who are tired of overly complicated purchase processes and product choices. Bank of America has streamlined the byzantine home-financing process (you remember, the one that helped sink the economy with those tricky adjustable rate mortgages a while back). Its "Clarity Commitment" reduces paperwork down to a single, one-sheet loan summary, presented in plain language.[27]

Playing on the themes of simplicity and eco-consciousness, BMW recently unveiled an extraordinary-looking, highly innovative concept car called the Lovos, short for "Lifestyle of Voluntary Simplicity." Designed by a young German, the car is clad with 260 slabs containing photovoltaic cells, which rotate to follow the path of the sun, allowing solar radiation to propel the vehicle. With all those rotating slabs, this peculiar car can, one critic says, "alternatively look either like a frightened porcupine or a svelte salmon."[28] The interior is warm and soft, in contrast to the bright-silver exterior, to offer a cocoon-like refuge from a troubled world. Prior to its massive recall woes, Toyota, too, was playing up connectedness to the natural environment; in marketing the 2010 Prius, it partnered with California's cash-strapped Department of Transportation to set up floral displays along highways. Regulations would not allow the Prius logo to be shown, but flowers were arranged in patterns previously used in Toyota's television commercials.[29] Simple but engagingly effective.

Mindfulness Made Easy

We noted earlier that even the most mindful consumer is unlikely to keep to the straight and narrow 100 percent of the time. Sometimes it simply is easier to grab that highly processed, planet-damaging product made by a company we do not admire. Increasingly, brands are offering a helping hand by nudging purchasers in the direction of the smart choices they want to make, treating them as actual thinking individuals rather than as some mindless mass of omnivorous beings. Those looking to put hyperconsumptive wastefulness behind them will find myriad eco-friendly alternatives to traditional products in every category. Consider, for example, purveyors of clothing and accessories: A time-honored, waste-free alternative to buying is to rent, and the Seattle-based company Avelle, formerly known as Bag Borrow or Steal, rents out more than three thousand styles of luxury handbags and jewelry: "Welcome to the Borrowing Revolution."[30] Fabrics are also getting an eco-makeover, enabling conscientious consumers to look fabulous without sacrificing their ideals. On the Corporate Logo Web site, Kirwei Lo wrote about the shift to responsible and sustainable apparel in late 2008:

> This trend is not just a fad. It's here to stay, and it goes well beyond organic cotton. While organic styles will continue to be popular, focus is also shifting to two other categories of sustainable apparel. The first is recycled fabrics—from post-consumer recycled soda bottles to pre-consumer recycled fabrics—and these blends have made a strong debut. Another important consideration is apparel manufactured by corporately responsible companies.[31]

Numerous manufacturers are following the example of Patagonia, which, since 1993, has used synthetic fleece made from plastic soda bottles—86 million, to date. "That's enough oil," the company notes, "to fill the forty-gallon gas tank of the diminutive Chevy Suburban 20,000 times."[32] Such statistics make buyers feel great about their role in helping to heal the damaged environment. In addition, Patagonia's Common Threads Program engages consumers by allowing them to return used products for recycling into new ones.

Mindful consumers feel especially pleased when they are not wasting raw materials and clogging landfills. They like knowing that everyday products can have ongoing uses via repurposing or rightsizing, and companies increasingly are stressing their efforts in this regard. Nike promotes its Reuse-A-Shoe project, which has ground up 25 million sneakers and turned them into tennis courts (the foam insoles), basketball courts (padding), and running tracks (just one of which requires 75,000 rubber soles).[33] To appeal to environmentally conscious techies, Apple has developed a seventeen-inch MacBook Pro constructed of recyclable aluminum and encased in

34 percent less packaging than usual.[34] Motorola has debuted a cell phone made from recycled plastic bottles. That company also makes it easy to recycle the products: Each phone comes with a prepaid envelope purchasers can use to send the device back when it is no longer wanted.[35]

In a major outreach to consumers, four Unilever brands (Knorr, AdeS, Omo, and Rexona) are partnering with Brazil's largest supermarket, Pão de Açúcar, to provide color-coded bags to facilitate sorting of recyclables that can be returned to in-supermarket recycling stations. The project, which began in 2001, has helped divert from landfills more than 22,000 tons of waste plastic, cardboard, toothpaste tubes, and glass. In addition, it has created more than four hundred jobs in sorting and reprocessing materials and even sponsors a group of senior citizens as "environmental instructors."[36]

GROWING UP: LET'S GET SERIOUS

Maturity means taking responsibility for one's actions. Real adults are expected to make good decisions, always keeping in mind the impact of those decisions not only on themselves but on others. Brands are helping these responsible consumers make better—and more mindful— choices. As we have seen, their offerings are increasingly eco-friendly, but they go further than that, also enabling people to develop their own personal self-sufficiencies and promoting old-fashioned virtues such as moderation and thrift.

Consideration for others means being aware of one's ecological impact. It is all very well to wear a fleece jacket made of recycled plastic bottles, but that does not solve the more pressing problem of personal energy consumption. Happily, more and more businesses are lending consumers a hand in that regard. In an interview, we asked C. J. O'Donnell, global marketing director for Jaguar Cars, Ltd., whether "going green" is merely a fad. Definitely not, he said: "Overall, consumer awareness regarding global warming is increasing. These consumer views are driving decisions regarding the environment and other aspects of social responsibility every day."[37] Heightened eco-awareness is apparent in the boardrooms of many corporations, and it accounts for the historic shift of Japanese giant Panasonic away from the glittering cavalcade of consumer electronics, such as ever-more-massive plasma TVs, and toward equipping homes with solar power and energy-saving technologies. The company aims to invest $1 billion in this endeavor by 2012.[38] Panasonic's new technologies will enable consumers to track their own electricity use and display that data on television sets; in addition, they will be able to monitor every appliance in the home, watching hawklike for energy wastefulness.[39]

As the New Consumer strives to grow up and embrace responsibility, information becomes critical: People want to know what is happening in real time—no more heads in the sand. Companies are eagerly responding. Like Panasonic, Google is committed to helping consumers reduce their carbon footprints. Among other initiatives, it has unveiled the PowerMeter, a free electricity-usage monitoring tool that enables homeowners to track their power consumption throughout the day.[40]

Too often, people's best intentions are stymied by confusion over which products and brands are the most responsible choices. Now retailers are stepping in with creative solutions: Home Depot's Eco-options labels identify products that have less impact on the environment than competing products in the assigned areas of Energy Efficiency, Water Conservation, Healthy Home, Clean Air, and Sustainable Forestry. Likewise, Walmart's new sustainability index promises to empower purchasers with an extraordinary amount of useful data. The retailer's hundred thousand suppliers around the world are being required to calculate and disclose the total environmental costs of their products; Walmart will use that data to create a single, simple rating that appears on the price tag. It is "the dawning of the age of ecological transparency in the marketplace," says the *Harvard Business Review,* which notes that suppliers that cannot bring their ratings up are likely to be cut, which gives them a powerful incentive to go green.[41]

"A green gun pointed at the head of consumer products companies"—that is how one industry observer describes Walmart's move. "While Wal-Mart did not explicitly say it would publish ingredients, such a disclosure would be an inevitable outcome of the green-rating process and a way to differentiate products." Immediately, manufacturers began scrambling to reveal what their products contain, overturning years of hard-fought secrecy. First Clorox disclosed its ingredients, followed by SC Johnson, which in 2009 created a special Web site (www.whatsinsidescjohnson.com) to list the contents of such household staples as Glade, Pledge, and Windex. Many expect Colgate-Palmolive and Procter & Gamble to follow suit, lest they seem to have something to hide—or risk being nudged off the shelves at the world's largest retailer. "Today's families want to know what's in the products they use in their homes," said SC Johnson chairman and chief executive Fisk Johnson. "For us, it's about living up to the trust our consumers put in us." To the astonishment of many environmental watchdogs, a new era of openness had arrived.[42]

As another example of the trend toward empowerment through knowledge, GoodGuide's new iPhone application lets customers scan barcodes in the store to learn about the health, environmental, and social responsibility ramifications of each of 60,000 products they might buy. Faced with a puzzling choice among several moisturizers, for example, a shopper might want to know which of two organic options also conforms to positive social practices in its manufacture and "life cycle." GoodGuide aggregates information about which products are scanned most frequently, helping the company to prioritize which items to rate next.[43]

Brands are reaching out to help customers make better personal decisions of all kinds, providing them with information that can be used in the pursuit of healthier, greener lifestyles. McDonald's has launched a Web site that allows restaurant goers in Europe to gauge the caloric content of their meals and, by using a special calculator, to tally how much they ought to be eating based on their age, size, and gender.

TerraCycle, a U.S. company that makes eco-friendly products from various nonrecyclable materials, is now asking consumers to get directly involved by bringing in waste. It has partnered with PETCO, OfficeMax, Home Depot, and Best Buy in setting up collection points in stores, with the goal of establishing 10,000 such sites. From all that waste, TerraCycle fabricates "upcycled" products, including pencil cases, lunch boxes, and corkboards.[44] In the United States and Britain, RecycleBank incentivizes households to recycle by paying them to do so: Participants receive credit for the weight of materials they recycle, then exchange those credits for coupons that can be redeemed at various businesses. This clever system benefits everyone: Municipalities save on disposal fees, recycling companies make money from processing, retailers gain kudos from happy customers.[45]

Korean consumer electronics giant Samsung has designed a prototype cell phone that can be recharged by solar panels built into the case. The Blue Earth phone will be made from recycled water bottles and is toxin-free.[46] The phone's "Eco Walk" function serves as a pedometer, showing how much the user is saving on carbon dioxide emissions by walking, not driving. It is all a response to the New Consumer's changing attitudes: "People believe it's no longer about someone else taking responsibility for them," says David Steel, senior vice president of Samsung, "but more and more about individuals taking responsibility for themselves."[47]

Banks, too, are empowering these new, more mindful consumers to make smarter, more satisfying choices. With a Barclaycard Breathe credit card, U.K. shoppers are able to spend as they normally would while simultaneously contributing to the fight against climate change. Barclay's makes such a responsible choice easy: From each purchase cardholders make, it donates 0.5 percent to government-approved projects that tackle global warming, such as installing solar panels in schools and buying and canceling carbon credits in developing countries.[48]

Act Local, Buy Fairly

Growing up and accepting responsibility go hand in hand with community involvement—supporting local businesses, for example. This is another reason brands are now emphasizing provenance, signaling to the mindful consumer that they genuinely care about such issues. As we saw, the New Consumer survey revealed strong interest in buying locally produced goods, especially among leading-edge Prosumers: A majority of global consumers (and more than three-quarters of U.S. Prosumers) reported it makes them "feel good to support local producers, artisans, and manufacturers." These buyers take pride in their local purchases, with many believing their efforts are improving the economic health of their communities.

Brands worldwide are responding to this upsurge in interest by making local linkages a prominent feature of their products and marketing. In the United States, Whole Foods is working to increase the proportion of local goods in its stores (partly in response to criticism from customers): "Be Loyal, Buy Local" is the new slogan. Its Authentic Food Artisan line is all local and handcrafted, and, through its Local Producer Loan Program, Whole Foods makes $10 million available annually for low-interest loans to small producers. Similarly, Walmart has upped its purchases of local produce and is working with state departments of agriculture and suppliers to develop growing areas for products that have never been tried there previously (e.g., corn in Mississippi, cilantro in South Florida). To reduce carbon outputs and support rural communities, Walmart has introduced a "Food Miles Calculator," which allows store buyers to enter information on each supplier and product, determine product pickup locations, and select which of the company's thirty-eight food distribution centers the product will reach. In this way, buyers can make intelligent decisions based on total food miles.

In 2006, U.K. supermarket chain Asda started a Collect & Save program under which customers earned rewards for collecting stamped receipts from participating independent retailers (including competing butchers and greengrocers). The program was all about supporting area merchants—and defending the burgeoning company against claims that it harms local retailers. Also in the United Kingdom, Tesco groceries pledged in 2009 to more than double sales of local products by 2011. Most fruits and veggies available at Tesco's Fresh & Easy locations in the western United States are locally sourced.

Conscious consumers also feel good about buying Fair Trade products, ones that, according to an advocacy group, are "about better prices, decent working conditions, local sustainability, and fair terms of trade for farmers and workers in the developing world."[49] Fair Trade brands are enjoying a boom, with Starbucks, Green Mountain Coffee Roasters, and Ten Thousand Villages receiving wide recognition for their efforts in this regard and many others making rapid strides. A 2008 study by Alter Eco showed that 71 percent of U.S. consumers are now aware of the term *Fair Trade*, a substantial increase from a decade prior. Fifty-six percent have purchased Fair Trade products, especially coffee; of these purchasers, almost half were motivated by a desire to help others. "This [finding] suggests that successful marketing of Fair Trade items should stress the existing perception of high quality, as well as ethical arguments," the study concludes.[50]

A Part of Something Big was founded by parents dissatisfied with humdrum approaches to school fundraising. The company's product catalogs showcase Fair Trade, earth-friendly, co-op, and microeconomic offerings. About 40 percent of proceeds go to the schools, with 43 percent going back to the producers. Every product is clearly labeled as to its producer and its cause. That $15 wooden spoon, for example, was made at tuition-free Berea College in Kentucky; its cause is to "help fund the college tuition for low income students in the rural South and support the preservation of the American Craft tradition."[51] Most participants want to support their children's schools; this company has figured out a way to let them do that while purchasing products that offer far more emotional appeal than the standard fundraising gift-wrap and chocolate bars.

PURPOSEFUL PLEASURE:
PLAYING UP THE POSITIVE

As customers strive to make better choices, brands are helping them down this more positive path by stressing the more meaningful and lasting benefits of their products and services. Pleasure has been redefined as something slower, more contemplative than a quick swipe of the plastic or the guzzling of a mass-produced sugary drink. Dom Perignon picked up on this with its Seven Sensualities program, a tasting experience featuring a seven-course meal matched to various aspects of a single champagne. Each event is limited to fourteen diners, who come away with a memorable experience—not just delicious food and drink, but a culinary education that remains with them long after the evening has ended.

Purposeful pleasure can arise from doing good, including being socially conscious and ecologically responsible. The company Three Green Moms understands that and reaches out to the conscious consumer with a clever, hip, and substantive product. The back-story is appealing: "Three Moms. Nine busy kids. One start up company." From a suburban home in Potomac, Maryland, the moms promote Lunch Skins, an alternative to wasteful plastic sandwich and snack baggies. Of European-made coated cotton of a type used in bakeries, the bags are stitched in the United States to give a welcome touch of localism and come in colorful patterns for "endless, custom combinations." Each dishwasher-safe Lunch Skin costs $8.95—not cheap, but the company notes that three months' of school lunches ordinarily consume 120 plastic baggies, sixty water bottles, and sixty plastic forks or spoons.[52] "How much does this cost? About $31 for three months of plastic"—a dollar more than the company's Less Trashy Lunch Kit, which includes two Lunch Skins, twenty pieces of cutlery made from corn starch, and one stainless steel water bottle that can be reused for years. The company boasts of its holistic eco-consciousness, including the fact that "we bike to our office or work from home (in our pjs and slippers sometimes)." With their colorful look (akin to the brilliant hues of today's revitalized Duck Tape), Lunch Skins make consumers happy even as they feel virtuous for helping to save the planet. Plus there's the fun element of product novelty, as other kids' parents look surprised and say, "Where did you get those? What a great idea!"[53]

Getting Closer

Today's consumers want to know that brands value them as individuals, just as brands want their customers to feel that special link that encourages them to actively support the brand. It is increasingly common for companies to build these linkages through on-site visits, during which customers can get an "insider" view and feel a sense of solidarity with fellow brand compatriots. In Amsterdam, Heineken has reopened an old brewery as "The Heineken Experience," where visitors can discover the nineteenth-century heritage of the company, take a ride through the brewing process, and bottle their own beer to take home.[54] For three bucks, ice cream devotees can tour the Ben & Jerry's production center in leafy Vermont, starting with a company-history "moo-vie" that dramatizes how Ben Cohen and Jerry Greenfield got started by subscribing to a five-dollar correspondence course about ice-cream making. Then comes a glimpse of roaring machinery on the factory floor, churning out 110 pints a minute—no cameras allowed here. And the last stop might be the Flavor Graveyard, on a hillside behind the bulk milk tanks, where such underperforming schlumps as Cantaloupe, Southern Pecan Pie, and Vermonty Python now push up daisies—killed off by heartless accountants thinking only of the bottom line. Some visitors are moved to bring flowers.[55]

Purposeful pleasure brings with it the possibility of interactive, committed relationships between customer and brand. Forward-thinking companies are inviting the public to participate with them in the creation of better products and even a better world. Dutch supermarket chain Albert Heijn recently asked customers to help improve its 700 stores, and more than 55,000 shoppers responded. The best suggestions were posted online, and their creators were rewarded with one-minute shopping sprees.[56] When Electrolux began hosting an annual Design Lab, thousands of students from across the world submitted ideas for household appliances as they might look in the year 2020.[57] Similarly, Procter & Gamble's Connect + Develop program looks to the general public for help with product design. More than 35 percent of the company's innovations now come from outside, and it has launched dozens of new products based on consumers' input—including Olay Regenerist, Swiffer Dusters, Crest SpinBrush, and Mr. Clean Magic Eraser.[58]

Recently we asked C. J. O'Donnell of Jaguar whether the old ways of mindless, over-the-top consumerism will ever return. He predicts an economic slump that persists until 2013—with underlying ramifications to extend much further than that: "Even then the dynamics of the market will have changed considerably."[59] In talking with Charles Schwab chief marketing officer Rebecca Saeger about what companies need to do to build lasting connections with the New Consumer, she told us that this is a valuable moment for business: "Corporations need to get back to what's important. People can easily distinguish today between how much is about *marketing* versus how much is about *being a better company*. Consumers don't trust companies—we are at a point where people trust themselves. It's not enough to say 'trust me'; we will have to stress *what we do* versus *what we say*."[60]

Both O'Donnell and Saeger agree that businesses are now operating in a profoundly changed world, but one that is full of opportunities. Already, brands are beginning to respond in remarkably creative ways. Having examined some of the new products and services on offer, we now look at the brand-communication revolution unfolding all around us.

Chapter 10

SPEAKING THE LANGUAGE OF MINDFUL CONSUMPTION

As virtually everyone is aware by now, brands are far more than the collective products and services sold under their names. Managed intelligently, they are living and ever-evolving entities that exist alongside consumers, communicating with them, learning from them, and growing with them—or, ideally, advancing slightly ahead of them.

Until the advent of modern retailing and marketing, most goods were commodities, not brands. People bought cow's milk; they did not choose from among Borden and Dean's, Horizon and Organic Valley. Milk was milk. And a company's net worth could be pinpointed just by tallying up the value of what it owned: inventory, machinery, land. Today, that notion seems almost absurd. Now it is *intangible* assets—including human capital (a.k.a. employees), intellectual property, knowledge, and *brand reputation*—that are the biggest determinants of value. In fact, intangible assets are believed to comprise 60 to 80 percent of the market capitalization of public companies today.[1]

What does all this have to do with marketing to the New Consumer? Everything. In the brave new Intangibles Economy, consumers are drawn to brands whose values they share (or aspire to share). To attract customers and retain their loyalty and cheerful participation, a brand must have a distinct persona and, in the new atmosphere of mindfulness, must communicate values in line with those of its target audience. As noted in chapter 7, nearly six in ten U.S. respondents to the New Consumer study (and 77 percent of U.S. Prosumers) said they prefer to buy from companies that *share their personal values*. A majority (57 percent of the U.S. sample and 70 percent of Prosumers) also said that, in recent years, it has become more important to them to *feel good about* the companies with which they do business.

Informed and responsive business planners understand this. We asked Christian McMahan, chief marketing officer of Heineken USA, for his opinion: Will consumers return to the old hyperconsumerist status quo in their behaviors or increasingly factor personal values into the consumption equation? "If by *status quo* you mean like they were before the recession, the answer may be never," he replied. "I think there is a permanent shift that has taken place in the minds of consumers. The companies that are going to be successful are the ones that best understand what this shift means to them and react quickly and effectively to be better positioned in this new world."[2]

As a road map through the new terrain, the Four Paradigms can help. We have seen how they apply to the development of products and services. Now we take a look at how they are reshaping brand communications in the era of the mindful spender.

EMBRACING SUBSTANCE: THE MESSAGE IS DOWN TO EARTH AND COMMUNITY FOCUSED

More and more, consumers gravitate toward products that feel deeply "real." So what makes a brand seem real? Influential ingredients include a strong sense of place (IKEA, Marlboro); a distinct point of view or passion (Apple, Nike); a larger purpose (Peace Cereal, Newman's Own); and an emphasis on integrity and action (Berkshire Hathaway, Google). In every case, what matters most is the emotional connection: how the consumer feels about the brand. Smart companies are working to enhance those connections by communicating the vital roles they play in the lives of individuals, local communities, and the broader society.

With its "10061.com" campaign (named for the SKU of its iconic yellow boot), Timberland took to the streets to connect directly with its urban base. Advertising agency Arnold Worldwide erected three blank leather billboards in the Bronx, Brooklyn, and Harlem sections of New York City. Local artists were invited to create murals on the leather canvases representing what life is like in each of these neighborhoods. After thirty days on display, the art installations were moved to local community centers. Adding further to the sense of interconnectedness, Timberland then dismantled the billboards and used the adorned leather to make limited-edition boots, which were auctioned off to support local charities.

Pete Favat, managing partner and chief creative officer at Arnold, told us, "In urban centers, it was already common for people to customize their yellow Timberland work boots with graffitilike designs. Each one totally original and personal. With 10061.com, we took that same concept and extended it in a way that brought people together and helped them celebrate their neighborhood communities and the vibrant cultures that exist there. Everything about the campaign was true to our customers and Timberland's place in their lives, and people responded to that."[3]

We're All in This Together

Today's consumers are less trusting, more skeptical, so marketers can no longer fake empathy; they truly have to understand what ordinary people are facing in their daily lives and respond accordingly. During times of real trouble, such as economic downturns, people are turned off by empty expressions of sympathy but open to words of solace and solidarity that have a practical (and verifiable) solution attached. Simply put, they are looking to brands for substantive help. That idea forms the cornerstone of Euro RSCG's "Talk to Chuck" campaign for Charles Schwab, which uses an eye-catching animation technique. The language is candid: "Without investors there is: no industry, no economy, no jobs, no growth. Enough is enough." The point is that investment firms have failed their individual investors by not thinking of the little guy first. In place of that old, discredited model, Schwab put forth an "Investors Rule" premise, and it democratized investing: All investors, rich or not, now pay the same flat rate of $8.95 per online equity trade—"Millions of investors. One price."[4]

Walmart is another brand that understands the new role businesses ought to play. As recession fears took hold in 2007 and 2008, the mega-retailer announced plans to roll back prices on many essentials 10 to 30 percent. Ordinary prescription drugs were offered at $4 for a thirty-day supply. The company helped ease the credit crunch by offering interest-free loans on purchases of $250 or more for eighteen months, and it ran ads claiming to save the average U.S. family $2,500 a year. As seen in its 2009 quarterly returns, Walmart emerged as a shining hero in recessionary times. That was due, in part, to its finally having learned that low prices are not enough. With its revamped logo—"Save money. Live better."—the company highlighted the positive role it plays in people's lives. Significantly, the brand was not proffering an aspirational fantasyland but, rather, "real" products sold by "real" people who live in the "real" world. Walmart now talks the language of interconnectedness and interdependency, humanized values that consumers crave.

Other companies have similarly embraced the "we're all in this together" ethos. As the economy tanked, Kmart expressed its solidarity with the down and out by offering a Smart Assist Savings Card to unemployed residents of hard-hit Michigan; cardholders received a 20 percent price reduction on Kmart's private label goods for six months.[5] In January 2009, Hyundai launched its Assurance Program, which spoke directly to customers' fears by allowing them to give their car back if they lost their job. This program was soon augmented with Assurance Plus: Anyone who bought or leased a Hyundai before the end of April 2009 and subsequently lost their job would be granted three months of payments, free. Hyundai's market share jumped from 3.1 percent to 4.3 percent between 2008 and 2009—but the company earned much more than cash: It gained in public favor.[6] "This is a recession of fear," Joel Ewanick, vice president of marketing for Hyundai Motor America, told *Advertising Age*. "We realized that the elephant in the room was the fear of losing your job. I feel the same way. We all do. The idea of giving people the option to give the car back if they were struggling...seemed a great way to make customers comfortable and increase our market share in an economy like this."[7] It was a rare opportunity, he added: "The last time a company like Hyundai could build brand and steal market share was almost forty years ago. And before that, you had to go back to 1930, when General Motors stole the leadership position away from Ford."[8]

There are all sorts of ways for brands to build goodwill. It can be as complicated as the Hyundai promotion or as simple as Samsung firing up electrical charging stations in airports to help travelers stay connected while in limbo. Among our favorite promotions in recent years was the Charmin-sponsored spiffed-up public restroom (complete with attendant) in New York's Times Square over the holiday shopping season. The brand has since extended the effort by developing an application for iPhone and BlackBerry that allows consumers to find a lavatory in a pinch. A relatively simple offering, but one that can prove invaluable to an individual in dire straits.

Supporting Local Communities

Increasingly, brands are emphasizing the good they do not just for individuals but also for communities. They know we want to feel connected; they know, too, that the kiss of death for any brand nowadays is to be perceived as cold, corporate, and remote. Even the biggest companies have scrambled to reposition themselves—in fact, their sprawling bigness may provide an extra incentive for them to emphasize the small. Let us look at several examples of the trend:

- Sportswear giant Nike introduced "Back Your Block" in 2009, a $650,000 grant program to support local organizations that help "young people through programs that focus on sport." A buzz-marketing campaign spearheaded by social marketing agency Mr. Youth sent forth a wave of 250 young influencers to get the word out about the competition. Competing organizations promoted themselves zealously on Facebook and Twitter.[9] Nearly 1,100 applications and more than 600,000 votes were submitted, culminating in the voters' choice of a couple hundred winners.[10] Among the victorious was Palo Alto, California-based Baskets 4 Hope, which uses basketball as a vehicle with which to "transform the prevalent culture of violence in the Bay Area" and inspire inner-city teens to live healthy and productive lives.[11]

- Kellogg also focused on sports with its Plant a Seed project aimed at getting kids more active. In 2009, the company devoted its first-ever Super Bowl commercial to urging viewers to go to the Frosted Flakes Web site and nominate some scruffy local playing fields for renovation. Thousands of nominations were received, one hundred finalists were picked, and fifty winners were chosen by public vote.[12]

- Nike has a natural relationship to sports; Kellogg, perhaps less so—though kid-focused food and beverage companies consider it in their best interest to be seen as combating childhood obesity. When you think KFC, it is highly unlikely that potholes come to mind. Yes, *potholes*. But that did not discourage the fast-food giant from unveiling a community-centric "Re-'Freshed' by KFC" campaign, in which the brand offered to patch some of America's 350 million potholes. The logic was somewhat cloudy, although the company tried to equate filling up diners and filling up holes, while also communicating the message that its chickens are delivered fresh, not frozen. Mayors competed to have their city be one of the four chosen. The payback for the company lay in the PR the promotion would garner; in addition to the media coverage, each patched pothole was emblazoned in chalk with the announcement "Re-'Freshed' by KFC." "This program is a perfect example

of that rare and optimal occurrence when a company can cre-
atively market itself and help local governments and everyday Americans across the country," KFC's vice president of
marketing explained.[13]

What each of these examples has in common is that the brand provided
concrete solutions to highly specific local problems, whether it involved
patching city potholes, reseeding a suburban playing field, or getting
kids off the street. There was a time when brand promotions focused
solely on "extras" given to individuals—for example, a trip to St. Barts
or a "Brand New Car!" This has changed in recent years as governments (local and national) have proved less capable of meeting local
needs and as consumers have begun to look to businesses and brands to
pick up the slack. As we discussed in our earlier book, *Good for Business*,
Euro RSCG's 2008 Future of the Corporate Brand study found that
72 percent of Americans believe businesses bear *as much responsibility
as governments* for generating positive social change. That is a heavy
burden but also an enormous opportunity for brands.

Giving People a Role to Play

We noted earlier the hunger among New Consumers for involvement
in a cause—in something "bigger than self." Brands can help them
get started. "Many people are anxious to help the world, but they
don't know where to begin," says a video spot for the online social
network V2V (for "volunteer to volunteer").[14] In 2008, Starbucks
joined forces with the network in a shared venture meant to foster "creativity, collaboration amongst new friends, and inspiration
to make our world a better place to live. Together, Starbucks and
V2V are 'Redefining Community.'"[15] The partners announced an
ambitious goal of generating more than a million hours of community service every year by 2015. Among the more than 23,000 people
who have already signed up is Liz Baker of Seattle, who has committed herself to several specific "Actions" (among the more than 2,200
Actions V2V has thus far undertaken), including knitting scarves
for the homeless, reusing shopping bags, gardening sustainably, and
recycling food scraps at her desk at work. "Community and family have always been two of the most important things to me," she
writes enthusiastically on the V2V Web site. "Seeing other people
get involved and take action inspires me to do more within my own
community and help others (local or not) improve their quality of
life."[16]

Starbucks excels at this kind of outreach. In collaboration with the Corporation for National and Community Service and HandsOn Network, it launched the "I'm In" campaign in January 2009—seeking to build on the enthusiasm surrounding President-elect Obama and his call for individual commitment. The initiative encouraged customers to pledge five hours or more of service to a local volunteer organization of their choice. Options included assisting at a food bank, assembling military care packages, reading to children at a hospital, and planting trees in a park, among many others. In return, Starbucks honored each person who pledged with one free tall coffee.[17] While that may not seem like much reward for five hours' anticipated work, nonetheless, an extraordinary 1.3 million hours of service were pledged.[18] New Consumers enjoy making connections with a brand while also feeling part of a broader movement.

Predicts marketing blogger Tim Leberecht:

> Only brands that give more than they take will be able to create sustained brand loyalty. ["I'm In"] provides a blueprint for *marketing with meaning* and presents the quintessential win-win-win situation: The embattled coffee chain will reinvigorate its grassroots image and underscore its ties to the local community; consumers are recognized in their desire to do something meaningful and are provided with an effective and user-friendly platform to take immediate action; and—last but not least—the brand-facilitated volunteering benefits the common good.[19]

Like Starbucks, Disney intends to use its massive reach to mobilize volunteerism and, at the same time, buff its brand reputation. With its much-publicized "Give a Day, Get a Disney Day" (in partnership with HandsOn Network), it aimed to inspire one million people to volunteer a day of service to a participating organization in their communities in 2010. In return, they would receive a free one-day ticket to a Disney theme park, redeemable within that calendar year.[20] Duncan Dickson of the University of Central Florida's Rosen School of Hospitality Management calls the endeavor "a smart marketing move"—Disney wins kudos even as it basks in free publicity from the nonprofits it is benefiting. Yes, it loses ticket revenue, but it earns money on sales of food and gifts to all those "free" customers—who might just bring their friends along. In a recession, "Anything that pushes the turnstiles is good for business," Dickson says.[21] Just six weeks into the promotion, some 600,000 people had already completed or scheduled their volunteer work.[22]

The Timberland Company has always been media savvy: In 1987, it became the first boot manufacturer to advertise on national television; in 1992, it ran an innovative "Give Racism the Boot" awareness campaign, and its "Beliefs" print campaign of 1998 showcased the company's philosophy of "pulling on your boots and making a difference."[23] Its latest effort is called Earthkeepers, an attempt to recruit a million people who will commit to taking small steps toward positive environmental change. These individuals, in turn, are expected to engage other Earthkeepers through interactive reporting tools such as blogs, photo galleries, videos, and podcasts. "Recycling, Earthkeeper style," read a recent tweet on Twitter. "Wartime fort tunnels in Belgium rehabbed into safe havens for hibernating bats."[24]

In explaining its campaign, Timberland took care to acknowledge its role in environmental depreciation and reach out to consumers for solutions: "Making outdoor boots, shoes and gear is what we do for a living. No more outdoors means no more living. For us—or anyone else. Of course, we realize that by making our products, we're part of the problem. We believe it's time for companies, like ours, to take a look at how the way they do business affects the environment and do something about it.... We know we don't have all the answers. So we hope you share yours."[25]

The horrendous aftermath of the earthquake in Haiti in January 2010 provided a focus for many other "common cause" corporate efforts. It would have been easy enough for corporations simply to donate money and goods to the relief effort—and many did. However, the more forward-thinking brands took the opportunity to invite customers to join the cause. American Airlines announced it would provide 250 frequent-flier miles to customers who donated fifty dollars or more to the stricken nation. Amazon.com posted a box on its home page that let site visitors easily give to Mercy Corps' relief efforts. In fact, so many companies jumped on board in the cause of Haiti, it seemed definitive proof of the new axiom that businesses are replacing government as the key solution provider in times of crisis.

Bringing the Local into Focus

We saw in the last chapter how brands are upping their "local" credentials by creating products using locally sourced ingredients, stocking shelves with locally produced goods, and so on. Here we look at how brands are communicating local roots and connections in their marketing efforts. Together with acting locally, communicating local linkages is an important component of authenticity.

TV viewers cannot escape the trend toward local-themed advertising right now. In 2006, Ocean Spray Cranberries (with Arnold Worldwide) began to express the brand's authentic roots with a campaign featuring two homespun growers engaged in banter as they stand knee deep in a New England cranberry bog. Sales jumped 10 percent.[26] In 2008–9, Ocean Spray took the concept further with a cartoon, "Cranberry Christmas," as well as a "Bogs Across America" tour that erected replica cranberry bogs in major cities. "Cranberries have become as much a part of holiday traditions as ice skating and decorating the tree," says Ken Romanzi, chief operating officer at Ocean Spray, who hopes " 'Cranberry Christmas' will take its place as a perennial holiday favorite."[27]

Companies wishing to stress localism would do well to look at the example of U.K. whisky distillers, which have long taken pride in their art and which effectively weave an entire mythology around their product: The cultural ancestry of Scotch whisky is as important to its brand identity as its taste. Worried about declining sales, distillers banded together in 1988 in an organization called Keepers of the Quaich (named for a traditional drinking bowl) to "advance the standing and prosperity of one of Britain's premier export industries, and to make more widely known its uniqueness, traditions, quality, service and benefits to the community it serves at home and in the markets of the world."[28] For its part, distiller Glenmorangie highlights the "Sixteen Men of Tain," highly skilled employees who produce the company's well-regarded product: "These sixteen individuals are the living embodiment of our founder's vision, the unofficial guardians of our malt, who still, to this day, use the time-honored, traditional skills that have passed from generation to generation. Together they ensure Glenmorangie is made in the same, unhurried and uncompromised way it always has been since 1843."[29] Great Britain has not entirely cornered the market on whisky authenticity. U.S.-based Jack Daniel's has long run ads that play up the company's roots in a town boasting a population of just 361. A current advertisement focuses on the brand's authentic production processes, with whiskey made (cue the gravelly voice) "The Tennessee Way. Which is not the easy way. But it was *his* way."

Marketers in every category are digging into heritage and narrative in order to develop a deeper brand story. They follow a famous example: Through coffee lore and provenance, Starbucks alchemized a basic commodity into a luxury. Coffee education and cultural learning forms part of the brand's mission, in store and online, and has contributed to one of the greatest entrepreneurial success stories in history. Starbucks exploded from 17 stores in 1987 to 8,337 in 2004.[30] (Expansion brought a blurring of mission focus, however—in 2008, the *Harvard Business Review* featured an article on how Starbucks' growth had destroyed its brand value; chief executive Howard Schultz is now back in the saddle and working to repair the recent brand damage.[31])

Many companies have tried to emulate the Starbucks model—the positive aspects, at least. One component of the strategy is to stress that there are *real people* behind the brand. Potato chip maker Burts Crisps, which promotes its products as "real food" entirely hand-cooked in England, slaps the name of the individual fryer on every bag. Its Web site offers tidbits about these humble workers (Linda's husband's worst habit is snoring; as a boy, Ian crashed his pedal car) and even invites customers to pepper them with questions.[32] An emphasis on folksy, homegrown goodness has helped the young brand "go supersonic," one industry observer notes, and it currently sells 12 million bags a year.[33]

Dole Organic bananas now carry a sticker with a three-digit Farm Code. Buyers can log onto a Web site to discover the story behind every bunch, including photographs of the crops and workers. In California, Top 10 Produce LLC invites "socially conscious consumers to play a role" by buying from small, independent growers. All of their products come with "a transparency enabling barcode" that the customer can scan with a mobile phone to learn about the farmer and whether the produce is locally grown. (There is even a map showing the location of the farm as compared with one's current location, based on the caller's cell phone's global positioning system.) Consumer reviews of fresh produce are also available, to shoppers and chefs alike.[34]

In the United Kingdom, Pipers Crisps potato chips come in an Anglesey Sea Salt variety, flavored with salt that boasts a compelling story all its own: "David and Alison Lea-Wilson harvest sea water from the Menai Straits at Brynsiencyn on Anglesey. Before the water arrives at the Anglesey Sea Salt company it has already passed through a mussel bed, nature's finest filter, and a sandbank. It is then filtered through charcoal."[35] Notice all the rich specificity—we are told exactly who is involved. And the process is made to sound almost poetic.

Just as we have seen a spike in so-called greenwashing (companies making false claims of environmental purity), so, too, are we seeing the rise of fake authenticity surrounding claims of being local. British financial conglomerate HSBC has taken to billing itself as "the world's local bank," despite its thousands of locations across the globe. In the United States, Dutch-owned Unilever's Hellmann's mayonnaise brand is claiming it is a local product because most of its ingredients come from somewhere within the 9.5 million square miles of North America. Now, that is seriously stretching the definition of *local*.[36]

In a bid to restore some of its lost authenticity, Starbucks has launched a chain of pseudolocal coffee shops under the name 15th Ave. Coffee & Tea. The coffeehouse design is "reminiscent of a European mercantile and draws inspiration from the original Starbucks location opened in Seattle's Pike Place Market thirty-eight years ago. It's eclectic and raw, featuring locally sourced and reused materials that are one-of-a-kind."[37] While many consumers are balking at the notion of a major corporation faking local, others consider the provenance of less importance than the experience. Posting on the *Fast Company* Web site, one visitor wrote:

> As far as this question goes—"But can it be authentic?"—I think it all depends on the experience a person has there. If you walk in and it feels just like the neighborhood coffee shop a few blocks away, then it's probably as authentic as it needs to feel. It's not like they'll be using fake, "comfortable" furniture or fake, home-made design elements. Of course, if employees are trained with the traditional Starbucks training manual/video and then told to pretend to be a local coffee shop, there could certainly be a disconnect that causes problems. But, as long as they provide a coffee shop that, from all discerning perspectives, is "real," then it seems to me that it's a pretty smart move by Starbucks.[38]

In the end, it will be up to the New Consumer to decide the relative value of a brand experience that *is* authentic versus one that simply *feels* authentic.

RIGHTSIZING: THE MESSAGE IS MODERATION

For many brands, communicating with the New Consumer means acknowledging the shift toward rightsizing with messages that stress simplicity and old-time values. That notion lies at the heart of an advertisement Euro RSCG created for Charles Schwab: "There are 17,000 mutual funds out there. How about seven that are right for me?" Industries considered inherently complicated—such as finance and healthcare—are particularly suited to a rightsizing approach. TV advertisements from Progressive Insurance that feature an upbeat cashier named "Flo" are set in a sparse space with white walls and shelving. The insurance products are shown as coming in tidy, clearly labeled boxes, which customers can mix and match to suit their preference. All the elements in these ads from Arnold Worldwide combine to make the process of buying insurance seem simple and friendly rather than complicated or intimidating.

Nissan has been pushing its small cars, including the low-cost Pixo, under the tagline "Welcome to Simplicity." In a press release, Pixo was called *practical, environmentally conscious, affordable, simple, straightforward,* and (seven times) *uncomplicated.*[39] In a television ad, the Pixo drives through an urban landscape overflowing with signage, including one that speaks to a central dilemma of our times: "Too Many Choices." But a view through the Pixo's windshield is shown to magically make the city go away. The voiceover intones, "Six colors, two models, zero complication. Simple."[40]

In a particularly thorough expression of the simplicity trend, there is Japanese household and consumer goods retailer MUJI, a company that focuses on minimalist design, recycling, and a deliberate absence of branding. Its Web site explains:

> MUJI is not a brand. MUJI does not make products of individuality or fashion, nor does MUJI reflect the popularity of its name in prices. MUJI creates products with a view toward global consumption of the future. This means that we do not create products that lure customers into believing that "this is the best" or "I must have this." We would like our customers to feel the rational sense of satisfaction that comes not with "this is the best," but with "this is enough." "Best" becomes "enough."[41]

The brand (for, even in the absence of paid efforts, the company clearly has become a brand) achieves cost savings through "the careful elimination and subtraction of gratuitous features and design unrelated to function." Unnecessary "bells and whistles," excessive decoration, needless packaging—and logos—are dispensed with.[42] MUJI outlets in Japan and fifteen other countries carry about seven thousand products that range from $4 striped socks to $115,000 prefab houses, enabling devoted consumers to live the MUJI lifestyle: riding a MUJI bike, eating MUJI food, even driving a MUJI car to a MUJI campground where they can set up a MUJI tent.[43] "Zen and the Art of Selling Minimalism," *BusinessWeek* calls the phenomenon, pointing to the brand's "legions of fanatical devotees" and predicting success as it invades the U.S. market, where consumers are "tired of in-your-face logos and over-the-top design."[44]

Communication via Packaging

Sometimes marketers use a visual shorthand to communicate with the New Consumer. As more people seek authenticity, store shelves are seeing a boom in packaging and merchandising cues that speak to naturality and artisanry. Marketers have all sorts of clever visual ways to associate their brands with Mother Nature (unbleached, recycled paper and other natural materials; muted colors), simplicity [handwritten notations (genuine or faux), clean lines, white space], realness (references to venerable processes, old-world methodologies, indigenous ingredients), and friendliness or approachability (childlike fonts and graphics; windows in packaging to show there is nothing to hide). All these gambits help set products apart from the standard-issue goods of big manufacturers.

A desire to communicate simplicity and product purity is behind the minimalist packaging popular in the bottled water category, and it is increasingly popping up in other categories as well. New Gatorade Thirst Quencher bottles now display only the large letter "G" overlaid with the brand's trademark lightning bolt on a transparent label. Coca-Cola, too, has redesigned some of its packaging, stripping away the folderol of recent years from its cans. "All the extra bits and doodads and extraneous graphics are gone," one observer notes approvingly. "Classic Coke imagery: the red, the ribbon, and the Coke script. 'Classic' is even in a simple lowercase sans serif. This is a confident design. Coca-Cola is acknowledging that we all know the product, so just drink it."[45]

"In a world competing for your attention it's great to see Coca-Cola removing the clutter from their new cans and going back to basics," comments a designer with U.K. firm Betley Whitehorne. "The result is a retro looking can but with a modern flavor which I think will look great on the shelves. Gone are the ghosts of ribbons past, drop shadows and bubbles leaving a cleaner, fresher look."[46]

Similarly pushing simplicity, The London Tea Company has lately debuted new-look packaging: A single sheet of cardboard, folded to make a cube, tells the story of the brand when unfolded. Excess glue or stitching is absent. Inside, a biodegradable pouch holds the tea bags together so there is no unnecessary waste in the form of tags or staples. The consumer is invited to focus on the product, not its box.[47]

To show off its new V8 Ready-to-Serve line of healthful soups and emphasize their back-to-basics simplicity, Campbell replaced its iconic steel cans with cartons (the type of packaging used for kids' drink boxes). The bright green cartons are literally a picture of health, each variety featuring a glamour shot of nutrient-rich vegetables. As the slogan has it, "Thinking inside the box just got really fresh." "To consumers," one critic observed, "the most interesting feature of the new V8 Soup was likely the packaging."[48] Such innovative design was meant to help Campbell hold onto its dominant position: It occupies pantry space in 85 percent of U.S. households, and eleven thousand servings of its soups are slurped up every minute.[49] Comfort foods do well in times of economic crisis and accompanying simplification: When the stock market had its worst day in seven years on September 28, 2008, only one Standard & Poor's 500 company actually went up: Campbell.[50]

GROWING UP: COMMUNICATING
THE NEW RESPONSIBILITY

In our recent interview with Christian McMahan of Heineken, we asked him if he saw any significant changes in thinking and outlook among suppliers, employees, or consumers. He replied definitively:

> Yes, yes, and yes. For us it, of course, all starts with the consumer. They are really driving toward a more value-based decision-making process, and brands that can clearly provide and communicate that are going to be in the best position to succeed. Statistics are showing they are spending significantly more time in their shopping behavior. They are much more engaged with the choices they are making. They are spending more time reading the packaging, comparing pricing, and at the end of the day they want to feel comfortable, to be able to rationalize the choices they make.[51]

It is all part of the new mindfulness. More and more, brands are stepping up with innovative responses to these changed consumer attitudes. Increasingly the tone is more grown-up, more responsible.

Campbell's Chunky Soup first built its brand image on ads depicting beefy football players extolling the heartiness of its line of offerings. But as the recession bit deep, the company (working with advertising agency Y&R) took a new direction: It crafted a more straightforward campaign aimed at the blue-collar working man who comes home at 5:30 to his family, for whom he is a responsible provider: "A man's got to eat. He just wants to eat better." Real working stiffs were featured, not actors. The decision was difficult, given the company's long-standing affiliation with the National Football League (since 1997), but the timing seemed right. The responsibility-based campaign suggests a trend toward taking men more seriously, as the recession spurs many of us to "grow up": "As a brand we need to be the everyday guy's advocate and celebrate him," says James Caporimo, executive vice president at Y&R New York. He points out that the commercials mark a clean break from the past, where male characters were "always the butt of the joke."[52]

Launched in 2006, Liberty Mutual's much-discussed "Responsibility Project" consists of TV ads and a series of short films dedicated to ordinary Americans being responsible and doing what is right. ("Doing the right thing says a lot about a person. And a company.") The company's Web site, continuously updated, hosts blogs and stories and offers visitors the chance to share opinions about what is the responsible thing to do in a variety of challenging situations.[53] Ads show people performing small kindnesses and, at the same time, being observed by others who do further kindnesses in turn—in pay-it-forward fashion. (Perhaps inevitably, these heartwarming commercials have given rise to funny YouTube parodies showing people being gratuitously mean to each other.) As updated for the recession in 2009, Liberty Mutual's campaign featured a fictional family, the Marlowes, wrestling with how they should handle difficult dilemmas. In one spot, they are seen secretly investigating their teenage daughter's computer.[54] "We shouldn't be doing this," the mother says worriedly. But when something alarming is discovered, the father asks, "Are you sure?"[55]

Unusually for an ad, the viewer is given little direction as to what to believe or think. Instead, the subtle campaign explores how difficult the making of hard decisions can be; it allows us to draw our own conclusions, treating the New Consumer as an intelligent adult. It is all remarkably open-ended. As Liberty Mutual explains online:

> As an insurance company, we like responsible people. Because people who believe in doing the right thing don't just make better people, they make better customers. But the idea of responsibility can be difficult to define. What does it mean? Why is it important? These aren't questions that can be easily addressed or agreed upon. There are a lot of differing opinions and beliefs involved. And while we may never uncover any definitive answers, we believe the questions are still worth asking.[56]

A Euro RSCG campaign for the venerable magazine the *Atlantic* played up the theme of responsibility as part of a broader effort to encourage more serious and substantive thinking and conversation.

The campaign—called "Think. Again."—was built around thought-provoking questions designed to intrigue consumers, such as "Which religion will win?" and "Is Google making us stupid?" (One was particularly apropos to the subject of this book: "Do we consume too much?") On a Web site, videos showed ordinary people commenting on these various questions, which had been posted in big neon letters in public places. "Our minds, dulled by sound bites and trivia, trudge along, unchallenged and unsatisfied," the site explained. "This is why we started The Atlantic Project: to illuminate questions that provoke us all to challenge assumptions, to get better answers, and to think again."[57] The campaign targeted the person who seeks more substantial pleasures and who, amid a culture of triviality and silliness, is ready to be a grown-up.

SEEKING PURPOSEFUL PLEASURE: COMMUNICATING SUBSTANTIVE VALUES

Forward-thinking companies are embracing humanized values now, including empathy, respect, fairness, and generosity. We associate such values with some iconic names—Whole Foods Market ("Whole Foods. Whole People. Whole Planet."), Starbucks (Fair Trade, profit sharing), and Google ("Don't be evil")—but hundreds of others are joining the effort too. They know that doing so makes excellent business sense. Euro RSCG's 2008 Value Study found that 82 percent of U.S. respondents (and 94 percent of Prosumers) felt that "to be successful, corporations of the future will need to show a more 'human' face (meaning they must care about people—employees, suppliers, customers, etc.—and take a more active role in community and social causes)."

We asked Heineken's McMahan how today's more brand-minded consumers are changing marketing communications. He replied:

> The exploding power of social media plays an increasingly important role, whether consumers like you or hate you. In the future it will become less and less about what companies tell consumers about their brands and much more about what consumers tell *each other*. Moving forward, marketers need to shift their energies away from the traditional thinking about brand communications and instead figure out how best to encourage consumers to engage in brand discussions of their own making.[58]

As McMahan suggests, ordinary people are no longer satisfied with being passive receptors of brand messaging; they now want to get involved—to be a valued partner of the brands they allow into their lives. Smart companies are forging meaningful personal connections by giving buyers a stake in the brand. Among the brands that consistently do this well is Ben & Jerry's, which even offers the public the chance to invent new products through its "Do the World a Flavor" contest.[59] Such participatory approaches have caught on widely. Dove, the leading personal wash brand in the United States (with a presence in one in three households), invites customers to go online and join "the Dove community.... Come on in and feel free to speak out. Tell others about yourself. Your perspective on things just might inspire someone else."[60] As the Dove Self-Esteem Fund Workshop Tour travels the country, it tailors its message to individual communities for greater street-level credibility. Participants in Missouri, for example, were told with concern that "54 percent of teen girls in Kansas City admit to talking badly about themselves."[61]

Dove has followed these and other teenagers to Facebook, creating a virtual community that is all about "promoting positive self esteem and helping women feel good about their unique inner and outer beauty.... Being a Dove fan means connecting with others interested in supporting this notion."[62] As it weaves a spell of togetherness, this thing called "Dove" transforms before our eyes. No longer is it an inert compound of fragrant chemicals hawked by faceless corporate giant Unilever. Instead, it becomes a friendly quasi-person, almost another member of the club. "Can I ask you, Dove, a question about hair shampoo/conditioner?" asks one visitor, as if to a trusted girlfriend. To which Dove helpfully replies, "Sure!"[63]

Subaru, too, is using marketing communications to emphasize humanized values and give consumers a chance to get involved. Thanks in part to a powerful marketing campaign, it became the best-performing car brand in the United States in 2009 (up 14 percent when the market slid 24 percent). Under chief marketing officer Tim Mahoney, Subaru revamped its approach to marketing and rolled out an appealing "Love" campaign (by Carmichael Lynch): "Love. It's what makes a Subaru a Subaru."[64] A "Share the Love" effort during two consecutive holiday seasons allowed each new Subaru owner or lessee to select a charity to receive $250 from the company. (The choices were Boys & Girls Clubs of America, Habitat for Humanity International, Meals On Wheels Association of America, National Wildlife Federation, and the American Society for the Prevention of Cruelty to Animals.)[65] In addition to driving home in a car they feel good about, these consumers had the added pleasure of making a difference for the charity of their choice.

A NEW BEGINNING?

As we have seen in this book, the long, wearisome decades of hyper-consumption shaped not just the way we think and feel but the very language we use. It is now customary to refer to human beings as *consumers* or even as *brands*. And an entire lexicon has been summoned into existence just to give verbal shape to our profligate excesses: *big-box store*, *Black Friday* (and now *Cyber Monday*), *bling*, *door-buster*, *McMansion*, *self-storage*, *shopaholic*, *supersized*, *warehouse club*. The bloated culture of excessive consumption—and its language, symbols, and styles—are so much a part of our everyday reality that it is difficult to remember that they have not always been around.

But now, thankfully, much is changing. And there might well come a time, not so far off, when the language of mindfulness becomes sufficiently ingrained in consumer culture to seem perpetually inter-twined with it, the way hyperconsumption has been for so long. Think how many terms connoting mindfulness have recently sprung into existence: *carbon footprint*, *downsizing*, *ecotourism*, *ethical consumption*, *Fair Trade*, *food miles*, *frugalista*, *green collar*, *locavore*, and *sustainable*, among others. Ten years ago, many of these terms would have been unfamiliar—perhaps bafflingly so. Now they are in constant use and spreading widely.

Future-focused brands are playing a role in this exciting trans-formation. And the more these brands contribute to the vibrant new language of rightsizing, restraint, and responsibility, the greater the likelihood of mindful consumption becoming ingrained within our collective psyches. Perhaps then we will see a new way of life emerge, one that keeps consumerism in happier and healthier balance. And perhaps then we will finally get back to enjoying more substantive fulfillment in our lives, with our families and friends, of course, but also with those brand partners that find profit not in being rapacious but in offering sensible solutions to our genuine needs.

Chapter 11

BEYOND CONSUMPTION: WHAT IS NEXT?

As we consider what will replace hyperconsumerism, we have found it helpful to undertake a STEEP (*social, technological, economic, environmental,* and *political*) analysis of current trends affecting consumer behavior. Understanding these trends and their implications for consumers and marketers helps us to see where these historic shifts more than likely will lead us.

STEEP ANALYSIS OF THE FACTORS DRIVING CONSUMPTION

Social Factors

- *The population turns gray.* In looking at trends that promise to have a significant impact on consumerism, it would be impossible to ignore the fact that the fastest-growing cohort in the world is seniors. In 2000, there were around 600 million people over age sixty on this planet; by 2050, that number is expected to soar to nearly two *billion*.[1] Our youth-obsessed culture is about to collide with unavoidable realities of aging, including the physical and mental challenges it brings. The older people become, the more cautious and mindful they grow, especially if finances are uncertain.

   Implication. Attitudes will swing away from the hedonistic impulsiveness of youth and toward the more mindful decision making of adults.
- *Wastefulness becomes uncool.* Consider the case of smoking: Long popular, it has now completely lost its cachet. Bans have been

imposed just about everywhere, and in early 2010, Finland
became the first country to announce a push to eradicate the
habit entirely. Hyperconsumption has started to undergo a
similar fall from grace. It is one thing to "burn money" when
there is plenty around and everyone has a chance to get some; it
is another matter when ordinary working people are struggling
to pay their bills. At the same time, ecological consciousness
is on the rise, with revulsion against mindless consumption
setting in.

Implication. Conspicuous consumption used to signal "I'm
rich enough not to care." Increasingly it will signal "I'm too
dumb to think about the consequences of my actions and too
self-absorbed to care."

- *We crave connectedness.* Lately, psychologists have pointed to
an epidemic of isolation and loneliness, for which they blame
shrinking family sizes, the hurried pace of modern life, and
the decline of nonelectronic entertainments. We noted earlier
the drop in friendships and the consensus that Internet
communication is weakening human bonds.

Implication. Marketers seeking to understand the new
mindfulness need to consider what impact a product or service
has on connectedness. Does it bring people together—or drive
them apart?

- *We want to get in on the action.* We have lived through the era of
the couch potato, mindlessly consuming whatever was thrust
upon us. But now the "push" culture has given way to "pull,"
with people reaching out to seize opportunities that seem
right for them. They create and share their own entertainment by uploading to YouTube, vote for contestants on reality
TV, phone in bilious comments to talk radio, offer their
opinions about products and services on Epinions and other
online forums, and create their own commercials for favorite brands. It is remarkable how much time and effort they
will offer up—for free. The open-source computer operating
system Linux was built by a global group of enthusiasts; the
14 million articles that make up Wikipedia have been written
by 85,000 volunteers; Lego relies on adult fans to develop its
Mindstorms toys.[2]

Implication. When people become actively involved in
shaping and even inventing products, the old producer-
consumer paradigm is transformed.

Technological Factors

- *Social media enables peer-to-peer communication.* In 2009 alone, the number of people using Facebook went from 150 million to 350 million; by October of that year, visitors to Twitter were up 1,271 percent from twelve months prior.[3] A Nielsen report pointed to the phenomenal growth in social networking, which by early 2009 had surpassed e-mail in popularity. Two-thirds of the global online population were accessing member community sites. "Social networking," they concluded, "will continue to alter not just the global online landscape, but the consumer experience at large."[4]

  Implication. Social media interactions are free from corporate interest and intervention. That is precisely what makes them more compelling than anything a corporation could devise. Peer to peer has overturned the old model of corporation to consumer.

- *Connectivity fosters transparency.* Along with many benefits, interactive technologies create risks for brands. It is much harder than before to control flows of information about the business. In the aftermath of the economic crisis, carpers will be on the lookout for bad guys and scapegoats. Traditional media, with its twenty-four-hour news cycle, and social media, with its viral speed, spread uncomfortable news about companies very far and very fast. Online reputation management has become a booming new industry.

  Implication. Making a virtue of today's high-risk environment, high-integrity corporations can use transparency to differentiate themselves and connect more strongly with mindful consumers.

- *Meters encourage mindfulness.* What gets measured gets managed. Technology is making it possible to monitor phenomena that formerly went ignored. Onboard computers in cars give real-time feedback on fuel consumption and tire pressure; smart meters in homes and businesses show energy consumption with great specificity. As meters become cheaper and more interconnected through wireless technology, many aspects of everyday living will become more measurable and manageable: body functions and indicators (heart rate, blood pressure, blood sugar, cholesterol, calorie intake), household metrics (food wastage, heating/cooling efficiency, water use), and environmental indicators (air quality, carbon dioxide).

Implication. As real-time meters become ubiquitous, consumers will become increasingly mindful of the cause-and-effect aspects of personal consumption.

Economic Factors

- *Lingering unemployment.* A lot of jobs are dependent on consumer spending, which accounted for two-thirds of U.S. gross domestic product before the Great Recession.[5] When the financial and economic crises hit, businesses shed jobs fast: Unemployment doubled from 5 to 10 percent in 2008–9, with more than 15 million Americans finding themselves out of work. Many of the jobs that were lost will never be restored, and headlines routinely predict a new, permanent condition of job scarcity.[6]

  Implication. The longer reduced incomes prevail, the more people will adjust their lifestyles, attitudes, and expectations to fit the straitened circumstances. The unemployed have lots of time and incentive to rethink how they are living.

- *Credit remains tight.* Before the recession, we saw a huge asset bubble in which billions were leveraged, driving asset prices up and enabling more credit to be created. A lot of that money evaporated in the meltdown. As consumers and government now strive to pay down debts, far less money will be in circulation than before; personal savings rates in the United States hit 6.9 percent in mid-2009, a sixteen-year high, leading the *Economist* to wonder "Are we witnessing a fundamental shift in American consumption?"[7]

  Implication. Tighter money will force consumers to think more carefully and purposefully about what they do with their personal funds.

- *Energy becomes really expensive.* Regardless of whether oil production has peaked, there is no doubt that demand has not; it will continue to grow as the earth's population increases (a 40 percent jump is expected by 2050) and as newly prosperous hordes in developing countries start to drive cars, use domestic appliances, and eat more bountiful food produced with high-energy inputs.[8] Whatever happens on the production side, higher aggregate demand plus the need for investment in new technologies and upgrading power distribution systems will push the cost of energy ever higher.

  Implication. Mindful consumers will seek more fuel-efficient cars, more energy-efficient products.

Environmental Factors

- *It's getting hot in here.* Arguments will continue to rage about climate change: whether there is global warming or not, whether human activity causes it, whether carbon dioxide is a problem, whether it is too late to make a difference anyway. Like the theory of evolution, climate change will remain perpetually disputed; nonetheless, influentials have embraced it, and it is emerging as a key paradigm for planning. Governments are getting on board, though without unanimity or perfect coordination. If China decides that climate change is both a strategic threat and a strategic opportunity, it could become the agenda setter on this issue while other countries are still arguing.

  Implication. Whether it is a mere mania or something far more cataclysmic, climate change will be a core concern for mindful consumers.

- *Sudden disappearances focus attention.* The media increasingly bombard us with reports of the natural world disappearing. More than 80 percent of the earth's forests have been cut down.[9] One in four mammal species is threatened with extinction; one in five sharks; half of all turtles.[10] Only 10 percent of large fish are left in the sea.[11] Climate change brings still more disappearances: There were 150 glaciers in Montana's Glacier National Park in 1850 but only 26 today.[12] According to much-publicized reports, the "vanishing islands" off the coast of India have left thousands homeless and threaten to displace tens of thousands more in the next dozen years as they are swallowed up by the sea.[13] All of these losses would seem to signal that something is seriously wrong with the planet.

  Implication. As these disappearances begin to happen closer to home, mindfulness about our pernicious impact on the environment will increase.

- *Resources are dwindling.* Every year, tens of millions of newly prosperous people join the ranks of consumers. As the U.S. National Intelligence Council put it in its *Global Trends 2025* report, "Unprecedented economic growth coupled with 1.5 billion more people will put pressure on resources—particularly energy, food, and water—raising the specter of scarcities emerging as demand outstrips supply."[14] Consider the matter of water alone: In the past fifty years, the use of water has tripled. Some 2.8 billion people already live in areas of high water stress, and their numbers are expected to rise to almost 4 billion by 2030. According to one report, the livelihoods of one in three people on the planet will be threatened by water scarcity within fifteen years.[15]

Implication. Governments will be forced to take the lead in encouraging people to be mindful in their consumption in order to minimize the risk of disruption.

Political Factors

- *Voters souring on selfish business.* As long as the going was good, people were happy to treat swashbuckling chief executives as celebrities and accept megabuck remuneration for corporate stars as part of the deal. A pell-mell push to "create shareholder value" was OK so long as there were jobs in it for workers too. The Enron, Tyco, and WorldCom scandals soon passed and did not radically change ordinary people's attitudes toward business. But things are different now: With wholesale greed and incompetence exposed on Wall Street, and millions suffering the consequences on Main Street, the mood has turned bitter. Social commentators have speculated that the star of free market capitalism may be falling. The derision with which many regarded communism and socialism in the 1990s is today finding a new target in unfettered free market capitalism.

  Implication. Skeptical consumers will look more critically beyond corporate public relations to see what brands really do, how they really behave.

- *Widespread distrust of government.* Politicians and parties emerged from the recession bloodied. None saw the crisis coming; many contributed to it by such means as encouraging loans to subprime borrowers or failing to enforce financial regulations. Polls show that support for Congress is as low as it has been in decades.[16] Voters complain about the pervasiveness of lobbying, factional strife, and short-term self-interest.

  Implication. Increasingly frustrated with the inability of mainstream political processes to address issues that concern them, mindful consumers will look to each other and to corporations as more effective agents.

RETHINKING VALUE

Taking into account all of the factors our STEEP analysis finds and others, it is abundantly clear that the conditions that permitted hyperconsumerism to flourish are disappearing. "I don't think we are ever going back to the way it was before," Jim Fielding told us in a telephone interview. The president of Disney Stores Worldwide sees impulse buying giving way to a new thoughtfulness. Customers come into his stores having researched products and prices online. "A few years ago, shopping was recreational," he says. "Now it's planned."[17]

The Great Recession has forced smart buyers and smart brands alike to plan far more carefully. They are asking a simple question with no simple answer: What is really worth paying for? In business speak, *value* often is used as a synonym for *low cost* or *cheap*. According to this mind-set, a "value shopper" looks for low prices and four-for-the-price-of-three deals. But increasingly, shoppers are reconsidering their definitions of *cost* and *value*. Back when credit was easy to obtain, the pleasures of choosing, buying, and owning were instant; by contrast, now that money is tight and people are both anxious and more conscientious, there is more pain in the prospect of buying (guilt, fear, "Can I really afford it?") and more pleasure in the prospect of *not* buying (feeling virtuous for having resisted the impulse, reducing waste)— yesterday's perceived value becomes today's cost.

The historic STEEP factors just outlined will continue to shift people's experiences of what is pleasure and what is pain, of what is value and what is cost. What was regarded as a worthwhile convenience before (say, a ready meal) could in the future be experienced as a pricey, lazy indulgence. What was previously regarded as too slow, dirty, and time consuming (e.g., growing vegetables) could in the future be experienced as creative and rewarding. We are already seeing this change: The U.S. Department of Labor's latest American Time Use Survey shows that, compared with 2005, Americans spent less time in 2008 buying goods and services and more time cooking or taking part in organizational, civic, and religious activities.[18] This activity goes to the heart of Mindful Consumption: investing more time, attention, and effort; spending less cash. As shoppers rethink what is important, reductivist scrambling for *value* is giving way to a quest for *values*.

GOING CO, GOING ANTI

"We consider ourselves co-producers, not consumers, because by being informed about how our food is produced and actively supporting those who produce it, we become a part of and a partner in the production process."[19] This statement of the Slow Food philosophy is highly relevant to the conscious consumerism now emerging: Talk of coproduction, codesign, and co-creation is everywhere now. Swiss-based consulting group ThinkStudio explores what it calls "The

Direct Economy" in which the consumer forms an active part of the value chain rather than merely being a "target." It lays out five levels of consumer involvement or interactivity:

1. *Passive consumption.* People get products and services without any real interaction and no real choice. They have to ask for what they want and take whatever is available.
2. *Self-service.* Consumers are given the ability to choose between various products laid out for them.
3. *Do It Yourself.* Consumers start getting involved in the value chain.
4. *Codesign.* Consumers start adding value by customizing the product and thereby defining their own needs, as opposed to buying a product defined by the product management team.
5. *Co-creation.* Consumers are involved in the design of the product or service itself.[20]

An astonishing number of consumers have shown interest in moving up from the basic level, Passive Consumption, to the more elevated and interesting stages. They are eager to become actively engaged in products and services that appeal to them, especially if brands encourage them to do so. Taking advantage of the opportunity, Nokia set up a "Concept Lounge" and invited consumers to submit their ideas for phones of the future; the winning design, submitted by a Turkish national, was developed into the Nokia 888 Concept Phone.[21] Philips has tapped the talents of "lead users" in creating innovative products, including video-telephony. Customers have helped Amazon and FedEx improve product delivery. Coffee lovers log onto MyStarbucksIdea.com to give input. And the "App Store" on Apple's iPhone has spurred thousands of inventors to come up with applications that work on the wildly successful mobile phone. The value-creating approach of whole business models is shifting to facilitate end user involvement as "going co" catches on.

At the same time, a less collaborative mind-set is spreading widely: "going anti," we might call it, as hyperconsumption spawns a furious backlash. Never before has there been so much negative attention directed at the consumer economy. Vancouver-based Kalle Lasn, a founder of *Adbusters* magazine and author of the books *Culture Jam* and *Design Anarchy*, says consumers fell under a "media trance" in their zombielike shopping craze.[22] "When you switch on a TV, you sort of zone out and start absorbing it all like a mindless consumer."[23] He advocates "subvertising" or "culture jamming" to disrupt familiar patterns of brainless consumption. As one strategy, *Adbusters* promotes

"Buy Nothing Day" as cold-turkey for shopaholics. Recently it ran a TV commercial in which a belching pig bursts out of a map of the United States as a voiceover intones, "We are the most voracious consumers in the world, a world that could die because of the way we North Americans live. Give it a rest."[24]

In a similar "anti" approach, San Francisco–based Billboard Liberation Front ("Marketing for the People") subversively alters the messages on outdoor advertising, such as tinkering with a Google logo to read "Goolag" in reference to the search engine's former agreement with China on restricting searches.[25] It has turned a billboard promoting Kent cigarettes into a meditation on the philosopher Kant and changed "now" to "no" in a sign that read "Business Intelligence. Now More Than Ever."[26] Such "culture jamming," "anti-branding," or "semiotic disobedience" hijacks the tools of marketing to communicate unexpected messages that snap viewers out of their consumer trance. It is intended to reclaim a little of the vast public space that has been bought up by corporations for branded messaging. "Let's face it," one anti-brander says. "Most of the advertisements are deceitful propaganda about the companies or their products to increase sale. How do we tell the companies what we really think about their product or their services?"[27]

Whether taking a "co" or "anti" tack, the new mindfulness means really thinking things through. It connotes awareness of ethical and big-picture issues, questioning consumer culture, wondering what is missing and what has gone wrong, trying to find out more, striving to be less passive and more active in making decisions, and sharing information and opinions. Smart brands will eagerly solicit and encourage such consumer involvement.

This is not to say that hundreds of millions of consumers will change their behavior overnight. The habits of hyperconsumption are too deeply engrained to disappear after just a few months of holding back. Christmas 2009 saw a toy craze of a scope not witnessed since Tickle Me Elmo thirteen years earlier: Customers pushed and shoved to buy $8 electronic hamsters called Zhu Zhu Pets—the price of which hit $60 in online trading. We will continue to see such frenzies, and even tragedies like the one at a Long Island Walmart in 2008, when a crowd of two thousand broke down the doors on Black Friday and trampled an employee to death. Even when told of the bloodshed, the crowd refused to leave the store; one astonished witness reported: "People were yelling, 'I've been on line since yesterday morning.'…They kept shopping."[28]

Yes, many of us will keep shopping, but others are already changing their habits profoundly. As the STEEP analysis showed, the external, structural conditions that foster new attitudes and behaviors are increasingly in place: economic crisis, tight cash and credit, energy and environmental concerns. Everything is changing: In the heyday of hyperconsumption, marketing was mostly about pushing consumers' hot buttons, masterfully cultivating the desire for *more, now*. It delivered instant gratification on both sides: a quick sale for the producer and retailer, and a brand-new object of desire wrapped and bagged to make the consumer feel dandy. In the new culture of Mindful Consumption, consumers feel best when they make smart choices that offer real substance, are appropriately matched to their genuine needs, and contribute to their sense of purpose.

Increasingly, brands and corporations are recognizing these needs and providing buyers with incentives to follow their better judgments. It makes good business sense to do so and is a compelling objective for the growing number of more conscious and conscientious people sitting in the executive suite. As Jim Fielding of Disney Stores told us of his five-year plan for the company, "I would love us to be seen as strong members of the local community wherever we are—good neighbors. May we leave our corner of the world a little better than we found it."[29]

APPENDIX: FINDINGS FROM EURO RSCG WORLDWIDE'S NEW CONSUMER STUDY

About the study: The New Consumer Study was fielded by Market Probe International in September and October 2009. The online survey was conducted in seven markets: Brazil (*n*=700), China (*n*=700), France (*n*=700), Japan (*n*=700), the Netherlands (*n*=700), the United Kingdom (*n*=700), and the United States (*n*=1,500). The study explores attitudes and behaviors related to consumption, with a focus on emerging signs of mindfulness.

Except where otherwise stated, percentages indicate how many respondents agree or strongly agree with each statement.

SHOPPING & SAVING

Smarter Shopping

I am a smarter shopper than I was a few years ago

	Total	Prosumers	Mainstream
Global:	69%	81%	66%
U.S.:	77%	87%	74%
Brazil:	76%	84%	74%
France:	69%	76%	67%
Netherlands:	58%	73%	54%
U.K.:	73%	85%	70%
China:	74%	84%	72%
Japan:	48%	70%	43%

I am a more demanding shopper than I was a few years ago

	Total	Prosumers	Mainstream
Global:	63%	79%	60%
U.S.:	64%	82%	60%
Brazil:	80%	88%	78%
France:	69%	81%	67%
Netherlands:	48%	70%	43%
U.K.:	64%	81%	61%
China:	79%	93%	76%
Japan:	36%	54%	32%

I do lots of consumer research online (e.g., seeking out product information, reviews and ratings, price comparisons)

	Total	Prosumers	Mainstream
Global:	62%	77%	59%
U.S.:	61%	82%	56%
Brazil:	70%	77%	69%
France:	51%	62%	48%
Netherlands:	61%	79%	56%
U.K.:	64%	83%	60%
China:	65%	71%	64%
Japan:	66%	74%	65%

The Internet has had little to no impact on my shopping

	Total	Prosumers	Mainstream
Global:	21%	16%	22%
U.S.:	19%	9%	21%
Brazil:	28%	23%	29%
France:	30%	29%	31%
Netherlands:	27%	23%	28%
U.K.:	17%	12%	17%
China:	17%	10%	19%
Japan:	10%	12%	9%

I trust customer reviews more than "expert" reviews

	Total	Prosumers	Mainstream
Global:	57%	68%	54%
U.S.:	57%	69%	54%
Brazil:	42%	46%	42%
France:	60%	71%	58%
Netherlands:	48%	62%	45%
U.K.:	57%	75%	53%
China:	84%	93%	82%
Japan:	49%	61%	46%

Reining in Spending

I often worry about money

	Total	Prosumers	Mainstream
Global:	56%	60%	55%
U.S.:	61%	63%	61%
Brazil:	66%	72%	65%
France:	58%	58%	58%
Netherlands:	37%	41%	36%
U.K.:	55%	65%	53%
China:	44%	56%	41%
Japan:	62%	63%	62%

I am putting more money into savings than I used to

	Total	Prosumers	Mainstream
Global:	31%	37%	30%
U.S.:	35%	43%	33%
Brazil:	34%	35%	34%
France:	25%	33%	24%
Netherlands:	33%	39%	32%
U.K.:	25%	24%	25%
China:	41%	48%	39%
Japan:	21%	30%	19%

I am having trouble saving as much money as I'd like

	Total	Prosumers	Mainstream
Global:	56%	58%	55%
U.S.:	61%	63%	61%
Brazil:	50%	44%	51%
France:	68%	67%	68%
Netherlands:	41%	49%	39%
U.K.:	60%	63%	59%
China:	43%	49%	42%
Japan:	62%	65%	61%

Saving money makes me feel good about myself

	Total	Prosumers	Mainstream
Global:	70%	73%	69%
U.S.:	87%	91%	86%
Brazil:	69%	71%	69%
France:	65%	69%	64%
Netherlands:	69%	75%	67%
U.K.:	71%	72%	71%
China:	59%	65%	57%
Japan:	53%	51%	53%

Buying luxury items makes me feel good about myself

	Total	Prosumers	Mainstream
Global:	30%	41%	27%
U.S.:	26%	38%	24%
Brazil:	34%	38%	33%
France:	15%	23%	14%
Netherlands:	25%	36%	23%
U.K.:	37%	55%	33%
China:	40%	57%	36%
Japan:	33%	44%	31%

I am getting a sense of satisfaction from reducing my purchases during the economic downturn

	Total	Prosumers	Mainstream
Global:	38%	46%	36%
U.S.:	49%	57%	47%
Brazil:	52%	49%	53%
France:	28%	30%	28%
Netherlands:	25%	34%	22%
U.K.:	39%	51%	36%
China:	38%	49%	36%
Japan:	24%	36%	21%

I won't go back to my old shopping patterns even when the economy rebounds

	Total	Prosumers	Mainstream
Global:	48%	54%	46%
U.S.:	52%	58%	50%
Brazil:	51%	46%	52%
France:	50%	53%	49%
Netherlands:	30%	42%	27%
U.K.:	44%	52%	42%
China:	45%	59%	42%
Japan:	58%	61%	57%

I am committed to reducing my use of credit cards over the long term

	Total	Prosumers	Mainstream
Global:	43%	48%	42%
U.S.:	60%	69%	57%
Brazil:	62%	57%	63%
France:	38%	40%	37%
Netherlands:	17%	23%	16%
U.K.:	45%	49%	45%
China:	42%	48%	41%
Japan:	21%	26%	20%

I am using coupons and/or seeking out other discounts
more often than I used to

	Total	Prosumers	Mainstream
Global:	62%	69%	60%
U.S.:	70%	78%	69%
Brazil:	55%	59%	55%
France:	58%	63%	57%
Netherlands:	56%	65%	54%
U.K.:	68%	74%	67%
China:	56%	68%	54%
Japan:	60%	67%	58%

In the past year, I have been asking myself the following
questions more often

"Do I really need this?"

	Total	Prosumers	Mainstream
Global:	51%	54%	50%
U.S.:	63%	67%	62%
Brazil:	44%	43%	44%
France:	47%	38%	49%
Netherlands:	45%	56%	43%
U.K.:	59%	69%	58%
China:	34%	40%	33%
Japan:	50%	48%	50%

*"Could I find the same item for less at another store or on
eBay?"*

	Total	Prosumers	Mainstream
Global:	47%	55%	45%
U.S.:	51%	63%	49%
Brazil:	34%	35%	34%
France:	51%	56%	50%
Netherlands:	39%	51%	36%
U.K.:	62%	71%	60%
China:	44%	57%	41%
Japan:	39%	45%	38%

"Can I afford it?"

	Total	Prosumers	Mainstream
Global:	45%	49%	45%
U.S.:	59%	63%	58%
Brazil:	35%	42%	33%
France:	46%	38%	48%
Netherlands:	41%	50%	38%
U.K.:	59%	63%	58%
China:	22%	26%	21%
Japan:	40%	44%	39%

"Can I wait until it's on sale?"

	Total	Prosumers	Mainstream
Global:	43%	46%	42%
U.S.:	56%	63%	55%
Brazil:	28%	31%	27%
France:	45%	37%	47%
Netherlands:	38%	44%	36%
U.K.:	46%	50%	45%
China:	35%	39%	34%
Japan:	35%	42%	33%

"Is it of solid, good quality? Will it last a long time?"

	Total	Prosumers	Mainstream
Global:	47%	55%	45%
U.S.:	51%	65%	48%
Brazil:	55%	61%	53%
France:	49%	45%	50%
Netherlands:	34%	43%	31%
U.K.:	49%	56%	47%
China:	47%	57%	45%
Japan:	38%	46%	37%

"Will I really get pleasure from buying this brand/ spending this money?"

	Total	Prosumers	Mainstream
Global:	35%	41%	33%
U.S.:	39%	49%	37%
Brazil:	37%	44%	36%
France:	34%	31%	35%
Netherlands:	29%	33%	28%
U.K.:	36%	47%	34%
China:	33%	44%	30%
Japan:	28%	31%	28%

"Could I make it myself?"

	Total	Prosumers	Mainstream
Global:	21%	27%	20%
U.S.:	24%	30%	22%
Brazil:	23%	27%	22%
France:	25%	30%	25%
Netherlands:	16%	19%	16%
U.K.:	25%	32%	24%
China:	14%	21%	13%
Japan:	20%	24%	18%

ASSESSING MODERN LIFE

Societal Issues

In many ways, I think society is moving in the wrong direction

	Total	Prosumers	Mainstream
Global:	58%	64%	57%
U.S.:	66%	73%	65%
Brazil:	61%	56%	62%
France:	70%	72%	69%
Netherlands:	53%	63%	51%
U.K.:	63%	69%	62%
China:	39%	50%	37%
Japan:	49%	59%	46%

As a society, we have gotten intellectually lazy

	Total	Prosumers	Mainstream
Global:	60%	69%	58%
U.S.:	76%	84%	74%
Brazil:	52%	54%	51%
France:	61%	69%	59%
Netherlands:	48%	57%	45%
U.K.:	73%	79%	72%
China:	50%	66%	47%
Japan:	43%	62%	39%

As a society, we have gotten physically lazy

	Total	Prosumers	Mainstream
Global:	67%	75%	65%
U.S.:	85%	91%	83%
Brazil:	56%	57%	56%
France:	66%	77%	64%
Netherlands:	55%	70%	51%
U.K.:	82%	89%	81%
China:	59%	66%	58%
Japan:	47%	59%	44%

I worry that society has become too shallow, focusing too much on things that don't really matter

	Total	Prosumers	Mainstream
Global:	69%	79%	67%
U.S.:	79%	91%	76%
Brazil:	66%	72%	65%
France:	77%	81%	76%
Netherlands:	62%	74%	59%
U.K.:	75%	80%	74%
China:	53%	68%	50%
Japan:	61%	72%	58%

I worry that people have become too disconnected from the natural world

	Total	Prosumers	Mainstream
Global:	59%	66%	57%
U.S.:	60%	69%	59%
Brazil:	64%	69%	63%
France:	50%	58%	49%
Netherlands:	43%	49%	41%
U.K.:	56%	61%	55%
China:	70%	82%	67%
Japan:	65%	69%	61%

Personal Concerns

I sometimes feel as though I'm wasting my life

	Total	Prosumers	Mainstream
Global:	38%	41%	37%
U.S.:	35%	36%	35%
Brazil:	43%	42%	43%
France:	41%	48%	40%
Netherlands:	17%	23%	16%
U.K.:	42%	42%	42%
China:	46%	52%	45%
Japan:	44%	49%	43%

I wish I could start fresh with an entirely different lifestyle

	Total	Prosumers	Mainstream
Global:	44%	49%	43%
U.S.:	36%	40%	35%
Brazil:	59%	55%	60%
France:	39%	46%	38%
Netherlands:	31%	38%	29%
U.K.:	38%	36%	39%
China:	70%	84%	68%
Japan:	48%	54%	46%

I sometimes feel "uncultured"; I wish I knew more about the arts, literature, other countries, etc.

	Total	Prosumers	Mainstream
Global:	40%	43%	40%
U.S.:	31%	34%	30%
Brazil:	55%	50%	56%
France:	44%	48%	43%
Netherlands:	18%	20%	17%
U.K.:	30%	31%	29%
China:	61%	71%	59%
Japan:	53%	56%	53%

In general, I feel more anxious than I did a few
years ago

	Total	Prosumers	Mainstream
Global:	54%	59%	52%
U.S.:	54%	60%	52%
Brazil:	50%	49%	50%
France:	62%	71%	60%
Netherlands:	29%	33%	28%
U.K.:	57%	65%	55%
China:	46%	55%	44%
Japan:	77%	80%	76%

I worry about my future or my family's future
more than I used to

	Total	Prosumers	Mainstream
Global:	55%	63%	54%
U.S.:	57%	64%	56%
Brazil:	74%	74%	74%
France:	65%	77%	62%
Netherlands:	34%	38%	34%
U.K.:	49%	60%	47%
China:	40%	50%	38%
Japan:	65%	75%	63%

I worry about health issues (current or
potential)

	Total	Prosumers	Mainstream
Global:	49%	54%	48%
U.S.:	55%	61%	53%
Brazil:	53%	52%	53%
France:	54%	63%	52%
Netherlands:	26%	28%	26%
U.K.:	42%	50%	40%
China:	61%	74%	59%
Japan:	47%	48%	47%

I worry about the mental health of my partner/
spouse

	Total	Prosumers	Mainstream
Global:	34%	38%	33%
U.S.:	22%	25%	22%
Brazil:	61%	59%	61%
France:	46%	48%	46%
Netherlands:	16%	20%	16%
U.K.:	22%	23%	21%
China:	44%	56%	42%
Japan:	36%	49%	33%

I worry about my own mental health

	Total	Prosumers	Mainstream
Global:	38%	42%	38%
U.S.:	31%	32%	31%
Brazil:	69%	70%	69%
France:	46%	53%	44%
Netherlands:	18%	18%	18%
U.K.:	26%	32%	25%
China:	41%	53%	38%
Japan:	45%	49%	45%

I spend too much time working and not enough time enjoying my life

	Total	Prosumers	Mainstream
Global:	36%	41%	35%
U.S.:	30%	35%	29%
Brazil:	52%	49%	52%
France:	39%	46%	38%
Netherlands:	26%	26%	26%
U.K.:	35%	41%	34%
China:	49%	66%	46%
Japan:	30%	36%	29%

I sometimes feel overwhelmed by family responsibilities

	Total	Prosumers	Mainstream
Global:	32%	37%	31%
U.S.:	37%	42%	35%
Brazil:	50%	49%	50%
France:	20%	26%	19%
Netherlands:	22%	24%	21%
U.K.:	32%	39%	30%
China:	35%	49%	32%
Japan:	25%	29%	24%

I feel I'm falling behind others financially and I'm not going to be able to catch up

	Total	Prosumers	Mainstream
Global:	32%	33%	31%
U.S.:	36%	41%	35%
Brazil:	40%	32%	42%
France:	20%	22%	19%
Netherlands:	19%	18%	19%
U.K.:	32%	31%	32%
China:	38%	44%	37%
Japan:	33%	36%	32%

Community & Connections

I sometimes feel I don't have enough close friendships

	Total	Prosumers	Mainstream
Global:	43%	46%	42%
U.S.:	46%	49%	45%
Brazil:	51%	52%	50%
France:	29%	28%	29%
Netherlands:	33%	38%	32%
U.K.:	45%	46%	45%
China:	50%	56%	49%
Japan:	45%	49%	44%

The main way I stay connected with my old friends and colleagues is through e-mail and/or social networking sites

	Total	Prosumers	Mainstream
Global:	50%	60%	48%
U.S.:	57%	70%	55%
Brazil:	64%	69%	62%
France:	48%	58%	46%
Netherlands:	35%	37%	34%
U.K.:	54%	65%	52%
China:	49%	63%	46%
Japan:	33%	46%	30%

I worry that digital communications is weakening human-to-human bonds

	Total	Prosumers	Mainstream
Global:	51%	53%	51%
U.S.:	54%	54%	54%
Brazil:	55%	55%	56%
France:	56%	53%	56%
Netherlands:	42%	48%	40%
U.K.:	48%	43%	49%
China:	55%	72%	51%
Japan:	45%	45%	45%

I have a close friendship with most of my neighbors

	Total	Prosumers	Mainstream
Global:	34%	38%	33%
U.S.:	26%	33%	24%
Brazil:	29%	31%	29%
France:	47%	52%	46%
Netherlands:	27%	28%	27%
U.K.:	30%	27%	30%
China:	63%	74%	61%
Japan:	24%	33%	22%

I worry we are losing the ability to engage in civil debate; people aren't as willing to consider other points of view anymore

	Total	Prosumers	Mainstream
Global:	57%	65%	55%
U.S.:	62%	72%	60%
Brazil:	64%	67%	63%
France:	64%	76%	62%
Netherlands:	46%	54%	44%
U.K.:	61%	69%	59%
China:	49%	63%	46%
Japan:	46%	50%	45%

Response to the Economic Downturn

I am concerned my relationship with my significant other won't survive the stress of the downturn

	Total	Prosumers	Mainstream
Global:	18%	21%	17%
U.S.:	14%	18%	13%
Brazil:	33%	25%	35%
France:	11%	14%	11%
Netherlands:	10%	11%	10%
U.K.:	13%	14%	12%
China:	26%	35%	25%
Japan:	25%	34%	23%

The recession has served to remind people of what's really important in life—and that's a good thing

	Total	Prosumers	Mainstream
Global:	56%	62%	55%
U.S.:	67%	73%	65%
Brazil:	63%	61%	63%
France:	50%	60%	48%
Netherlands:	47%	55%	45%
U.K.:	59%	63%	58%
China:	61%	73%	58%
Japan:	33%	37%	32%

Over the long term, this economic downturn will be a good thing for my country

	Total	Prosumers	Mainstream
Global:	31%	37%	30%
U.S.:	33%	38%	32%
Brazil:	43%	40%	44%
France:	21%	22%	20%
Netherlands:	31%	37%	30%
U.K.:	29%	40%	26%
China:	44%	56%	41%
Japan:	16%	28%	13%

Over the long term, this economic downturn will be a good thing for me and my family

	Total	Prosumers	Mainstream
Global:	24%	31%	23%
U.S.:	26%	31%	25%
Brazil:	40%	36%	42%
France:	16%	23%	15%
Netherlands:	22%	28%	20%
U.K.:	21%	29%	19%
China:	31%	42%	29%
Japan:	11%	25%	8%

I worry about the stress this downturn is placing on my family

	Total	Prosumers	Mainstream
Global:	37%	42%	36%
U.S.:	41%	50%	39%
Brazil:	52%	46%	54%
France:	43%	55%	41%
Netherlands:	16%	17%	16%
U.K.:	32%	40%	30%
China:	34%	48%	31%
Japan:	35%	38%	35%

THE MOVE TOWARD MINDFULNESS

Looking for Change

I am actively trying to figure out what really makes me happy

	Total	Prosumers	Mainstream
Global:	50%	63%	48%
U.S.:	48%	61%	45%
Brazil:	75%	78%	74%
France:	53%	65%	51%
Netherlands:	33%	44%	30%
U.K.:	42%	53%	40%
China:	64%	80%	61%
Japan:	41%	61%	36%

I would like to be part of a truly important cause

	Total	Prosumers	Mainstream
Global:	51%	62%	48%
U.S.:	57%	72%	54%
Brazil:	76%	79%	76%
France:	41%	51%	39%
Netherlands:	29%	40%	26%
U.K.:	26%	54%	41%
China:	66%	84%	62%
Japan:	34%	45%	31%

I would like to lead a more spiritual life

	Total	Prosumers	Mainstream
Global:	40%	47%	39%
U.S.:	51%	58%	49%
Brazil:	64%	59%	65%
France:	21%	28%	19%
Netherlands:	19%	23%	19%
U.K.:	27%	26%	27%
China:	59%	75%	56%
Japan:	29%	45%	25%

I would like to feel more connected to a religion or life philosophy

	Total	Prosumers	Mainstream
Global:	30%	34%	29%
U.S.:	39%	44%	38%
Brazil:	54%	49%	55%
France:	16%	23%	14%
Netherlands:	13%	14%	13%
U.K.:	20%	20%	20%
China:	40%	54%	37%
Japan:	18%	26%	15%

Rightsizing

Most of us would be better off if we lived more simply

	Total	Prosumers	Mainstream
Global:	67%	71%	66%
U.S.:	78%	84%	76%
Brazil:	68%	63%	69%
France:	73%	76%	73%
Netherlands:	51%	62%	48%
U.K.:	68%	69%	68%
China:	72%	85%	70%
Japan:	48%	51%	47%

I wish my house were less cluttered

	Total	Prosumers	Mainstream
Global:	46%	47%	45%
U.S.:	47%	47%	47%
Brazil:	42%	42%	43%
France:	36%	42%	34%
Netherlands:	21%	20%	21%
U.K.:	47%	46%	47%
China:	81%	92%	79%
Japan:	45%	48%	44%

I think I would be happier if I owned less "stuff"

	Total	Prosumers	Mainstream
Global:	25%	28%	25%
U.S.:	31%	36%	30%
Brazil:	33%	30%	35%
France:	14%	21%	13%
Netherlands:	13%	12%	13%
U.K.:	25%	22%	26%
China:	30%	40%	28%
Japan:	24%	32%	22%

In recent years, I have thrown out or thought about throwing out lots of stuff to declutter my life and my home

	Total	Prosumers	Mainstream
Global:	50%	58%	48%
U.S.:	57%	69%	54%
Brazil:	40%	44%	40%
France:	47%	49%	47%
Netherlands:	44%	56%	41%
U.K.:	55%	59%	45%
China:	52%	62%	49%
Japan:	45%	55%	43%

I sometimes feel bad about myself when I buy too much

	Total	Prosumers	Mainstream
Global:	43%	47%	42%
U.S.:	46%	49%	45%
Brazil:	49%	48%	50%
France:	29%	33%	28%
Netherlands:	39%	43%	38%
U.K.:	44%	53%	42%
China:	37%	45%	35%
Japan:	51%	58%	50%

I have wasted lots of money on things I don't need

	Total	Prosumers	Mainstream
Global:	39%	45%	38%
U.S.:	47%	51%	45%
Brazil:	39%	36%	40%
France:	34%	41%	32%
Netherlands:	29%	41%	26%
U.K.:	46%	52%	45%
China:	38%	48%	36%
Japan:	32%	39%	30%

I respect/admire people who live simply (minimal purchases, debt free, etc.)

	Total	Prosumers	Mainstream
Global:	70%	76%	68%
U.S.:	79%	84%	78%
Brazil:	69%	68%	69%
France:	73%	79%	72%
Netherlands:	69%	75%	67%
U.K.:	72%	79%	71%
China:	69%	74%	60%
Japan:	52%	58%	51%

I respect/admire people who live a high-luxury lifestyle (lots of indulgences, expensive possessions, etc.)

	Total	Prosumers	Mainstream
Global:	19%	24%	17%
U.S.:	15%	21%	13%
Brazil:	31%	31%	32%
France:	11%	17%	10%
Netherlands:	10%	12%	9%
U.K.:	17%	22%	16%
China:	35%	45%	33%
Japan:	15%	24%	13%

In recent years, I have moved or thought about moving to a smaller or more affordable home

	Total	Prosumers	Mainstream
Global:	25%	30%	24%
U.S.:	29%	35%	28%
Brazil:	42%	41%	43%
France:	19%	19%	19%
Netherlands:	17%	23%	16%
U.K.:	26%	25%	26%
China:	21%	29%	19%
Japan:	19%	29%	16%

In recent years, I have moved or thought about moving to a smaller, less expensive town

	Total	Prosumers	Mainstream
Global:	24%	28%	23%
U.S.:	29%	33%	28%
Brazil:	40%	37%	41%
France:	26%	28%	26%
Netherlands:	13%	15%	13%
U.K.:	20%	24%	19%
China:	21%	29%	19%
Japan:	15%	27%	12%

I no longer want lots of "bells and whistles" on products I buy; I'd rather just have the functions I really need

	Total	Prosumers	Mainstream
Global:	68%	65%	69%
U.S.:	66%	58%	67%
Brazil:	67%	68%	67%
France:	78%	79%	78%
Netherlands:	73%	72%	73%
U.K.:	65%	56%	67%
China:	81%	82%	81%
Japan:	50%	48%	50%

I would rather spend money on an experience (e.g., traveling or going to a concert) than on a luxury item

	Total	Prosumers	Mainstream
Global:	51%	56%	50%
U.S.:	52%	55%	51%
Brazil:	52%	56%	52%
France:	68%	68%	68%
Netherlands:	42%	45%	41%
U.K.:	44%	49%	43%
China:	54%	65%	52%
Japan:	48%	56%	46%

Slowing Down

In recent years, I have adopted or thought about adopting a "slower" lifestyle

	Total	Prosumers	Mainstream
Global:	41%	46%	40%
U.S.:	40%	48%	38%
Brazil:	50%	47%	51%
France:	34%	33%	34%
Netherlands:	35%	37%	35%
U.K.:	37%	40%	36%
China:	51%	56%	50%
Japan:	42%	54%	39%

In recent years, I have switched or thought about switching to a less-stressful job

	Total	Prosumers	Mainstream
Global:	30%	35%	28%
U.S.:	26%	35%	25%
Brazil:	55%	56%	55%
France:	31%	37%	30%
Netherlands:	16%	17%	15%
U.K.:	26%	35%	25%
China:	30%	29%	30%
Japan:	27%	39%	25%

In recent years, I have started or thought about starting a home vegetable or fruit garden

	Total	Prosumers	Mainstream
Global:	39%	44%	37%
U.S.:	43%	48%	41%
Brazil:	55%	59%	54%
France:	46%	48%	46%
Netherlands:	16%	20%	16%
U.K.:	45%	59%	42%
China:	32%	40%	31%
Japan:	29%	35%	27%

In recent years, I have started or thought about starting a "quiet" hobby such as gardening, knitting, or pottery

	Total	Prosumers	Mainstream
Global:	38%	43%	37%
U.S.:	37%	46%	35%
Brazil:	49%	51%	49%
France:	41%	46%	40%
Netherlands:	25%	27%	25%
U.K.:	38%	43%	37%
China:	48%	54%	47%
Japan:	30%	34%	29%

I am looking forward to a holiday season that is less about shopping and more about family and simple pleasures

	Total	Prosumers	Mainstream
Global:	62%	70%	61%
U.S.:	73%	79%	71%
Brazil:	59%	61%	59%
France:	62%	72%	60%
Netherlands:	45%	56%	43%
U.K.:	60%	66%	59%
China:	72%	85%	69%
Japan:	55%	63%	53%

Growing Up

Even though I'm an adult, I don't always feel like a real "grown up"

	Total	Prosumers	Mainstream
Global:	48%	56%	46%
U.S.:	50%	58%	49%
Brazil:	46%	44%	47%
France:	38%	48%	36%
Netherlands:	38%	49%	35%
U.K.:	52%	64%	49%
China:	50%	61%	47%
Japan:	58%	67%	56%

I am making an effort to improve the person I am

	Total	*Prosumers*	*Mainstream*
Global:	71%	84%	68%
U.S.:	78%	91%	75%
Brazil:	84%	89%	83%
France:	69%	81%	66%
Netherlands:	56%	71%	52%
U.K.:	62%	76%	59%
China:	83%	93%	81%
Japan:	56%	79%	51%

I am making an effort to improve the way I live

	Total	*Prosumers*	*Mainstream*
Global:	72%	84%	69%
U.S.:	78%	92%	75%
Brazil:	85%	88%	85%
France:	73%	88%	70%
Netherlands:	56%	71%	53%
U.K.:	65%	83%	62%
China:	80%	92%	78%
Japan:	60%	71%	57%

I am less concerned about what others think of me than I used to be

	Total	*Prosumers*	*Mainstream*
Global:	59%	65%	57%
U.S.:	66%	74%	65%
Brazil:	70%	65%	71%
France:	56%	56%	56%
Netherlands:	53%	65%	50%
U.K.:	58%	64%	57%
China:	58%	69%	56%
Japan:	39%	54%	36%

Mindful Shopping

I am shopping more carefully and mindfully than I used to

	Total	Prosumers	Mainstream
Global:	72%	80%	70%
U.S.:	80%	86%	79%
Brazil:	70%	78%	69%
France:	70%	81%	68%
Netherlands:	62%	75%	59%
U.K.:	72%	77%	71%
China:	73%	82%	72%
Japan:	67%	75%	65%

Compared with a few years ago, it is more important to me to feel good about the companies with which I do business

	Total	Prosumers	Mainstream
Global:	50%	61%	47%
U.S.:	57%	70%	54%
Brazil:	70%	71%	70%
France:	47%	57%	45%
Netherlands:	36%	49%	33%
U.K.:	46%	63%	43%
China:	58%	71%	55%
Japan:	24%	39%	21%

I prefer to buy from companies that share my personal values

	Total	Prosumers	Mainstream
Global:	57%	70%	54%
U.S.:	59%	77%	56%
Brazil:	71%	77%	69%
France:	54%	66%	52%
Netherlands:	40%	57%	36%
U.K.:	47%	55%	46%
China:	69%	85%	66%
Japan:	55%	64%	52%

I prefer to buy from companies with a reputation for having a purpose other than just profits (e.g., Newman's Own, The Body Shop)

	Total	*Prosumers*	*Mainstream*
Global:	49%	60%	46%
U.S.:	56%	69%	54%
Brazil:	56%	66%	54%
France:	51%	64%	48%
Netherlands:	27%	38%	25%
U.K.:	46%	58%	43%
China:	74%	88%	71%
Japan:	20%	35%	16%

I am more interested today in how and where products are made

	Total	*Prosumers*	*Mainstream*
Global:	51%	62%	48%
U.S.:	54%	66%	52%
Brazil:	60%	66%	59%
France:	61%	72%	58%
Netherlands:	34%	45%	31%
U.K.:	41%	49%	39%
China:	59%	74%	56%
Japan:	41%	58%	36%

I am paying more attention to the quality and freshness of the food I buy

	Total	*Prosumers*	*Mainstream*
Global:	76%	83%	75%
U.S.:	78%	88%	76%
Brazil:	79%	85%	77%
France:	81%	87%	80%
Netherlands:	66%	74%	64%
U.K.:	71%	80%	69%
China:	89%	93%	88%
Japan:	66%	71%	65%

I pay more attention to the color, feel, and overall design of products than I used to

	Total	Prosumers	Mainstream
Global:	43%	55%	40%
U.S.:	47%	63%	44%
Brazil:	36%	38%	35%
France:	38%	52%	35%
Netherlands:	27%	37%	25%
U.K.:	39%	60%	35%
China:	65%	80%	62%
Japan:	44%	54%	42%

I research the safety of the products I buy more
than I used to (e.g., checking to see whether there
is BPA in plastic bottles, lead paint on toys)

	Total	Prosumers	Mainstream
Global:	47%	57%	44%
U.S.:	41%	60%	37%
Brazil:	63%	70%	61%
France:	52%	60%	50%
Netherlands:	26%	33%	24%
U.K.:	29%	34%	29%
China:	83%	92%	81%
Japan:	38%	51%	35%

I avoid shopping at stores that don't treat their
employees fairly

	Total	Prosumers	Mainstream
Global:	51%	62%	49%
U.S.:	52%	65%	49%
Brazil:	69%	76%	67%
France:	57%	63%	56%
Netherlands:	38%	49%	35%
U.K.:	41%	50%	40%
China:	68%	83%	64%
Japan:	34%	44%	31%

As a consumer, I have a responsibility to censure unethical companies by avoiding their products

	Total	Prosumers	Mainstream
Global:	65%	75%	63%
U.S.:	67%	79%	64%
Brazil:	76%	82%	75%
France:	74%	79%	73%
Netherlands:	51%	67%	47%
U.K.:	54%	65%	52%
China:	83%	93%	80%
Japan:	51%	61%	49%

Going Green

I buy environmentally friendly products

	Total	Prosumers	Mainstream
Global:	52%	61%	50%
U.S.:	45%	57%	42%
Brazil:	72%	79%	70%
France:	56%	65%	54%
Netherlands:	31%	39%	30%
U.K.:	44%	50%	42%
China:	78%	90%	76%
Japan:	49%	56%	47%

I am paying more attention than in the past to the environmental and/or social impact of the products I buy

	Total	Prosumers	Mainstream
Global:	54%	63%	52%
U.S.:	54%	68%	51%
Brazil:	61%	66%	60%
France:	64%	77%	62%
Netherlands:	37%	49%	35%
U.K.:	51%	55%	50%
China:	72%	84%	69%
Japan:	38%	44%	37%

Making environmentally friendly choices makes me feel good

	Total	Prosumers	Mainstream
Global:	64%	74%	62%
U.S.:	65%	73%	63%
Brazil:	80%	91%	78%
France:	65%	74%	63%
Netherlands:	49%	62%	46%
U.K.:	54%	68%	52%
China:	80%	91%	78%
Japan:	55%	61%	54%

I am willing to pay a slightly higher price for socially or environmentally responsible products

	Total	Prosumers	Mainstream
Global:	45%	54%	43%
U.S.:	38%	48%	35%
Brazil:	62%	70%	60%
France:	54%	60%	52%
Netherlands:	30%	41%	28%
U.K.:	35%	46%	33%
China:	77%	87%	75%
Japan:	28%	36%	26%

I am making an effort to buy fewer disposable goods (e.g., paper plates, paper towels, disposable razors)

	Total	Prosumers	Mainstream
Global:	54%	62%	52%
U.S.:	48%	61%	45%
Brazil:	60%	61%	60%
France:	59%	69%	46%
Netherlands:	46%	54%	43%
U.K.:	51%	61%	49%
China:	75%	85%	73%
Japan:	48%	52%	47%

I feel good about reducing the amount of waste I create

	Total	Prosumers	Mainstream
Global:	72%	78%	70%
U.S.:	73%	82%	71%
Brazil:	79%	85%	78%
France:	63%	69%	62%
Netherlands:	58%	65%	56%
U.K.:	74%	78%	74%
China:	85%	93%	83%
Japan:	66%	70%	65%

The most successful and profitable businesses in the future will be those that practice sustainability

	Total	Prosumers	Mainstream
Global:	64%	75%	63%
U.S.:	70%	81%	67%
Brazil:	77%	83%	76%
France:	59%	70%	57%
Netherlands:	50%	65%	46%
U.K.:	61%	73%	59%
China:	81%	93%	79%
Japan:	52%	57%	51%

The Appeal of Local

It is important to me to buy locally produced goods

	Total	Prosumers	Mainstream
Global:	45%	52%	44%
U.S.:	51%	63%	48%
Brazil:	42%	40%	42%
France:	58%	65%	56%
Netherlands:	25%	36%	23%
U.K.:	45%	53%	43%
China:	36%	44%	34%
Japan:	55%	59%	55%

It makes me feel good to support local producers, artisans, and manufacturers

	Total	Prosumers	Mainstream
Global:	57%	63%	55%
U.S.:	69%	76%	67%
Brazil:	68%	66%	68%
France:	57%	66%	55%
Netherlands:	41%	54%	38%
U.K.:	65%	74%	63%
China:	41%	48%	39%
Japan:	44%	46%	43%

Locally produced goods tend to be of higher quality

	Total	Prosumers	Mainstream
Global:	31%	34%	31%
U.S.:	38%	44%	37%
Brazil:	31%	24%	33%
France:	50%	56%	49%
Netherlands:	18%	20%	18%
U.K.:	34%	41%	33%
China:	21%	21%	21%
Japan:	17%	26%	15%

I have more confidence in the safety of locally produced goods

	Total	Prosumers	Mainstream
Global:	31%	33%	30%
U.S.:	34%	40%	33%
Brazil:	40%	34%	42%
France:	32%	40%	30%
Netherlands:	14%	16%	13%
U.K.:	28%	30%	28%
China:	40%	45%	39%
Japan:	21%	26%	20%

Locally produced foods tend to be more healthful (e.g., fresher, fewer preservatives)

	Total	Prosumers	Mainstream
Global:	53%	60%	52%
U.S.:	55%	66%	52%
Brazil:	74%	79%	73%
France:	60%	64%	59%
Netherlands:	30%	37%	28%
U.K.:	46%	54%	45%
China:	58%	61%	57%
Japan:	45%	51%	44%

Buying locally produced goods is easier on the environment (e.g., reduces transportation/"food miles")

	Total	*Prosumers*	*Mainstream*
Global:	57%	62%	56%
U.S.:	57%	67%	55%
Brazil:	60%	56%	61%
France:	65%	69%	65%
Netherlands:	43%	55%	30%
U.K.:	66%	76%	64%
China:	62%	65%	61%
Japan:	48%	47%	49%

I would rather give my money to small businesses than large corporations

	Total	*Prosumers*	*Mainstream*
Global:	44%	48%	43%
U.S.:	63%	70%	61%
Brazil:	26%	22%	27%
France:	53%	55%	52%
Netherlands:	41%	54%	37%
U.K.:	62%	65%	61%
China:	14%	13%	14%
Japan:	28%	34%	27%

I improve the economic health of my community when I buy from local producers, artisans, and manufacturers

	Total	*Prosumers*	*Mainstream*
Global:	57%	63%	56%
U.S.:	66%	71%	65%
Brazil:	69%	71%	69%
France:	59%	65%	58%
Netherlands:	43%	55%	40%
U.K.:	52%	58%	51%
China:	47%	53%	46%
Japan:	53%	54%	52%

NOTES

1 THE BIRTH OF CONSUMERISM

1. Grant McCracken, *Culture and Consumption: New Approaches to the Symbolic Character of Consumer Goods and Activities* (Bloomington: Indiana University Press, 1990), 11–12.
2. Thorstein Veblen, *The Theory of the Leisure Class* (Whitefish, MT: Kessinger Publishing Reprint, 2004), 42.
3. John White, *The Golden Cow: Materialism in the Twentieth-Century Church* (Madison, WI: Inter-Varsity Press, 1979).
4. Samuel Strauss, "Things Are in the Saddle," *The Atlantic Monthly* (November 1924): 577–579.
5. Ibid., 579.
6. Simon Jenkins, "There Are Rewards for Us All in This Crunch," *The Sunday Times*, October 12, 2008, www.timesonline.co.uk/tol/comment/colum-nists/guest_contributors/article4926560.ece (accessed November 12, 2009).
7. "Text from Bush News Conference," Associated Press, December 20, 2006.
8. Dana Stevens, "The Century of the Self (2003)," *The New York Times*, August 12, 2005.
9. "Employment Status of the Civilian Noninstitutional Population, 1940 to Date," Bureau of Labor Statistics, www.bls.gov/cps/cpsaat1.pdf (accessed January 25, 2010).
10. Victor Lebow, "Price Competition in 1955," *Journal of Retailing* 31, no. 1 (Spring 1955): 7–8, www.scribd.com/doc/965920/LebowArticle (accessed November 29, 2009).
11. John Lewis, "The History of John Lewis Newcastle," www.johnlewis.com/Shops/DSTemplate.aspx?Id=18 (accessed November 17, 2009).
12. Richard H. Robbins, *Global Problems and the Culture of Capitalism* (Boston: Allyn & Bacon Publishing Inc., 2002), 13, quoting Rosalind H. Williams, *Dream Worlds: Mass Consumption in Late Nineteenth Century France* (Berkeley: University of California Press, 1991), 67.

13. David W. Dunlap, "Return of a White Marble Palace; Buildings Agency to Occupy Old Home of Stewart's and The Sun," *The New York Times*, September 24, 1997, www.nytimes.com/1997/09/24/nyregion/return-white-marble-palace-buildings-agency-occupy-old-home-stewart-s-sun.html.

14. Wired New York, "Ladies' Mile Historic District," http://wirednewyork.com/forum/showthread.php?t=5184 (accessed November 3, 2009).

15. Robbins, *Global Problems and the Culture of Capitalism*, 22–23, quoting Michael B. Miller, *The Bon Marche—Bourgeois Culture and the Department Store, 1869–1920* (Princeton, NJ: Princeton University Press, 1981), 183.

16. Selfridges & Co., "History," www.selfridges.com/index.cfm?page=1303 (accessed November 17, 2009).

17. Amsterdam.info, "Bijenkorf Amsterdam," www.amsterdam.info/shopping/bijenkorf/ (accessed December 1, 2009).

18. Kurt Andersen, "New Right Now," www.metropolismag.com, January 1, 2003, www.metropolismag.com/story/20030101/new-right-now (accessed December 17, 2009).

19. New World Encyclopedia, "Bernays, Edward L.," www.newworldencyclopedia.org/entry/Edward_L._Bernays (accessed November 19, 2009).

20. Edward L. Bernays, *Propaganda* [1928] (New York: Ig Publishing, 2005), 74–75.

21. Ibid., 37.

22. Robbins, *Global Problems and the Culture of Capitalism*, 18.

23. William Shakespeare, *The Tragedy of King Lear*, Vol. XLVI, Part 3, The Harvard Classics (New York: P.F. Collier & Son, 1909–14); Bartleby.com, www.bartleby.com/46/3/24.html (accessed November 15, 2009).

24. Dmitri Iglitzin and Steven Hill, "Henry Ford and the Minimum Wage," *The Huffington Post*, January 8, 2007, www.huffingtonpost.com/steven-hill/henry-ford-and-the-minimu_b_38140.html (accessed November 18, 2009).

25. BBC, World War 2: Food and Shopping, "Rationing," www.bbc.co.uk/schools/primaryhistory/world_war2/food_and_shopping/ (accessed December 19, 2009).

26. Richard C. Bayer, *Capitalism and Christianity: The Possibility of Christian Personalism* (Washington, DC: Georgetown University Press, 1999), 22.

27. William H. Young, *The 1950s: American Popular Culture Through History* (Santa Barbara, CA: Greenwood Press, 2004), 25.

28. Television History—The First 75 Years, "Television Facts and Statistics—1939 to 2000," www.tvhistory.tv/facts-stats.htm (accessed November 18, 2009).

29. U. S. Bureau of the Census, "Conversion from Analog to Digital TV"—Feb. 17, 2009, www.census.gov/Press-Release/www/releases/archives/facts_for_features_special_editions/012025.html (accessed November 23, 2009).

30. History.com, This Day in History, "NBC Airs First Official TV Commercial," July 1, 1941, www.history.com/this-day-in-history.do?action=Article&id=3414 (accessed November 23, 2009).

31. Young, *The 1950s*, 41.
32. The Museum of Broadcast Communications, "Quiz Show Scandals," www.museum.tv/eotvsection.php?entrycode=quizshowsca (accessed January 25, 2010)
33. Neil Postman, *Amusing Ourselves to Death: Public Discourse in the Age of Show Business* (New York: Penguin Books, 1985).
34. Federal Reserve Bank of Boston, "Credit History: The Evolution of Consumer Credit in America," *The Ledger* (Spring/Summer 2004), www.bos.frb.org/education/ledger/ledger04/sprsum/credhistory.htm (accessed November 18, 2009).
35. GMnext.com, http://wiki.gmnext.com/wiki/index.php/File:UNC1957-0031.jpg (accessed January 25, 2010).
36. Jennifer Rosenberg, "The First Credit Card," About.com: 20th Century History, http://history1900s.about.com/od/1950s/a/firstcreditcard.htm (accessed November 18, 2009).
37. CreditCards.Org.UK., Credit Card Guide: Visa Card and Amex Card, "What Is Visa?" www.creditcards.org.uk/visa-and-amex.html (accessed November 18, 2009).
38. Rosenberg, "The First Credit Card."
39. "Cheapskate Wisdom from…Mad Magazine," Time.com, http://money.blogs.time.com/2009/06/23/cheapskate-wisdom-from-%E2%80%A6-mad-magazine/ (accessed January 3, 2010).
40. Libby Purves, "The Seventies Are Back, With Less Good Cheer," Timesonline.com, July 21, 2008, www.timesonline.co.uk/tol/comment/columnists/libby_purves/article4368530.ece (accessed November 18, 2009).

2 EATING THE WORLD

1. Stephanie Coontz, *The Way We Never Were: American Families and the Nostalgia Trap* (New York: Basic Books, 1992), 24.
2. Encyclopedia.com, "The Baby Boom," www.encyclopedia.com/doc/1G2-3468301958.html (accessed December 13, 2009).
3. U.S. Energy Information Administration, "EIA World Nominal Oil Price Chronology: 1970–2007," http://tonto.eia.doe.gov/country/time-line/oil_chronology.cfm (accessed December 13, 2009).
4. U.S. Department of State, "History of the U.S. Trade Deficit," About.com, http://economics.about.com/od/foreigntrade/a/trade_deficit_h.htm (accessed November 2009).
5. "The U.S. Unemployment Rate January 1948 to December 2009," The Misery Index, www.miseryindex.us/urbymonth.asp (accessed January 26, 2010).
6. "The U.S. Misery Rate 1948 to 2009," The Misery Index, www.misery-index.us/customindexbyyear.asp (accessed January 26, 2010).
7. Centers for Disease Control, National Center for Health Statistics, "Advance Report of Final Divorce Statistics, 1989 and 1990," April 18,

1995, www.cdc.gov/nchs/PRESSROOM/95facts/fs_439s.htm (accessed December 13, 2009).

8. PBS.org, *American Experiences: Jimmy Carter,* "The Crisis of Confidence Speech," July 15, 1979, www.pbs.org/wgbh/amex/carter/filmmore/ps_crisis.html (accessed December 13, 2009).

9. Margaret Thatcher Foundation, "Conservative General Election Manifesto 1979," April 11, 1979, www.margaretthatcher.org/archive/displaydocument.asp?docid=110858 (accessed December 2, 2009).

10. "Ronald Reagan TV Ad: 'It's Morning Again in America,' " YouTube.com, www.youtube.com/watch?v=EU-IBF8nwSY (accessed January 28, 2010).

11. Library of Economics and Liberty, *The Concise Encyclopedia of Economics: Milton Friedman,* www.econlib.org/library/Enc/bios/Friedman.html (accessed November 20, 2009).

12. Ibid.

13. Maria Moschandreas, *Business Economics* (London: Thomson Learning, 2000), 376.

14. Wikipedia contributors, "Neoliberalism," *Wikipedia, The Free Encyclopedia,* http://en.wikipedia.org/w/index.php?title=Neoliberalism&oldid=347754635 (accessed December 2, 2009).

15. Duke Law Library & Technology, "GATT/WTO," www.law.duke.edu/lib/researchguides/gatt.html (accessed December 2, 2009).

16. "Ivory Soap Celebrates 125 Years of Keeping America Clean," P&G.com Press Release, June 22, 2004, http://phoenix.corporate-ir.net/phoenix.zhtml?c=104574&p=irol-newsArticle&ID=628856&highlight= (accessed December 4, 2009).

17. Ruth Mortimer, "Sunlight Soap Did so Much More than Just Cleaning: The Soap Brand Is a National Treasure Despite Being Washed Out of the UK Market," *Brand Strategy,* June 1, 2003. Lifebuoy Soap, "Sunlight Soap," www.lifebuoy.co.uk/ (accessed December 4, 2009).

18. Wikipedia contributors, "Nike, Inc.," *Wikipedia, The Free Encyclopedia,* http://en.wikipedia.org/w/index.php?title=Nike,_Inc.&oldid=348451822 (accessed December 4, 2009).

19. "Company News: Suchard Drops Out," *The New York Times,* June 25, 1988, www.nytimes.com/1988/06/25/business/company-news-suchard-drops-out.html (accessed December 4, 2009).

20. NBC.com, "About the Show," www.nbc.com/Vintage_Shows/Miami_Vice/about/index.shtml (accessed December 3, 2009).

21. NBC.com, "Classic TV: About the Shows," www.nbc.com/classic-tv/about/miami-vice.shtml (accessed December 3, 2009).

22. "Video: Cool Cops, Hot Show," *Time,* September 16, 1985, www.time.com/time/magazine/article/0,9171,959822-2,00.html#ixzz0dAEZSgcv (accessed December 4, 2009).

23. NationMaster.com, "Home Ownership (Most Recent) by Country," www.nationmaster.com/graph/peo_hom_own-people-home-ownership (accessed November 12, 2009).

24. Richard H. Robbins, *Global Problems and the Culture of Capitalism* (Boston: Allyn & Bacon Publishing Inc., 2002), 25, quoting George Nash, *The Life of Herbert Hoover: The Humanitarian (1914–1917)* (New York: W. W. Norton, 1998).

25. Robbins, *Global Problems and the Culture of Capitalism*, 25.

26. Ibid.

27. Steven Mintz and Susan Kellogg, *Domestic Revolutions: A Social History of American Family Life* (New York: The Free Press, 1988), 183.

28. Wikipedia contributors, "Homeownership in the United States," *Wikipedia, The Free Encyclopedia*, http://en.wikipedia.org/w/index.php?title=Homeownership_in_the_United_States&oldid=336463770 (accessed December 13, 2009).

29. BBC News, "1979: Council Tenants Will Have 'Right to Buy,'" *On This Day*, December 20, 1979, http://news.bbc.co.uk/onthisday/hi/dates/stories/december/20/newsid_4017000/4017019.stm (accessed December 13, 2009).

30. Jon Mooallem, "The Self-Storage Self," *The New York Times*, September 2, 2009, www.nytimes.com/2009/09/06/magazine/06self-storage-t.html?pagewanted=all (accessed December 13, 2009).

31. ABCNews.com, "America's Homes Get Bigger and Better: As the American Family Shrinks, Houses Grow," *Good Morning America*, December 27, 2005, http://abcnews.go.com/GMA/Moms/story?id=1445039 (accessed December 23, 2009).

32. "The Second Home Ownership Market: Baby Boomers Buying Vacation Homes," Condo Hotel Center, 2004, www.condohotelcenter.com/articles/a80.htm (accessed January 28, 2010).

33. Library Index, "The American Consumer—Contemporary Consumer Spending," www.libraryindex.com/pages/1306/American-Consumer-CONTEMPORARY-CONSUMER-SPENDING.html (accessed December 12, 2009).

34. "Room to Swing a Cat? Hardly," *BBC News Magazine*, August 15, 2009, http://news.bbc.co.uk/2/hi/uk_news/magazine/8201900.stm (accessed January 26, 2010).

35. "Electric Dreams," BBC, www.bbc.co.uk/electricdreams/about.shtml (accessed December 30, 2009).

36. "Safe as Houses," *The Economist*, December 30, 2009, www.economist.com/businessfinance/displaystory.cfm?story_id=14438245 (accessed January 1, 2010).

37. Ruth Simon and James R. Hagerty, "One in Four Borrowers Is Underwater," *The Wall Street Journal*, November 24, 2009, http://online.wsj.com/article/SB125903489722661849.html (accessed December 1, 2009).

38. Tamara Weston, "Top 10 Toy Crazes: Pet Rocks," *Time*, December 14, 2009, www.time.com/time/specials/packages/article/0,28804,1947621_1947626_1947687,00.html (accessed January 4, 2010).

39. "Edwards Lecture Features Dreyer," *Newsletter of Boston Theological Institute* 28, no. 29 (April 1999), www.bostontheological.org/publications /pdf/1998–1999/apr211999.pdf (accessed December 22, 2009).

40. Paul Krassner, *The Best of the Realist* (Philadelphia: Running Press, January 1985), 159.

41. Ray Wright, *Consumer Behavior* (London: Thomson Learning, 2006), http://books.google.com/books (accessed December 22, 2009).

42. Helen Kaiao Chang, "Why $5 Million Is the New $1 Million," MSNBC. com, September 13, 2007, www.msnbc.msn.com/id/20586948/ (accessed December 22, 2009).

43. Martha C. White, "Americans Have Less Debt, More Savings," WalletPop, October 8, 2009, www.walletpop.com/blog/2009/10/08/americans-have-less-debt-more-savings/ (accessed December 22, 2009).

44. Dave Tilford, "Why Consumption Matters," Sierra Club, www.sierraclub.org/sustainable_consumption/tilford.asp (accessed November 30, 2009).

45. Overheard in New York, "Retail Therapy Soothes Even the Most Troubled Upper East Side Soul," www.overheardinnewyork.com/archives/006988.html (accessed December 22, 2009).

46. "2010 Chevy Suburban 3/4 Ton," Chevrolet.com, www.chevrolet.com/suburban3-4ton/features-specs/ (accessed January 25, 2010).

3   CONSUMERISM HITS THE WALL

1. "China's Middle Class Growing Fast," BBC News, March 30, 2004, http://news.bbc.co.uk/2/hi/business/3582015.stm (accessed December 8, 2009).

2. Organisation for Economic Co-Operation and Development, "Economic Survey of India, 2007," *Economic Outlook*, No. 81, June 2007.

3. Ramachandra Guha, "A Father Betrayed," *The Guardian*, August 14, 2007, www.guardian.co.uk/world/2007/aug/14/india.features111 (accessed December 8, 2009).

4. Matthew Kirdahy, "CEO Turnover Increased in 2007," Forbes.com, March 7, 2008, www.forbes.com/2008/03/07/executive-ceo-tenure-lead-manage-cx_mk_0307turnover.html (accessed December 8, 2009).

5. Alan Greenspan, "Remarks by Chairman Alan Greenspan," Francis Boyer Lecture, American Enterprise Institute for Public Policy Research, Washington, D.C., Federal Reserve Board, December 5, 1996, www.federalreserve.gov/boardDocs/speeches/1996/19961205.htm (accessed December 8, 2009).

6. Amazon.com, "Book Searches," www.amazon.com/gp/search/ref=sr_n r_n_1?rh=i%3Astripbooks%2Cn%3A!1000%2Ck%3Adow%2Cn%3A3 &bbn=1000&keywords=dow&ie=UTF8&qid=1257348822&rnid=1000 (accessed December 15, 2009).

7. American Rhetoric.com, "American Rhetoric: Movie Speech, Wall Street (1987)," www.americanrhetoric.com/MovieSpeeches/moviespeechwall-street.html (accessed December 8, 2009).

8. Po Bronson, "Gen Equity," *Wired*, 7, no. 7 (July 1999), www.wired.com/wired/archive/7.07/pilgrims.html (accessed December 8, 2009).

9. Bain & Company, "Global Luxury Goods Market Growing At 9% Per Year—Despite Uncertain Signals," November 14, 2007, www.bain.com/bainweb/About/press_release_detail.asp?id=26081&menu_url=for_the_media.asp (accessed December 8, 2009).

10. David Brooks, "The Next Culture War," *The New York Times*, September 28, 2009, www.nytimes.com/2009/09/29/opinion/29brooks.html (accessed December 8, 2009).

11. William A. Galston, "The 'New Normal' for the U.S. Economy: What Will It Be?" The Brookings Institution, September 1, 2009, www.brookings.edu/opinions/2009/0901_economy_galston.aspx (accessed December 8, 2009).

12. Ibid.

13. Bill Robinson, "Expert View: All the Signs Point to the End of the Years of Plenty," *The Independent on Sunday*, August 7, 2005.

14. John Tierney, "The Voices in My Head Say 'Buy It!' Why Argue?" *The New York Times*, January 16, 2007, www.nytimes.com/2007/01/16/science/16tier.html?_r=1.

15. Brian Knutson, Scott Rick, G. Elliott Wimmer, Drazen Prelec, and George Loewenstein, "Neural Predictors of Purchases," *Neuron* 53, no. 153, January 4, 2007, www.cell.com/neuron/abstract/S0896-6273(06)00904-4.

16. ThinkExist.com, "E.F. Schumacher Quotes," http://thinkexist.com/quotation/infinite-growth-of-material-consumption-in-a/348253.html (accessed December 8, 2009).

17. U.S. Census Bureau, "Trade in Goods with China," Foreign Trade Statistics, www.census.gov/foreign-trade/balance/c5700.html (accessed December 8, 2009).

18. Europa, "EU—China Summit," May 18, 2009, http://europa.eu/rapid/pressReleasesAction.do?reference=STAT/09/72&format=HTML&aged=0&language=EN&guiLanguage=en (accessed December 8, 2009).

19. Robert Skidelsky, "The World Finance Crisis & the American Mission," *New York Review of Books* 56, no. 12, July 16, 2009, www.nybooks.com/articles/22898 (accessed December 8, 2009).

20. Joe Klein, "The Full Obama Interview," October 23, 2008, Time.com, http://swampland.blogs.time.com/2008/10/23/the_full_obama_interview/ (accessed December 8, 2009).

21. "Wages and Benefits: Real Wages 1964–2004," www.workinglife.org/wiki/Wages+and+Benefits:+Real+Wages+(1964–2004) (accessed January 28, 2010).

22. Carter Dougherty and Katrin Bennhold, "For Europe's Middle-Class, Stagnant Wages Stunt Lifestyle," *The New York Times*, May 1, 2008, www.nytimes.com/2008/05/01/business/worldbusiness/01middle.html (accessed March 23, 2010).

23. Christian E. Weller, "Economic Snapshot for November 2007," Center for American Progress, November 7, 2007, www.americanprogress.org/issues/2007/11/econ_snapshot.html (accessed December 8, 2009).

24. United States Government Accountability Office, "Credit Cards: Increased Complexity in Rates and Fees Heightens Need for More Effective Disclosures to Consumers," September 2006, www.gao.gov/new.items/d06929.pdf (accessed December 8, 2009).

25. Bureau of Labor Statistics, U.S. Department of Labor, "The Employment Situation—November 2009," December 4, 2009, www.bls.gov/news.release/pdf/empsit.pdf (accessed December 22, 2009).

26. Office for National Statistics, "Employment Rate Unchanged at 72.5%," November 2009, www.statistics.gov.uk/cci/nugget.asp?ID=12 (accessed December 29, 2009).

27. Organization for Economic Co-Operation and Development, "Governments Must Act Decisively on Jobs, says OECD's Gurría," September 16, 2009, www.oecd.org/document/62/0,3343,en_2649_3745 7_43701438_1_1_1,00.html (accessed December 20, 2009).

28. Nancy Trejos, "Consumers Keep Paying Off Credit Cards, Building Up Savings," *The Washington Post*, October 8, 2009, www.washington-post.com/wp-dyn/content/article/2009/10/07/AR2009100703680.html (accessed December 29, 2009).

29. Marilyn Geewax, "Americans' Savings Offer Little Shelter for Rainy Day," NPR, November 15, 2009, www.npr.org/templates/story/story.php?storyId=120397501 (accessed December 20, 2009).

30. Associated Press, "U.S. Savings Rate Hits Lowest Level Since 1933," MSNBC.com, January 30, 2006, www.msnbc.msn.com/id/11098797/ (accessed December 22, 2009).

31. Shane Goldmacher, "Schwarzenegger Promotes Ana Matosantos to Finance Director," *Los Angeles Times*, December 15, 2009, http://articles.latimes.com/2009/dec/15/local/la-me-state-budget15-2009dec15 (accessed March 23, 2010).

32. Associated Press, "Federal Deficit Reaches All-Time High of $1.42 Trillion," FoxNews.com, October 16, 2009, www.foxnews.com/politics/2009/10/16/federal-deficit-reaches-time-high-trillion/ (accessed December 8, 2009).

33. "Global Economic Shock Worse than Great Depression," April 7, 2009, *The Huffington Post*, www.huffingtonpost.com/2009/04/07/global economic-shock-wor_n_184283.html (accessed December 8, 2009).

34. U.S. Department of State, "Second Arab Oil Embargo, 1973–1974," www. state.gov/r/pa/ho/time/dr/96057.htm (accessed December 8, 2009).

35. 1979 Energy Crisis, http://1979_energy_crisis.totallyexplained.com/ (accessed December 8, 2009).

36. "Historical Crude Oil Prices (Table)," InflationData.com, July 15, 2009, www.inflationdata.com/inflation/Inflation_Rate/Historical_Oil_Prices_Table.asp (accessed December 8, 2009).

37. Ibid.

38. "How Much Does Gas Cost Where You Live?" FlowingData.com, http://flowingdata.com/2008/06/13/how-much-does-gas-cost-where-you-live/, June 13, 2008 (accessed December 12, 2009).

39. Jad Mouawad, "Rising Demand of Oil Provokes New Energy Crisis," *The New York Times*, November 9, 2007, www.nytimes.com/2007/11/09/business/worldbusiness/09oil.html?_r=1 (accessed December 8, 2009).

40. Association for the Study of Peak Oil and Gas, "Peak Oil Primer," *Energy Bulletin*, www.energybulletin.net/primer.php (accessed January 3, 2010).

41. The7thFire.com, www.the7thfire.com/peak_oil/peak_oil_is_a_scam_to_promote_world_depopulation.htm (accessed January 3, 2010).

42. Dave Tilford, "Why Consumption Matters," Sierra Club, www.sierraclub.org/sustainable_consumption/tilford.asp (accessed December 15, 2009).

43. Gunther Latsch, "Are GM Crops Killing Bees?" Spiegel Online International, March 22, 2007, www.spiegel.de/international/world/0,1518,473166,00.html (accessed December 8, 2009).

44. *National Geographic*, "Greendex 2009: Consumer Choice and the Environment—A Worldwide Tracking Survey" (May 2009), www.nationalgeographic.com/greendex/assets/Greendex_Highlights_Report_May09.pdf (accessed December 20, 2009).

4   EMBRACING SUBSTANCE

1. ThinkExist.com, "Bo Derek Quotes," http://thinkexist.com/quotes/with/keyword/shopping/ (accessed December 11, 2009).

2. Carol Midgley, "Unhappy? That's Rich," *London Times*, January 31, 2006.

3. Kimberly Palmer, "Consumer Values vs. Civic Values," *U.S. News & World Report*, August 23, 2007, www.usnews.com/usnews/biztech/articles/070823/23alphaconsumer.htm (accessed January 20, 2010).

4. "Consultation on Today's Social Evils Reveals Deep Unease about Greed, Individualism and Decline of Community," Joseph Rowntree Foundation, April 20, 2008, www.jrf.org.uk/media-centre/consultation-todays-social-evils-reveals-deep-unease-about-greed-individualism-and-decl (accessed December 11, 2009).

5. John Seabrook, *Nobrow: The Culture of Marketing, The Marketing of Culture* (New York: Vintage, 2001).

6. Marketing Campaign Case Studies, "Hummer Campaign," January 27, 2009, http://209.85.229.132/search?q=cache:http://marketing-case-studies.

blogspot.com/2009/01/hummer-campaign.html (accessed January 10, 2010).

7. Jennifer Senior, "Is Urban Loneliness a Myth? Alone Together," *New York Magazine*, November 23, 2008, http://nymag.com/news/features/52450/ (accessed January 10, 2010).

8. U.S. Census Bureau, "Americans Marrying Older, Living Alone More, See Households Shrinking, Census Bureau Reports," May 25, 2006, www.census.gov/Press-Release/www/releases/archives/families_households/006840.html (accessed January 10, 2010).

9. Office for National Statistics, "Proportion of People Living Alone Doubled Since 1971," April 15, 2009, www.statistics.gov.uk/pdfdir/stalone0409.pdf (accessed January 10, 2010).

10. "Americans Deal with Loneliness," *Trends Magazine* (October 2006), www.trends-magazine.com/trend.php/Trend/1273/Category/45 (accessed January 11, 2010).

11. Dan Ariely, "The 2009 Time 100: Nicholas Christakis," *Time*, April 30, 2009, www.time.com/time/specials/packages/article/0,28804,1894410_1893209_1893472,00.html (accessed December 11, 2009).

12. Reid Mihalko, "What Is a Cuddle Party?" Cuddle Party, www.oc-cuddle.com/html/what_is_a_cuddle_party_.html (accessed January 10, 2010).

13. Ibid.

14. Michael Schaffer, "The Family Dog: Why We Treat Out Pets Like Royalty," *The Boston Globe*, March 29, 2009, www.boston.com/bostonglobe/ideas/articles/2009/03/29/the_family_dog/ (accessed December 11, 2009).

15. Ibid.

16. American Animal Hospital Association, "2004 Pet Owner Survey," www.aahanet.org/media/graphics/petownersurvey2004.pdf (accessed January 11, 2010).

17. Christian Menno, "Don't Call It a Pet Store," Bow Wow Meow Press, http://buzzysbowwowmeow.com/news/48/ (accessed January 11, 2010).

18. American Pet Products Association, "Industry & Trends," www.americanpetproducts.org/press_industrytrends.asp (accessed January 11, 2010).

19. "75% Say Americans Are Getting Ruder," Rasmussen Reports, September 22, 2009, www.rasmussenreports.com/public_content/lifestyle/general_lifestyle/september_2009/75_say_americans_are_getting_ruder (accessed January 11, 2010).

20. "The Collapse of Civility," Ponder Anew, September 14, 2009, http://ponderanew.wordpress.com/2009/09/14/the-collapse-of-civility/ (accessed December 12, 2009).

21. "Who Says We're Rude," Rude Busters!, www.rudebusters.com/who-says.htm (accessed January 11, 2010).

22. "Land of the Rude: Americans in New Survey Say Lack of Respect Is Getting Worse," Public Agenda, April 3, 2002, www.publicagenda.

org/press-releases/land-rude-americans-new-survey-say-lack-respect-getting-worse (accessed January 11, 2010).

23. Louise Kramer, "Adding a Personal Touch to Hotel Etiquette," *The New York Times*, October 1, 2006, www.nytimes.com/2006/10/01/jobs/01homefront.html (accessed January 11, 2010).

24. Guatam Naik, "A Baby, Please. Blond, Freckles—Hold the Colic," *The Wall Street Journal*, February 12, 2009, http://online.wsj.com/article/SB123439771603075099.html (accessed January 8, 2010).

25. BrainyQuote, "Henry David Thoreau," www.brainyquote.com/quotes/quotes/h/henrydavid161619.html (accessed January 10, 2010).

26. ThinkExist.com, "John Ruskin Quotes," http://thinkexist.com/quotation/every_increased_possession_loads_us_with_a_new/171171.html (accessed January 11, 2010).

27. WorldofQuotes.com, "Socrates," www.worldofquotes.com/author/Socrates/1/index.html (accessed January 11, 2010).

28. Edward Wachtman and Sheree Johnson, "Discover Your Persuasive Story," *Marketing Management* 18, no. 2 (March–April 2009): 22.

29. "Thursday Quote: Owens Lee Pomeroy," The Daily Mayo, www.daily-mayo.com/?p=175 (accessed March 23, 2010).

30. Tim Dickinson, "The Machinery of Hope," *Rolling Stone*, March 20, 2008, www.rollingstone.com/news/coverstory/obamamachineryofhope/page (accessed December 3, 2009).

31. Ibid.

32. Richard Stengel, "Exclusive Interview: The Obamas on the Meaning of Public Service," *Time*, September 10, 2009, www.time.com/time/nation/article/0,8599,1921296-2,00.html (accessed December 30, 2009).

33. Michael Scherer, "Obama's Inaugural Internet Call to Service," *Time*, January 15, 2009, www.time.com/time/politics/article/0,8599,1872152,00. html (accessed January 5, 2010).

34. Corporation for National & Community Service, "Fact Sheet," April 2009, www.americorps.gov/pdf/factsheet_cncs.pdf (accessed December 11, 2009).

35. "Americorps Applications Skyrocketing," YSA service wire, July 20, 2009, http://servicewire.org (accessed April 28, 2010).

36. Break Away, "What Is an Alternative Break?" http://alternativebreaks.org/Alternative_Breaks.asp (accessed January 3, 2010).

37. Kerry Hubert, "Are There Too Many Breakfast Cereals? People Who Dislike Free Markets Think So, and Blame Wicked Advertising," *Fortune*, March 3, 1997, http://money.cnn.com/magazines/fortune/fortune_archive/1997/03/03/222740/index.htm (accessed January 11, 2010).

38. Eric Schlosser, "Fast Food Nation," *The New York Times*, January 21, 2001, www.times.com/books/first/s/schlosser-fast.html (accessed January 5, 2010).

39. Rob Stein, "Obesity Epidemic Slows," *The Washington Post*, January 13, 2010, http://voices.washingtonpost.com/checkup/2010/01/obesity_epidemic_slows_emba.html (accessed March 23, 2010).

40. Slow Food, www.slowfood.com/ (accessed January 11, 2010).
41. "Thousands Crowd More Than 300 'Time for Lunch' Demonstrations Across All 50 States to Demand Real Food," Slow Food USA, September 9, 2009, www.slowfoodusa.org/index.php/about_us/news_post/thousands_crowd_more_than_300_time_for_lunch_demonstrations_across_all_50_s/ (accessed December 11, 2009).
42. "New Endangered Food Products Boarded to Slow Foods USA's Ark of Taste," Slow Food USA, September 9, 2009, www.slowfoodusa.org/index.php/about_us/news_post/new_endangered_food_products_hoarded to slow_food_usas_ark_of_taste/ (accessed January 5, 2010).
43. Slow Travel, www.slowtrav.com/ (accessed January 5, 2010).
44. Mintel International Group, "Holistic Tourism," MarketResearch.com, February 1, 2007, www.marketresearch.com/map/prod/1467363.html (accessed January 5, 2010).

5   RIGHTSIZING

1. William Wordsworth, "The World Is Too Much With Us," Poets.org, www.poets.org/viewmedia.php/prmMID/15878 (accessed December 3, 2009).
2. Ralph Waldo Emerson, "Ode, Inscribed to William H. Channing," Ralph Waldo Emerson—Texts, www.emersoncentral.com/poems/ode_inscribed_to_william_h_channing.htm (accessed December 3, 2009).
3. "Increasing Stress Making Millions Ill, Survey Finds," *The Guardian*, February 15, 2006, www.guardian.co.uk/uk/2006/feb/15/health.healthandwellbeing (accessed December 1, 2009).
4. American Psychological Association, "Stress in America 2009," July 2009, www.apa.org/news/press/releases/stress-exec-summary.pdf (accessed December 3, 2009).
5. Ben Harder, "Raw Data: Are Antidepressant Drugs Actually Worth Taking?" *Discover*, October 10, 2008, http://discovermagazine.com/2008/oct/10-are-antidepressant-drugs-actually-worth-taking (accessed December 3, 2009).
6. Liz Szabo, "Number of Americans Taking Antidepressants Doubles," *USA Today*, August 4, 2009, www.usatoday.com/news/health/2009-08-03-antidepressants_N.htm (accessed November 20, 2009).
7. Tyler Woods, "Preschoolers Leading the Growth in Use of Antidepressants," EmaxHealth, September 18, 2009, www.emaxhealth.com/1357/25/33655/preschoolers-leading-growth-use-antidepressants.html (accessed December 20, 2009).
8. Wikipedia contributors, "Ronald Inglehart," *Wikipedia, The Free Encyclopedia*, http://en.wikipedia.org/w/index.php?title=Ronald_Inglehart&oldid=339052552 (accessed January 4, 2010).
9. Ronald Inglehart, "Globalization and Postmodern Values," *The Washington Quarterly* 23, no.1 (Winter 2000), http://muse.jhu.edu/

journals/washington_quarterly/v023/23.1inglehart.html   (accessed January 4, 2010).

10. Mary Jane Boland, "Ronald Inglehart," *New Zealand Listener* 216, no. 3576, November 22, 2008, www.listener.co.nz/issue/3576/columnists/12264/ronald_inglehart.html (accessed January 4, 2010).

11. Tori DeAngelis, "Consumerism and its Discontents," *Monitor on Psychology* 35, no. 6 (June 2004): 52, www.apa.org/monitor/jun04/discontents.html (accessed December 20, 2009).

12. Ibid.

13. Ibid.

14. "Record-Breaking Number of New Products Flood Global CPG Shelves," AllBusiness, January 23, 2007, www.allbusiness.com/services/business-services/3999534-1.html (accessed December 20, 2009).

15. T. M. Shine, "The Last Word: I'm No Decider," *The Week*, January 9, 2009, www.theweek.com/article/index/92141/The_last_word_Im_no_decider (accessed December 17, 2009).

16. ThinkExist.com, "Henry David Thoreau Quotes," http://thinkexist.com/quotation/simplicity-simplicity-simplicity-i_say-let_your/208295.html (accessed January 6, 2010).

17. "Luxury or Necessity? Things We Can't Live Without," Pew Research Center Publications, http://pewresearch.org/pubs/323/luxury-or-necessity (accessed December 20, 2009).

18. "The Difficulty of Choosing a New Camera," AutoPuzzles, May 27, 2009, www.autopuzzles.com/forum/index.php?PHPSESSID=94102eca9045d41ea2c8d6df4a09e474&topic=1957.msg15656 (accessed December 20, 2009).

19. "Hard to Use Products: Dumb Users or Dumb Designers?" Dvorak Uncensored, March 6, 2006, www.dvorak.org/blog/2006/03/06/hard-to-install-products-dumb-users-or-dumb-designers/ (accessed December 20, 2009).

20. Virginia Postre, "Consumer Vertigo," Reason.com, June 2005, http://reason.com/archives/2005/06/01/consumer-vertigo/ (accessed December 20, 2009).

21. T. M. Shine, "The Last Word: I'm No Decider," *The Week*, January 9, 2009, www.theweek.com/article/index/92141/The_last_word_Im_no_decider (accessed December 17, 2009).

22. Amazon.com, "The Paradox of Choice: Why More Is Less," www.amazon.com/Paradox-Choice-Why-More-Less/dp/product-description/0060005696 (accessed December 20, 2009).

23. Interview by Euro RSCG Worldwide with Barry Schwartz, professor of social theory and social action, Swarthmore College, on December 10, 2009.

24. Ibid.

25. "Nicolas Cage Losing His Treasures," *People* 72, no. 23, December 7, 2009, www.people.com/people/archive/article/0,,20325559,00.html (accessed December 20, 2009).

26. "Half of Americans Repeatedly Struggle with Debt: One in Four Shows Signs of Money Abuse," *Atlanta Inquirer*, April 6, 2002.

27. "You Might Be a Shopaholic," MSN.Money, http://moneycentral.msn.com/content/SavingandDebt/P58684.asp (accessed December 20, 2009).

28. "Are You One of America's 18,000,000 Shopaholics?" Stopping Overshopping, www.stoppingovershopping.com/ (accessed December 22, 2009).

29. April Lane Benson, "Holidays Beckon: What's an Overshopper to Do?" *Psychology Today*, November 10, 2009, www.psychologytoday.com/blog/buy-or-not-buy/200911/holidays-beckon-whats-overshopper-do (accessed December 22, 2009).

30. "Here's What Clients Are Saying," Stopping Overshopping, www.stoppingovershopping.com/compulsive_shoppers.htm (accessed December 20, 2009).

31. Melissa Healy, "It's a Problem. But a Disorder?" *Los Angeles Times*, July 21, 2008, http://articles.latimes.com/2008/jul/21/health/he-shopillness21?pg=2 (accessed December 20, 2009).

32. Lisa Grace Marr, "Shop Till You Drop Is Tragic, Not Funny," *The Hamilton Spectator* (Ontario, Canada), November 26, 2009, www.thespec.com/article/679731 (accessed December 20, 2009).

33. "How Can I Manage Compulsive Shopping and Spending Addiction," www.indiana.edu/~engs/hints/shop.html (accessed December 20, 2009).

34. Dick Meyer, "Aggressive Ostentation," CBSNews.com, January 13, 2006, www.cbsnews.com/stories/2006/01/13/opinion/meyer/main1206612_page2.shtml?tag=contentMain;contentBody (accessed December 21, 2009).

35. Boulder-Area Group Discussions, www.bagd.org/ (accessed December 20, 2009).

36. Rasna Warahp, "Money and Happiness: Are Kenyans' Priorities Right?" *Daily Nation* (Kenya), October 4, 2009.

37. Ruth Limkin, "An Antidote for Modern Melancholy," *The Courier Mail* (Australia), March 17, 2008.

38. John Quelch Blog, "How Recession Will Accelerate Consumer Downsizing," *Harvard Business Review*, October 15, 2008, http://discussionleader.hbsp.com/quelch/2008/10/how_recession_will_accelerate.html (accessed December 20, 2009).

39. Gail Blanke, "Throw Out Fifty Things—Clear the Clutter, Find Your Life," www.throwoutfiftythings.com/ (accessed January 3, 2010).

40. The Fresh Ideas Group, "The Fresh Ideas Group's 2009 Consumer Trends Forecast," December 12, 2008, www.freshideasgroup.com/work/focus_group.php?id=205 (accessed January 4, 2010).

41. Elizabeth Olsen, "Shrinking the World, or at Least Your Corner," *The New York Times*, April 13, 2008, www.nytimes.com/2008/04/13/jobs/13starts.html (accessed December 19, 2009).

42. Ibid.
43. Interactives, "Garbage," www.learner.org/interactives/garbage/solidwaste. html (accessed December 21, 2009).
44. Ibid.
45. The Yankelovich Monitor 2009/2010, "Striking a New Deal: Embedding Responsibility," presented to Euro RSCG Worldwide by Ann Clurman, November 17, 2009.
46. "Less Is More," *The Economist* (U.S. Edition), February 28, 2009.
47. Green Living, "United States Recycling Statistics," http://greenliving. lovetoknow.com/United_States_Recycling_Statistics (accessed December 21, 2009).
48. Nick Chambers, "San Francisco Reaches Highest Recycling Rate in U.S. at 72%," *Red, Green and Blue*, May 12, 2009, http://redgreenand-blue.org/2009/05/12/san-francisco-reaches-highest-recycling-rate-in-united-states-at-72-percent/ (accessed December 21, 2009).
49. Amazon.com, "BookSearch," www.amazon.com/s/ref=nb_ss?url=search-alias%3Dstripbooks&field-keywords=+mgan+nicolay&x=0&y=0 (accessed December 20, 2009).
50. Crazy Crayons, "National Crayon Recycle Program," http://crazycray-ons.com/recycle_program.html (accessed January 4, 2010).
51. Richard Stengel, "For American Consumers, a Responsibility Revolution," *Time*, September 10, 2009, www.time.com/time/nation/ article/0,8599,1921444-1,00.html (accessed December 20, 2009).
52. The Futures Company, *A Darwinian Gale 2010*, http://www. darwiniangale.com/ (accessed December 15, 2009).
53. Pippa Smith, "Duffy: 'My Life Is So Glam Now—But It Means Nothing to Me,'" *Mirror* February, 8, 2008, www.mirror.co.uk/celebs/celebs-on-sunday/2008/08/02/duffy-my-life-is-so-glam-now-but-it-means-nothing-to-me-115875-20680113/ (accessed December 20, 2009).
54. Jenn Abelson, "Lead Laws Put Thrift Stores in Lurch," *The Boston Globe*, February 27, 2009, www.boston.com/community/moms/articles/ 2009/02/27/lead_law_puts_thrift_stores_in_lurch/ (accessed December 20, 2009).
55. Sherri Begin Welch, "Thrift Stores on the March; Salvation Army's Growing Resale Chain Will Test Waters with Fast-Moving Outlet," *Crain's Detroit Business*, March 9, 2009.
56. Mercedes Cardona, "Americans Save More, Spend Less. Will It Last?" *Daily Finance*, August 29, 2009, www.dailyfinance.com/2009/08/29/ americans-save-more-spend-less-will-it-last/ (accessed December 20, 2009).
57. Sheryl Kay, "Dot's Thrift Shop Adds More Room to Roam," *St. Petersburg Times* (Florida), June 26, 2009, www.tampabay.com/news/ business/retail/article1013000.ece (accessed January 4, 2010).
58. Amy Hardin Turosak, "Green Shopping: Don't Say 'Eww,' to Thrift Stores," *Christian Science Monitor*, March 2, 2009, www.csmonitor.

com/Commentary/Opinion/2009/0302/p09s03-coop.html   (accessed
December 20, 2009).

59. Ibid.

60. Heather Sanders, "The Diaper Drama—Environment," *Diaper Pin*,
www.diaperpin.com/clothdiapers/article_diaperdrama4.asp (accessed
December 20, 2009).

61. Erica Firment, "How to Stop Using Paper Towels," Librarian Avengers,
http://librarianavengers.org/2009/07/how-to-stop-using-paper-towels/
(accessed January 3, 2010).

62. Christian Wolmar, "Let's Wipe Out Toilet Paper," *The Guardian*, March
9, 2004, www.guardian.co.uk/commentisfree/2009/mar/04/stop-using-
toilet-paper (accessed January 3, 2010).

63. Virginia Linn, "Products to Eliminate Wastefulness in the Bathroom,"
Pittsburgh Post-Gazette, September 19, 2007, www.post-gazette.com/
pg/07262/818551-30.stm (accessed January 3, 2010).

64. Liz Hunt, "Tiger Woods: The Wags Who Deserve a Medal," *The Daily
Telegraph* (London), December 2, 2009, www.telegraph.co.uk/comment/
columnists/lizhunt/6706887/Tiger-Woods-The-Wags-who-deserve-a-
medal.html (accessed December 22, 2009).

65. Jonathan Chevreau, "The Death of Thrift," *The Financial Post* (Canada),
May 10, 2008, www.financialpost.com/personal-finance/wealthy-
boomer/story.html?id=c916b78e-2fbe-4c3c-99da-7c7e86ad7eb1 (accessed
January 3, 2010).

66. Kimberly Palmer, "'Frugalista' Debate: One Blogger Stakes Claim," *U.S.
News & World Report*, September 18, 2009, www.usnews.com/money/
blogs/alpha-consumer/2009/09/18/frugalista-debate-one-blogger-
stakes-claim (accessed December 3, 2009).

67. Kelly Evans, "Americans Are Saving More, Amid Rising Confidence,"
The Wall Street Journal, June 27, 2009, http://online.wsj.com/article/
SB124601913090460255.html (accessed December 3, 2009).

68. Mercedes Cardona, "Americans Save More, Spend Less. Will It Last?"
Daily Finance, August 29, 2009, www.dailyfinance.com/2009/08/29/amer-
icans-save-more-spend-less-will-it-last/ (accessed December 21, 2009).

69. Sarah Gilbert, "Recession Tales, Frugal Becomes Fashion," WalletPop,
November 6, 2009, www.walletpop.com/blog/2009/11/06/recession-
tales-frugal-becomes-fashion/ (accessed December 20, 2009).

70. Daniel Gross, "Thrift Is the New Fashion," *Newsweek*, November 3,
2008.

71. Sarah Gilbert, "Recession Tales, Frugal Becomes Fashion," WalletPop,
November 6, 2009, www.walletpop.com/blog/2009/11/06/recession-
tales-frugal-becomes-fashion/ (accessed December 20, 2009).

72. Bonnie Erbe Scripps, "When Wedding Is a Big Show, Marriage Often
Doesn't Last," *Deseret News* (Salt Lake City), May 8, 2005, http://findar-
ticles.com/p/articles/mi_qn4188/is_20050508/ai_n14617455/ (accessed
January 3, 2010).

73. "New Wedding Trends for 2009 Impact the Way Couples Plan Their Big Day," Business Wire, June 30, 2009.

74. "Bridal Registries Reflect Our Casual Lifestyles," Women's Web, January 9, 2005, www.womensweb.ca/k2news/index.php?Action=Full&NewsID=236 (accessed December 20, 2009).

75. "Green Wedding Ideas," Ecomall, www.ecomall.com/greenshopping/greenwedding.htm (accessed December 20, 2009).

76. Abigal Van Buren, "Dear Abby: Opening Presents Brings Chaos at Kids' Birthday Party," *The Bradenton Herald* (Florida), January 21, 2008.

77. Anna Jane Grossman, "$10,000 for Child's Birthday Party?" CNN.com, www.cnn.com/2008/LIVING/04/18/lw.pricey.bday.parties/index.html (accessed December 20, 2009).

78. "Bailey Baio Celebrates Her 1st in Classic Style," Over the Top Productions, November 14, 2008, http://overthetopcouture.blogspot.com/ (accessed December 21, 2009).

79. Van Buren, "Opening Presents Brings Chaos at Kids' Birthday Party."

80. Colleen Kottke, "Birthday Blowout," *The Reporter* (Fond du Lac, Wisconsin), May 21, 2008.

81. Birthdays Without Pressure, www.birthdayswithoutpressure.com (accessed December 21, 2009).

82. "Kids Learn to Party with Less Waste and More Fun," National Public Radio (NPR), April 21, 2009, www.npr.org/templates/story/story.php?storyId=103315784 (accessed December 21, 2009).

83. "Green Goods: Verterra Dinnerware," ABC7 Green Right Now, December 31, 2008, www.verterra.com/press_details.php?id=56 (accessed December 22, 2009).

84. Becky Striepe, "Earth Friendly Disposable Dinnerware from Fallen Leaves," *Eat. Drink. Better,* October 22, 2009, http://eatdrinkbetter.com/2009/10/22/earth-friendly-disposable-dinnerware-from-fallen-leaves/ (accessed December 22, 2009).

6 GROWING UP

1. Robert Fulford, "The Teenage-ification of Manhood," *National Post,* October 17, 2009, http://network.nationalpost.com/np/blogs/fullcomment/archive/2009/10/17/robert-fulford-the-teenage-ification-of-manhood.aspx (accessed December 8, 2009).

2. "Transition to Adulthood Delayed, Marriage and Family Postponed, Study Finds," University of Pennsylvania, January 12, 2004, www.upenn.edu/pennnews/article.php?id=573 (accessed December 8, 2009).

3. Fulford, "The Teenage-ification of Manhood."

4. Lev Grossman, "Grow Up? Not So Fast," *Time,* January 16, 2005, www.time.com/time/magazine/article/0,9171,1018089,00.html (accessed January 20, 2010).

5. "Are You a Twit? (That's Teenage Woman in Her Thirties)," *Daily Mirror*, July 14, 2009, www.mirror.co.uk/life-style/real-life/2009/07/14/are-you-a-twit-that-s-teenage-woman-in-her-thirties-115875-21517749/ (accessed December 8, 2009).

6. Sarah R. Hayford and Frank F. Furstenberg, Jr., "Delayed Adulthood, Delayed Desistance? Trends in the Age Distribution of Problem Behaviors," NIH Public Access, June 1, 2008, www.ncbi.nlm.nih.gov/pmc/articles/PMC2714655/ (accessed January 10, 2010).

7. "Estimated Median Age at First Marriage, by Sex: 1890 to Present," U.S. Bureau of the Census, January 2009, www.census.gov/population/socdemo/hh-fam/ms2.xls (accessed January 30, 2010).

8. Adam Sternbergh, "Up with Grups," *New York*, March 26, 2006, http://nymag.com/news/features/16529/index2.html (accessed December 11, 2009).

9. Roy Long, "The Perils of Peter Pan Syndrome," FoxNews.com, October 1, 2009, www.foxnews.com/opinion/2009/10/01/uwire-peter-pan-syndrome-college/ (accessed January 10, 2010).

10. "Why I Am Leaving Guyland," *Newsweek*, September 8, 2008, www.newsweek.com/id/156372/page/2 (accessed December 20, 2009).

11. Michael Chabon, "Manhood for Amateurs: The Wilderness of Childhood," *The New York Review of Books*, July 16, 2009, www.nybooks.com/articles/22891 (accessed January 20, 2010).

12. Wallace Immen, "Meaning Means More than Money at Work," *The Globe and Mail* (Canada), February 27, 2009.

13. "Some Hands-on Techniques to Save Resources and Money," Verdant.net, www.verdant.net/handson.htm (accessed February 3, 2010).

14. Matthew B. Crawford, www.matthewbcrawford.com (accessed January 12, 2010).

15. Fred A. Bernstein, "Are McMansions Going Out of Style?" *The New York Times*, October 2, 2005, www.nytimes.com/2005/10/02/realestate/02nati.html?_r=1&pagewanted=2 (accessed December 6, 2009).

16. Ibid.

17. Wendy Koch, "Americans Are Moving on Up to Smaller, Smarter Homes," *USA Today*, March 17, 2009, www.usatoday.com/life/lifestyle/home/2009-03-16-small-homes_N.htm (accessed January 8, 2010).

18. Bernstein, "Are McMansions Going Out of Style?"

19. Posts, "Downsizing Our Home," Unclutterer, http://unclutterer.com/2007/08/27/downsizing-our-home/ (accessed December 8, 2009).

20. Tumbleweed, Tiny House Company, "Philosophy," www.tumbleweed-houses.com/ (accessed December 8, 2009).

21. "Interest in Small Living Is Growing South of the Border," *The Toronto Star*, December 15, 2007, www.thestar.com/living/article/284731 (accessed December 8, 2009).

22. Tyson, "Tiny Testimonial," *Small Living Journal*, July 27, 2009, http://smalllivingjournal.com/what-about-a-tiny-home-appeals-to-you-personally/dirtsmith/tiny/ (accessed December 8, 2009).

23. "'Serve God, Save the Planet' Author to Speak at Trinity UMC in Birmingham on August 23," North Alabama Conference of the United Methodist Church, July 27, 2009, www.northalabamaumc.org/news/detail/552 (accessed December 8, 2009).

24. "Freeconomist Lives in Non-Material World," *Somerset Guardian*, December 1, 2009, www.thisissomerset.co.uk/guardian/news/Freeconomist-lives-non-material-world/article-1566173-detail/article.html (accessed December 7, 2009).

25. "Less Is More," *The Economist*, February 28, 2009.

26. Richard Stengel, "For American Consumers, a Responsibility Revolution," *Time*, September 10, 2009, www.time.com/time/nation/article/0,8599,1921444,00.html (accessed December 8, 2009).

27. Jeremy Caplan, "Shoppers Unite! Carrotmobs Are Cooler than Boycotts," *Time*, May 15, 2009, www.time.com/time/business/article/0,8599,1898728,00.html (accessed December 8, 2009).

28. Carrotmob, http://carrotmob.org/faq/ (accessed January 20, 2010).

29. Deborah E. Popper and Frank J. Popper, "An America without Farmers?" Prairie Writers, April 8, 2004, www.landinstitute.org/vnews/display.v/ART/2004/04/08/4076b2169776a (accessed December 8, 2009).

30. National Institute of Food and Agriculture, United States Department of Agriculture, www.csrees.usda.gov/qlinks/extension.html (accessed December 8, 2009).

31. "Rod Dreher: One Way to Cope? Grow Your Own," *The Dallas Morning News*, February 20, 2009 (accessed January 20, 2010).

32. Bruce Horovitz, "Recession Grows Interest in Seeds, Vegetable Gardening," *USA Today*, February 20, 2009, www.usatoday.com/money/industries/food/2009-02-19-recession-vegetable-seeds_N.htm (accessed January 8, 2010).

33. Institute of Urban Homesteading, www.sparkybeegirl.com/iuh.html (accessed January 9, 2010).

34. Alex Williams, "Duck and Cover: It's the New Survivalism," *The New York Times*, April 6, 2008, www.nytimes.com/2008/04/06/fashion/06survival.html?pagewanted=1&_r=2 (accessed December 8, 2009).

35. Sarah Rich, "Tales of the Self-Sufficient City," World Changing.com, January 31, 2007, www.worldchanging.com/archives/005961.html (accessed December 8, 2009).

36. Rosie Boycott, "London's Unsung Eco Heroes," *The Evening Standard* (London), December 3, 2009, www.thefreelibrary.com/LONDON'S+UNSUNG+ECO+HEROES%3B+In+the+third+part+of+our+series+on...-a0213422226 (accessed December 8, 2009).

37. Adam Fisher, "Humanure: Goodbye, Toilets. Hello Extreme Composting," *Time*, December 4, 2009, www.time.com/time/nation/article/0,8599,1945764,00.html (accessed December 20, 2009).

38. Linda L. Creighton, "Get Rid of the Leaf Blower," *U.S. News & World Report*, December 17, 2006, http://health.usnews.com/usnews/health/articles/061217/25leaf.planet.htm (accessed December 10, 2009).

39. "Deere 2Q Profit Tumbles 38 Percent," *The Seattle Times*, http://seattletimes.nwsource.com/html/businesstechnology/2009241201_apusearnsdeere.html (accessed February 3, 2010).

40. Stengel, "For American Consumers, a Responsibility Revolution."

41. "Living Locally to Leave a Smaller Footprint," *Sunday Tasmanian* (Australia), August 10, 2008.

42. James E. McWilliams, "The Locavore Myth," Forbes.com, August 3, 2009, www.forbes.com/forbes/2009/0803/opinions-energy-locavores-on-my-mind.html (accessed December 8, 2009).

43. Billy Baker, "For Local Freegans, Dumpsters Yield Bountiful Harvest," *The Boston Globe*, December 3, 2009, www.boston.com/news/local/breaking_news/2009/12/for_local_freeg.html (accessed December 30, 2009).

44. Freegan.Info, "Intro to Freegan Philosophy," http://freegan.info/?page_id=253 (accessed December 10, 2009).

45. Ibid.

46. "Overcoming Consumerism," Verdant.net, www.verdant.net (accessed December 8, 2009).

47. Harvey Jones, "Now It's All Gone Horribly Wrong, We're Finding Ourselves Flying Back in Time," LoveMoney.com, March 11, 2009, www.lovemoney.com/news/manage-your-finances/the-return-of-traditional-values-3211.aspx (accessed December 8, 2009).

48. "The Fresh Ideas Group's 2009 Consumer Trends Forecast," Fresh Ideas Group, 2008, www.freshideasgroup.com/work/focus_group.php?id=205 (accessed December 10, 2009).

49. Betsy Lowther, "'G Word' Host: It's Easy Being Green," *The Boston Globe*, May 22, 2009, www.boston.com/ae/tv/articles/2009/05/22/g_word_host_its_easy_being_green/ (accessed December 8, 2009).

50. Joseph Epstein, "When Prudence Was a Virtue," *Newsweek*, January 26, 2009, www.newsweek.com/id/180054 (accessed December 8, 2009).

51. Sarah Gilbert, "Recession Tales, Frugal Becomes Fashion," WalletPop, November 6, 2009, www.walletpop.com/blog/2009/11/06/recession-tales-frugal-becomes-fashion/ (accessed December 9, 2009).

52. Patricia Nicol, "Grandmother Knows Best," *The Sunday Times* (London), May 3, 2009, http://women.timesonline.co.uk/tol/life_and_style/women/the_way_we_live/article6185896.ece (accessed December 8, 2009).

53. W. Hodding Carter, "Extreme Frugality: Doing the Unthinkable," *Gourmet*, February 5, 2009, www.gourmet.com/food/2009/02/extreme-frugality-introduction (accessed December 8, 2009).

54. Interview by Euro RSCG Worldwide with Rebecca Saeger, executive vice president and chief marketing officer, Charles Schwab Corporation, February 1, 2010.

55. "The Knot Top 10 Trends for 2009 Weddings," *The Knot*, January 12, 2009, www.theknotinc.com/press-releases-home/2009-press-releases/2009–01-12-top-2009-trends.aspx (accessed December 10, 2009).

56. Interview by Euro RSCG Worldwide with Alex Castellanos, political media strategist and partner, National Media, Inc., January 9, 2009.

57. Sternbergh, "Up with Grups."

58. "Dress Code: It's Casual Come Friday," *Sun Sentinel*, March 21, 1993, http://articles.sun-sentinel.com/1993-03-21/business/9302010020_1_dress-code-casual-fridays-fashion-statement (accessed December 8, 2009).

59. "'Business Casual' Most Common Work Attire," Gallup.com, www.gallup.com/poll/101707/business-casual-most-common-work-attire.aspx (accessed February 3, 2010).

60. Katie Arcieri, "Too Casual Fridays?" *Capital* (Annapolis), May 1, 2008.

61. Isaac Bonnell, "Warm Weather No Excuse for Sloppy Work Wear; It's Casual, Not Couch Potato—Even in Bellingham," *Bellingham Business Journal*, August 2008, http://findarticles.com/p/articles/mi_hb6548/is_2008_August/ai_n28565895/ (accessed December 7, 2009).

62. Sandy Dumont, "Expert Image Consultant Announces the Premiere of Her New Book: Business Casual Is Dead, Long Live Classy Casual," Fabulously 40 & Beyond, February 27, 2008, http://fabulously40.com/view/blog/user/imageconsultantsandydumont/dv/7 (accessed December 10, 2009).

63. Susan Gunelius, "When Is Casual Too Casual?" Women on Business, August 3, 2009, www.womenonbusiness.com/when-is-casual-too-casual/ (accessed December 10, 2009).

64. Ibid.

65. Ben Stein, "Father's Day: Time to Accessorize," CBS News, June 15, 2008, www.cbsnews.com/stories/2008/06/15/sunday/main4181710.shtml (accessed January 3, 2010).

66. Ray A. Smith, "Tie Association, a Fashion Victim, Calls It Quits as Trends Change," *Wall Street Journal*, June 4, 2008, http://online.wsj.com/article/SB121253690573743197.html (accessed January 3, 2009).

67. Ibid.

68. Ibid.

69. Stefanie Scarlett, "Necktie Hangs In as Closet Staple," *The Journal Gazette* (Fort Wayne, IN), June 5, 2008, www.journalgazette.net/apps/pbcs.dll/article?AID=/20080605/FEAT/806050331/0/APO (accessed January 2, 2010).

70. Adam Geller, "Men Tossing Their Ties," *Washington Times*, June 16, 2008, www.washingtontimes.com/news/2008/jun/16/men-tossing-their-ties/?page=4 (accessed January 2, 2010).

71. "Old Standby, The Tie, Making Comeback," CBS News, December 27, 2007, www.cbsnews.com/stories/2007/12/27/earlyshow/living/beauty/main3649577.shtml (accessed December 19, 2009).

72. "Customize Your Tie," Pink, www.us.thomaspink.com/fcp/content/PersonallyPinkTies/filter (accessed December 4, 2009).

7 SEEKING PURPOSEFUL PLEASURE

1. TED conference, "Joachim de Posada Says, Don't Eat the Marshmallow Yet" (February 2009), www.ted.com/talks/joachim_de_posada_says_don_t_eat_the_marshmallow_yet.html (accessed January 5, 2010).

2. Jonah Lehrer, "Don't! The Secret of Self-Control," *The New Yorker*, May 18, 2009, www.newyorker.com/reporting/2009/05/18/090518fa_fact_lehrer?currentPage=all (accessed January 5, 2010).

3. Adam Smith, *Wealth of Nations* (New York: Oxford University Press, 2008), 201.

4. Willie Henderson, *Evaluating Adam Smith: Creating the Wealth of Nations* (New York: Routledge, 2006), 67.

5. Alan L. Grey (ed.), *"Class and Personality in Society"* (New Brunswick, NJ: Transaction Publishers, 2009), 87.

6. Scott I. Rick, Cynthia E. Cryder, and George Loewenstein, "Are You a Tightwad or a Spendthrift? And What Does This Mean for Retailers?" Knowledge@Wharton, September 19, 2007, http://knowledge.wharton.upenn.edu/article.cfm?articleid=1811 (accessed January 5, 2010).

7. BrainyQuote, "Ashton Kutcher Quotes," www.brainyquote.com/quotes/authors/a/ashton_kutcher.html (accessed January 5, 2010).

8. Janelle Brown, *All We Ever Wanted Was Everything* (New York: Spiegel & Grau, 2008).

9. Interview by Euro RSCG Worldwide with Dr. Neal Hinvest, research fellow, University of Bath, December 10, 2009.

10. Andrew C. Revkin, "Are You on a Hedonic Treadmill?" Dot Earth Blog, NYTimes.com, August 31, 2009, http://dotearth.blogs.nytimes.com/2009/08/31/are-you-on-a-hedonic-treadmill/ (accessed January 5, 2010).

11. Interview by Euro RSCG Worldwide with Scott Rick, assistant professor of marketing, Ross School of Business, University of Michigan, December 11, 2009.

12. Karl Greenberg, "Marketers of the Next Generation: Hummer H2's Liz Vanzura," *Brandweek*, April 7, 2003, www.allbusiness.com/marketing-advertising/branding-brand-development/4683369–1.html (accessed January 5, 2009).

13. "Internet Use Triples in Decade, Census Bureau Reports," U.S. Census Bureau News, June 3, 2009, www.census.gov/Press-Release/www/releases/archives/communication_industries/013849.html (accessed January 6, 2010).

8 TRIGGERS FOR CHANGE

1. Joe Klein, "Why Barack Obama Is Winning," *Time*, October 22, 2008, www.time.com/time/politics/article/0,8599,1853025-4,00.html(accessed January 8, 2010).

2. Jeremy Cato, "Driving It Home," *The Globe and Mail*, January 28, 2009, www.theglobeandmail.com/blogs/driving-it-home/forcing-consumers-to-do-the-right-thing/article968403/ (accessed January 5, 2010).
3. Interview by Euro RSCG Worldwide with Christian McMahan, chief marketing officer, Heineken USA, January 27, 2010.
4. "What Is Carrotmob?" Carrotmob.org, http://carrotmob.org/about/ (accessed December 20, 2009).
5. Interview by Euro RSCG Worldwide with Jim Fielding, president, Disney Stores Worldwide, January 5, 2010.
6. Interview by Euro RSCG Worldwide with Scott Rick, assistant professor of marketing, Ross School of Business, University of Michigan, December 11, 2009.
7. George Osborne, "Nudge, Nudge, Win, Win," *The Guardian*, July 14, 2008, www.guardian.co.uk/commentisfree/2008/jul/14/conservatives.economy (accessed December 20, 2009).

9   SATISFYING THE SUBSTANCE SHOPPER

1. Interview by Euro RSCG Worldwide with Carlos Abrams-Rivera, vice president of marketing, Nabisco Snacks, Kraft Foods, Inc., January 27, 2010.
2. Bill Breen, "Who Do You Love?" *Fast Company*, May 1, 2007, www.fastcompany.com/magazine/115/features-who-do-you-love.html (accessed February 2, 2010).
3. "Sustainable Tourism," whl.travel, www.whl.travel/sustainable_tourism (accessed January 29, 2010).
4. Michael Bauer, "Between Meals," *San Francisco Chronicle*, March 21, 2007, www.sfgate.com/cgi-bin/blogs/mbauer/detail?blogid=26&entry_id=14369 (accessed February 2, 2010).
5. Sara Liss, "A Florida Psychologist Asks: Kabbalah with Your Sushi?" *Forward*, May 4, 2007, www.forward.com/articles/10633/ (accessed February 2, 2010).
6. "The Ancient Tarlogie Springs," Glenmorangie World, www.glenmorangie.com/_swf/glenworld/fiche_provenance.swf (accessed February 1, 2010).
7. Zach Smith, "Iowa Wrestlers Bring Their Own Tradition, Fashion to Mats," University Wire, March 5, 2009.
8. "Hudson's Bay Co. Goes for Simpler Look for '10 Games Apparel," *SportsBusiness Daily*, October 2, 2009, www.sportsbusinessdaily.com/article/133799 (accessed February 2, 2010).
9. "Adidas Originals Celebrates '60 Years of Soles and Stripes,'" Adidas Press Releases, September 20, 2008, www.press.adidas.com/Portaldata/1/ Resources/sport_heritage/pressreleases/adidas_originals_ss09_press_release_en.pdf (accessed February 2, 2010).

10. Jessica Bruder, "The Etsy Wars," CNNMoney.com, July 15, 2009, http://money.cnn.com/2009/07/13/smallbusiness/etsy_wars.fsb/ (accessed February 3, 2010).

11. Ibid.

12. "Consumers Are Discovering the Delights of Authentic Fare," *Design Week*, May 28, 2009, http://trendwatching.com/about/inmedia/articles/2009_consumers_are_discovering_the.html (accessed February 2, 2010).

13. Alexander von Keyserlingk, "A Vida Portuguesa in Lisboa," Slowretail Blog, May 2, 2009, http://slowretailen.wordpress.com/2009/05/02/a-vida-portuguesa-in-lisboa/ (accessed February 3, 2010).

14. "New Flavor: Absolut New Orleans—Mango with Black Pepper," July 18, 2007, Absolutads.com, www.absolutads.com/?s=new+orleans&type=news (accessed February 2, 2010).

15. "Absolut Unveils Absolut Boston," Bostonist.com, August, 30, 2009, http://bostonist.com/2009/08/30/absolut_unveils_absolut_boston.php (accessed February 2, 2010).

16. "Express Yourself in the Company of Others," Harley Owners Group, www.harley-davidson.com/wcm/Content/Pages/HOG/HOG.jsp?locale=en_US (accessed February 2, 2010).

17. Michael C. Juliano, "Duracell Pedals into 2010," Newstimes.com, November 25, 2009, www.newstimes.com/default/article/Duracell-pedals-into-2010-266581.php (accessed February 2, 2010).

18. "Duracell Invites Consumers to Power in the New Decade at the Duracell Smart Power Lab in New York City's Times Square," P&G Press Release, November 19, 2009, www.pginvestor.com/phoenix.zhtml?c=104574&p=irol-newsArticle&ID=1357596&highlight=duracell (accessed February 2, 2010).

19. Jacques Torres Chocolate, www.jacquestorres.com (accessed February 8, 2009).

20. "The Home of Homestyle Gets a Homestyle Restyle," Bob Evans Restaurants, www2.bobevans.com/website/homepage.nsf/download/031309_GracelandRestyle.pdf/$File/031309_GracelandRestyle.pdf?open (accessed January 29, 2010).

21. "Bob Evans Farm Festival Underway in Rio Grande, Ohio," WSAZ.com, October 9, 2009, www.wsaz.com/home/headlines/63906612.html (accessed January 29, 2010).

22. Lush review by Aiofe O., Yelp.com, April 8, 2009, www.yelp.ie/biz/lush-dublin (accessed February 10, 2010).

23. "Five," Häagen-Dazs.com, www.haagen-dazs.com/products/five.aspx (accessed February 2, 2010).

24. "Welcome to Duck Brand.com," DuckBrand.com, www.duckbrand.com/Info/FAQ.aspx (accessed January 28, 2010).

25. "Duck® Brand Duct Tape: Saving the Day and Dishing out Pay," Business Wire, May 1, 2007, www.allbusiness.com/services/business-services/4326863-1.html (accessed January 28, 2010).

26. "Virginia Man Wins $5,000 for Story of How Duct Tape Saved the Day," Business Wire, January 15, 2008, http://findarticles.com/p/articles/mi_m0EIN/is_2008_Jan_15/ai_n24230128/ (accessed January 29, 2010).

27. "Our Commitment," Bank of America, http://homeloans.bankofamerica.com/en/our-commitment.html.go (accessed February 2, 2010).

28. Jeremy Korzeniewski, "BMW Lovos Concept Makes Chris Bangle Look Drab," September 25, 2009, www.autoblog.com/2009/09/25/bmw-lovos-concept-makes-chris-bangle-look-drab/ (accessed January 28, 2010).

29. Kunur Patel, "Toyota Now Planting Flowers, Fixing Roads in Broke California," AdAge.com, August 8, 2009, http://adage.com/adages/post?article_id=138550 (accessed January 28, 2010).

30. "The New Bag Borrow or Steal," Avelle, www.bagborroworsteal.com (accessed December 17, 2009).

31. Kirwei Lo, "Style Watch: 2009 Apparel Trends Review," Corporate Logo, November 4, 2008, http://74.125.93.132/search?q=cache:8ar9iVlexSMJ:www.corporatelogo.com/articles/style-watch-2009-apparel-trends-preview.html+Kirwei+Lo+and+Style+Watch:+2009+Apparel+Trends+Review&cd=1&hl=en&ct=clnk&gl=us&ie=UTF-8 (cached—accessed February 9, 2010).

32. "Fabric: Recycled Polyester," Patagonia, www.patagonia.com/web/us/patagonia.go?slc=en_US&sct=US&assetid=2791 (accessed January 29, 2010).

33. "Trash Today, Track Tomorrow," Nike Grind, www.nikereuseashoe.com/where-it-goes/sports-surfaces (accessed February 3, 2010).

34. Chris Holt, "Expo: 17-inch MacBook Pro Gets Unibody Makeover," Macworld.com, January 6, 2009, www.macworld.com/article/137947/2009/01/17inchmacbookpro.html (accessed February 2, 2010).

35. Jennifer LeClaire, "Motorola Phone Made from Recycled Plastic Bottles," Mobile Tech Today.com, January 6, 2009, www.mobile-tech-today.com/story.xhtml?story_id=63862 (accessed February 4, 2010).

36. "Brazil: Recycling Consumer Waste," Unilever, www.unilever.com/sustainability/casestudies/environment/brazilrecyclingconsumerpackagingwaste.aspx (accessed January 29, 2010).

37. Interview by Euro RSCG Worldwide with C. J. O'Donnell, global marketing director, Jaguar Cars, Ltd., January 27, 2010.

38. Tim Mullaney and Mariko Yasu, "Panasonic Will Invest $1 Billion in 'Green Home' Plan," Bloomberg.com, December 2, 2009, www.bloomberg.com/apps/news?pid=20601101&sid=ajhto3eO4fpM (accessed January 28, 2010).

39. Ibid.

40. "About Google PowerMeter," Google.org, www.google.com/powermeter (accessed January 28, 2010).

41. Daniel Goleman, "Wal-Mart Exposes the De-Value Chain," Harvard Business Review, July 17, 2009, http://blogs.hbr.org/

leadinggreen/2009/07/walmarts-transparency-exposes.html?cm_mmc=npv-_-DAILY_STAT-_-JUL_2009-_-STAT0717 (accessed January 29, 2010).

42. Alex Salkever, "What's Really in Glade, Windex and Pledge? SC Johnson Will Finally Tell You," DailyFinance.com, November 23, 2009, www.dailyfinance.com/story/whats-really-in-glade-windex-and-pledge-sc-johnson-will-final/19251627/ (accessed January 29, 2010).

43. "GoodGuide iPhone App—Now with Barcode Scanning," GoodGuide.com, www.goodguide.com/about/mobile (accessed February 4, 2010).

44. "TerraCycle Collects Non-Recyclables," moreinspiration.com, May 6, 2009, http://media.terracycle.net/10-01-06—inspiration/10-01-06—inspiration.html (accessed January 27, 2010).

45. Bonnie DeSimone, "Rewarding Recyclers, and Finding Gold in the Garbage," *The New York Times*, February 21, 2006, www.nytimes.com/2006/02/21/business/businessspecial2/21recycle.html (accessed January 28, 2010).

46. Martyn Williams, "LG, Samsung Develop Solar-Powered Cell Phones," *PCWorld*, February 12, 2009, www.pcworld.com/article/159507/lg_samsung_develop_solarpowered_cell_phones.html (accessed January 27, 2010).

47. Andy Patrizio, "Samsung's Aggressive Green Tech Strategy," InternetNews.com, August 26, 2009, www.internetnews.com/bus-news/article.php/3836221 (accessed January 29, 2010).

48. "Barclaycard Breathe," Barclay's, www.barclaycardbreathe.co.uk/ (accessed January 3, 2010).

49. "Fairtrade in General," Fairtrade Foundation, www.fairtrade.org.uk/what_is_fairtrade/faqs.aspx (accessed January 28, 2010).

50. "Alter Eco Fair Trade Study," Alter Eco Fair Trade (October 2008), www.altereco-usa.com/altereco-fairtrade-study2008usa.pdf (accessed January 16, 2010).

51. "Let's Face It," A Part of Something Big, www.partofsomethingbig.com/ (accessed January 28, 2010).

52. "Green Your Lunch This School Year," Little Green Blog, August 12, 2009, http://littlegreenbooties.blogspot.com/2009/08/go-green-with-your-lunch-this-school.html (accessed February 3, 2010).

53. "Our Story," 3 Green Moms.com, www.3greenmoms.com/Our_Story.html (accessed November 2, 2009).

54. "Heineken Experience," Heineken Experience.com, www.heinekenexperience.com/home.html (accessed February 4, 2010).

55. "Ben & Jerry's Factory Tour," BenJerry.com, www.benjerry.com/scoop-shops/factory-tours/ (accessed January 28, 2010).

56. "Customer-Made," Trendwatching.com, May 2006, www.trendwatching.com/trends/CUSTOMER-MADE.htm (accessed February 4, 2010).

57. Ibid.

58. Ibid.

59. Interview by Euro RSCG Worldwide with C. J. O'Donnell, global marketing director, Jaguar Cars, Ltd, January 27, 2010.
60. Interview by Euro RSCG Worldwide with Rebecca Saeger, executive vice president and chief marketing officer, Charles Schwab Corporation, February 1, 2010.

10 SPEAKING THE LANGUAGE OF MINDFUL CONSUMPTION

1. Denise Caruso, "The Real Value of Intangibles," Strategy+Business. com, August 26, 2008, www.strategy-business.com/article/08302?rssid= finance&gko=47f49 (accessed February 2, 2010).
2. Interview by Euro RSCG Worldwide with Christian McMahan, chief marketing officer, Heineken USA, January 27, 2010.
3. Interview by Euro RSCG Worldwide with Pete Favat, managing partner and chief creative officer, Arnold Worldwide, March 26, 2010.
4. "Print Advertising," aboutschwab.com, www.aboutschwab.com/advertising/talk-to-chuck/advertising-print.html (accessed February 2, 2010).
5. "Kmart Introduces Smart Assist Savings Card in Michigan to Provide Needed Relief to Unemployed and Their Families," Kmart News Release, June 30, 2009, www.kmartcorp.com/pubrel/kmart/06302009. pdf (accessed February 2, 2010).
6. Jean Halliday, "Marketer of the Year: Hyundai," *Advertising Age*, November 9, 2009, http://adage.com/moy09/article?article_id=140380 (accessed February 2, 2010).
7. Ibid.
8. Melanie Warner, "Hyundai's Advertising Strategy: Wait for the Fire Sales," BNET.com, September, 30, 2009, www.bnet.com/2403-13240_23-346169.html (accessed February 2, 2010).
9. Steve Hall, "Nike Supports Local Community with 'Back Your Block,'" AdRants, July 1, 2009, www.adrants.com/2009/07/nike-supports-local-community-with-back.php (accessed January 30, 2010).
10. "You Stepped Up!" Back Your Block, www.nikebackyourblock.com/ (accessed February 2, 2010).
11. "2009 Award Winners," Nike Back Your Block, www.nikebackyourblock.com/ (accessed February 13, 2010).
12. Kenneth Hein and Elaine Wong, "Is Community Service the New Green?" BrandWeek.com, January 31, 2009, www.brandweek.com/bw/content_display/news-and-features/direct/e3i3b5ee64b200b60e1fb1-b0015c6d77f29 (accessed January 30, 2010).
13. "KFC Colonel and Road Repair Crew Take Advertising to the Streets to Re-'Fresh' America's Pothole-Stricken Roadways," KFC Newsroom, March 25, 2009, www.kfc.com/about/newsroom/032509.asp (accessed January 30, 2010).

14. "V2V," Global Volunteer Network, www.v2v.net/ (accessed January 30, 2010).
15. "Starbucks V2V," V2V, www.v2v.net/ (accessed January 30, 2010).
16. Liz Baker, "Starbucks V2V: Redefining Community," www.v2v.net/people/liza (accessed January 30, 2010).
17. "Starbucks/Volunteer Connection/HandsOn Network's I'm In! Campaign," Community Foundation, January 21, 2009, www.commfound.org/content/starbucksvolunteer-connectionhandson-networks-im-campaign (accessed February 2010).
18. "Thank You," Starbucks Pledge 5, http://pledge5.starbucks.com/ (accessed February 2, 2010).
19. Tim Leberecht, "Marketing with Meaning: Starbucks 'I'm In' Campaign," DesignMind, January 18, 2009, http://designmind.frogdesign.com/blog/marketing-with-meaning-starbucks-im-in-campaign.html (accessed January 29, 2010).
20. "Program Overview," Disney Parks, http://disneyparks.disney.go.com/disneyparks/en_US/WhatWillYouCelebrate/index?name=Give-A-Day-Get-A-Disney-Day (accessed January 30, 2010).
21. Beth J. Harpaz, "Disney Offers Free Entry to 1 Million Volunteers," ABCNews/Travel, September 30, 2009, http://abcnews.go.com/Travel/wireStory?id=8700087 (accessed January 30, 2010).
22. Jason Cochran, "Disney Says 600,000 Have Already Signed Up to Volunteer for Free Days," WalletPop.com, February 11, 2010 (accessed February 13, 2010).
23. "Corporate Timeline," About Timberland, www.timberland.com/corp/index.jsp?page=corpTimeline (accessed January 30, 2010).
24. HootSuite, "Recycling Earthkeeper Style," Earthkeepers Twitter, November 4, 2009, http://twitter.com/earthkeepers (accessed February 2, 2010).
25. "About Earthkeepers," Earthkeepers.com, http://earthkeeper.com/blog/about-2/ (accessed January 30, 2010).
26. Laurie Petersen, "Breakaway Brands: Ocean Spray Tells It Straight from the Bog," MarketingDaily, Mediapost.com, www.mediapost.com/publications/index.cfm?fa=Articles.showArticle&art_aid=49302 (accessed January 29, 2010).
27. "Ocean Spray's Cranberry Christmas a Ratings Success," Arnold News, Press Release, December 18, 2008, www.arn.com/arn.cfm (accessed January 29, 2010).
28. "Keepers of the Quaich," Ulf Buxrud, www.buxrud.se/society.htm (accessed February 2, 2010).
29. "Glenmorangie World: The Sixteen Men of Tain," Glenmorangie Distillery, www.glenmorangie.com/home.php#/glenworld/people.php?resolution=1280 (accessed January 31, 2010).
30. "Starbucks Timeline & History," Starbucks.com, October 2004, www.starbucks.com/aboutus/timeline.asp (accessed January 29, 2010).

31. John Quelch, "How Starbucks Growth Destroyed Brand Value," July 2, 2008, Harvard Business Review Blog, http://blogs.hbr.org/ quelch/2008/07/how_starbucks_growth_destroyed.html?utm_ source=feedburner&utm_medium=feed&utm_campaign=Feed%253A+ harvardbusiness%252Fquelch+(John+Quelch+on+HarvardBusiness.org) (accessed January 29, 2010).

32. "WhoBurts—Meet the Fryers," BurtsChips.com, www.burtschips.com/ (accessed February 2, 2010).

33. Rebecca Burn-Callander, "'We're Bigger than Pringles,' Says Burts Crisps Co-founder," August 15, 2009, www.realbusiness.co.uk/news/ sales-and-marketing/5675636/were-bigger-than-pringles-says-burts-crisps-cofounder.thtml (accessed January 30, 2010).

34. "Produce Brand Uses Barcodes and Transparency to Promote Social Change," Current.com, October 27, 2009, http://current.com/items/ 91297986_produce-brand-uses-barcodes-and-transparency-to-promote-social-change.htm (accessed January 30, 2010).

35. "Anglesey Sea Salt," Pipers Crisps.com, www.piperscrisps.com/angelsey-salt.phtml (accessed February 14, 2010).

36. Jim Hightower, "Corporados Pretending to Be Local," Undernews.com, October 2, 2009, http://prorev.com/2009/10/corporados-pretending-to-be-local.html (accessed February 14, 2010).

37. "Fact Sheet: 15th Ave. Coffee & Tea," Starbucks.com, July 23, 2009, http://news.starbucks.com/news/fact+sheet+15th+ave+coffee+and+tea. htm (accessed February 14, 2010).

38. Kit Eaton, "How Do You Disguise a Starbucks Store? Like This…" FastCompany.com, July 29, 2009, www.fastcompany.com/blog/kit-eaton/ technomix/how-do-you-disguise-starbucks-store (accessed February 14, 2010).

39. "Nissan Pixo: Simplicity Is the Key," Nissan News, April 9, 2009, www.newsroom.nissan-europe.com/EU/en-gb/Media/PressKit. aspx?mediaid=2424 (accessed March 23, 2010).

40. "New Nissan Pixo Commercial—Welcome to Simplicity," YouTube.com, www.youtube.com/watch?v=qOtkUGi_3f0 (accessed January 30, 2010).

41. "The Future of MUJI," MUJI Global, www.muji.com/message/ (accessed February 2, 2010).

42. "The Philosophy," About MUJI, www.muji.us/about-muji/ (accessed January 31, 2010).

43. Matt Tyrnauer, "Mad for MUJI," *Vanity Fair* (November 2007).

44. "Zen and the Art of Selling Minimalism," *BusinessWeek*, April 9, 2007, www.businessweek.com/magazine/content/07_15/b4029069.htm? chan=innovation_innovation+%2B+design_top+stories (accessed January 30, 2010).

45. JonSel, "The Real Thing. Really," Under Consideration.com, June 28, 2007, www.underconsideration.com/brandnew/archives/the_real_thing. php (accessed January 30, 2010).

46. Anthony Burrill, "Coca Cola Can Redesign," BwLOG.com, February 18, 2008, www.betleywhitehorne.com/bwlog/2008/02/coca-cola-can-re-design/ (accessed January 30, 2010).

47. "Our Packaging," London Tea Co., www.londontea.co.uk/packaging.html (accessed January 30, 2010).

48. Tom Vierhile, "Steady Growth in Soup and Side Dishes—March 2009," Prepared Foods Network, March 1, 2009, www.preparedfoods.com/Articles/Article_Rotation/BNP_GUID_9-5-2006_A_10000000000000547891 (accessed February 2, 2010).

49. "Campbell Outlines Plans for U.S. Soup Business, Expansion Efforts in Emerging Markets," Campbell's, July 1, 2008, http://investor.shareholder.com/campbell/ReleaseDetail.cfm?releaseid=319256 (accessed January 30, 2010).

50. Vierhile, "Steady Growth in Soup and Side Dishes—March 2009."

51. Interview with Christian McMahan.

52. Stuart Elliot, "A Soup Swaps Football Helmets for Hard Hats," *The New York Times*, August 31, 2009, www.nytimes.com/2009/08/31/business/media/31adcol.html (accessed January 30, 2010).

53. "About the Project," The Responsibility Project, www.responsibility-project.com/about/ (accessed January 29, 2010).

54. Stuart Elliot, "An Insurer's Family Drama," *The New York Times*, March 29, 2009, www.nytimes.com/2009/03/30/business/media/30adcol. html (accessed January 30, 2010).

55. "Liberty Mutual Launches New Adverting Campaign," YouTube.com, www.youtube.com/watch?v=-Yxr8yQyo1s (accessed February 12, 2010).

56. "About the Project," The Responsibility Project.

57. "TheAtlantic.project," ThinkAgain.TheAtlantic.com, http://thinkagain.theatlantic.com/ (accessed February 10, 2010).

58. Interview with Christian McMahan.

59. "Do the World a Flavor," BenJerry.com, www.benjerry.com/scoop-shops/factory-tours/factory/ (accessed February 2, 2010).

60. "Welcome to the Dove Community," Dove, www.dove.us/#/connections/ (accessed February 2, 2010).

61. "The State of Self-Esteem in Your City: Kansas City, MO," Dove, www.dove.us/#/makeadifference/tour.aspx (accessed February 2, 2010).

62. "Dove Self-Esteem Fund: Get Involved," Facebook.com, www.facebook.com/DoveSelfEsteemFund?v=app_7146470109 (accessed February 2, 2010).

63. "Dove: Wall," Facebook.com, www.facebook.com/dove#/dove?v=wall (accessed January 29, 2010).

64. Diana T. Kuryiko, "How Subaru Defies the Recession," *Automotive News*, December 21, 2009, www.autonews,com/apps/pbcs.dll/article?AID=/20091221/RETAIL03/312219959/1018 (accessed February 2, 2010).

65. "Subaru Hands over Proceeds from 'Share the Love' First-of-Its-Kind Cause-Related Campaign," PRNewswire, February 12, 2009,

http://media.subaru.com/index.php?s=43&item=53 (accessed February 3, 2010).

11   BEYOND CONSUMPTION: WHAT IS NEXT?

1. Sharon O'Brien, "Aging Population: Seniors Are Fastest Growing Population Worldwide," About.com, http://seniorliving.about.com/od/lifetransitionsaging/a/seniorpop.htm (accessed January 14, 2010).
2. Brendan I. Kocrncr, "Geeks in Toyland," *Wired* (February 2006), www.wired.com/wired/archive/14.02/lego.html (accessed December 11, 2009).
3. LeeAnn Prescott, "Twitter's Stalled Growth Could Spell Bad News for Twitter Ecosystem," VentureBeat, November 23, 2009, http://venture-beat.com/2009/11/23/twitters-stalled-growth-could-spell-bad-ncws-for-twitter-ecosystem/ (accessed January 14, 2010).
4. "Social Networks and Blogs Now Fourth Most Popular Online Activity, Ahead of Personal Email, Nielsen Reports," Nielsen, March 9, 2009, http://en-us.nielsen.com/main/news/news_releases/2009/march/social_networks (accessed January 14, 2010).
5. Annie Baxter, "Consumer Spending Accounts for Two-Thirds of U.S. Economy," MPR News, October 30, 2008, http://minnesota.publicradio.org/display/web/2008/10/29/gdp_numbers_consumer_spending/ (accessed January 14, 2010).
6. Editorial, "Jobless Recovery," *The New York Times*, November 8, 2009, www.nytimes.com/2009/11/08/opinion/08sun1.html (accessed January 2, 2010).
7. "The Sharp Rising Personal Savings Rate," Economist Online, June 28, 2009, http://economistonline.blogspot.com/2009/06/sharp-rising-personal-savings-rate.html (accessed January 14, 2010).
8. "2008 World Population: Data Sheet," Population Reference Bureau, 2008, www.prb.org/pdf08/08WPDS_Eng.pdf (accessed January 3, 2010).
9. "Forest Holocaust," National Geographic.com, www.nationalgeographic.com/eye/deforestation/effect.html (accessed January 3, 2010).
10. "Species Disappearing at an Alarming Rate," MSNBC.com, November 17, 2004, www.msnbc.msn.com/id/6502368/?GT1=5809 (accessed December 14, 2009).
11. "Big Fish Stocks Fall 90 Percent Since 1950, Study Says," *National Geographic News*, May 15, 2003, http://news.nationalgeographic.com/news/2003/05/0515_030515_fishdecline.html (accessed January 3, 2010).
12. Bjorn Carey, "Glaciers Disappear in Before & After Photos," LiveScience.com, March 24, 2006, www.livescience.com/environment/060324_glacier_melt.html (accessed December 13, 2009).
13. Subhra Priyadarshini, "Vanishing Islands: Displaced Climate Casualties Underlying Truth," *The Telegraph* (Calcutta), October 30, 2006, www.telegraphindia.com/1061030/asp/knowhow/story_6929967.asp (accessed February 5, 2010).

14. "Global Trends 2025: The National Intelligence Council's 2025 Project," National Intelligence Council, www.dni.gov/nic/NIC_2025_project. html (accessed January 14, 2010).

15. "Developed and Emerging Nations Focusing on Worldwide Water Shortages," Jutia Group.com, April 20, 2009, http://jutiagroup. com/2009/04/20/developed-and-emerging-nations-focusing-on-worldwide-water-shortage/ (accessed January 14, 2010).

16. "Polls Show Voter Dissatisfaction with U.S. Congress," RT.com, September 4, 2009, http://rt.com/Top_News/2009-09-04/polls-voter-dissatisfaction-congress.html (accessed January 3, 2010).

17. Interview by Euro RSCG Worldwide with Jim Fielding, president, Global Disney Stores, January 5, 2010.

18. Damien Cave, "In Recession, Americans Doing More, Buying Less," *The New York Times*, January 2, 2010, www.nytimes.com/2010/01/03/business/economy/03experience.html (accessed January 13, 2010).

19. "Our Philosophy," Slow Food.com, www.slowfood.com/about_us/eng/philosophy.lasso (accessed January 13, 2010).

20. Xavier Laurent Comtesse, "Direct Economy: An Essay for a Better Understanding of the Future," ThinkStudio.com, www.thinkstudio. com/text/directeconomy_en2.pdf (accessed February 6, 2010).

21. "Nokia 888 Concept Phone," MobilePhone Review.com, July 24, 2007, www.mobilephone-review.com/nokia/nokia-888-concept-phone/ (accessed January 14, 2010).

22. "Culture Jam: The Uncooling of America," Disenchantmentville. com, www.disenchantmentville.com/books/culturejam.shtml (accessed January 14, 2010).

23. Kono, "Kalle Lasn: Clearing the Mindspace," *Adbusters*, March 4, 2009, www.adbusters.org/blogs/adbusters_blog/kalle_lasn_clearing_mindscape.html (accessed January 14, 2010).

24. "Buy Nothing Day," YouTube, www.youtube.com/watch?v=ZEpsshQ5_NI (accessed January 14, 2010).

25. "Semiotic Disobedience: Shit Disturbers in an Age of Image Overload," www.slideshare.net/danieldrache/semiotic-disobedience-shitdisturbers-in-an-age-of-image-overload (accessed January 14, 2010).

26. "Billboard Liberation Front's Photostream," flickr.com, www.flickr. com/photos/24301298@N08/page5/ (accessed January 14, 2010).

27. "Being a Creative Critique: 40 Best Spoof Ads," Desizn Tech, August 14, 2009, http://desizntech.info/2009/08/being-a-creative-critique-40-best-spoof-ads/ (accessed January 14, 2010).

28. Robert D. McFadden and Angela Macropoulos, "Wal-Mart Employee Trampled to Death," *The New York Times*, November 28, 2008, www.nytimes.com/2008/11/29/business/29walmart.html?pagewanted=1&_r=1 (accessed January 12, 2010).

29. Interview with Jim Fielding.

INDEX